MORE PRAISE FOR
Sustainable Leadership

·

"**Modern educational** leadership is driven by moral purpose, and in *Sustainable Leadership,* Hargreaves and Fink give us a first-class primer on how to make such leadership ubiquitous."

—DAVID HOPKINS, *HSBC Chair of International Leadership and formerly chief advisor to the Secretary of State on School Standards, Department for Education and Skills, England*

"**When leaders** depart from their initial values and purposes, their organizations change in untoward ways. In *Sustainable Leadership,* the authors convince us that when leaders focus on what is truly important and sustainable, organizations will thrive. This is, thank God, no cookbook. It is a distinctive contribution to the literature."

—SEYMOUR B. SARASON, *professor of psychology, emeritus, Yale University*

Andy Hargreaves
Dean Fink

Sustainable
Leadership

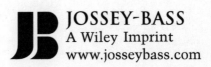

JOSSEY-BASS
A Wiley Imprint
www.josseybass.com

Published by Jossey-Bass
A Wiley Imprint
989 Market Street, San Francisco, CA 94103-1741   www.josseybass.com

Excerpt from the Nobel Lecture by Wangari Maathai © The Nobel Foundation 2004. F. R. Scott's poem "Villanelle for Our Time" reprinted with the permission of William Toye, literary executor for the Estate of F. R. Scott.

Jossey-Bass books and products are available through most bookstores. To contact Jossey-Bass directly call our Customer Care Department within the U.S. at 800-956-7739, outside the U.S. at 317-572-3986, or fax 317-572-4002.

Jossey-Bass also publishes its books in a variety of electronic formats. Some content that appears in print may not be available in electronic books.

Library of Congress Cataloging-in-Publication Data
Hargreaves, Andy.
  Sustainable leadership / Andy Hargreaves, Dean Fink. — 1st ed.
    p. cm. — (Jossey-Bass leadership library in education)
  Includes bibliographical references and index.
  ISBN-13: 978-0-7879-6838-0 (alk. paper)
  ISBN-10: 0-7879-6838-2 (alk. paper)
  1. School management and organization. 2. Educational leadership.
  I. Fink, Dean, 1936– . II. Title. III. Series.
  LB2805.H32 2006
  371.2—dc22   2005013835

Printed in the United States of America
FIRST EDITION
PB Printing 10 9 8 7 6 5 4

THE JOSSEY-BASS
Leadership Library in Education

·

Andy Hargreaves
Consulting Editor

THE JOSSEY-BASS LEADERSHIP LIBRARY IN EDUCATION is a distinctive series of original, accessible, and concise books designed to address some of the most important challenges facing educational leaders. The authors are respected thinkers in the field who bring practical wisdom and fresh insight to emerging and enduring issues in educational leadership. Packed with significant research, rich examples, and cutting-edge ideas, these books will help both novice and veteran leaders understand their practice more deeply and make schools better places to learn and work.

ANDY HARGREAVES is the Thomas More Brennan Chair in Education in the Lynch School of Education at Boston College and the author of numerous books on culture, change, and leadership in education.

For current and forthcoming titles in the series, please see the last pages of this book.

To our children,
Stuart, Lucy, Danielle, and Tracy,
environmentalists, educators, and advocates
whose contributions to the public good
will live on long after this book and its authors
have been forgotten

Contents

Acknowledgments

Much of this book arises out of research conducted for and funded by the Spencer Foundation of the United States under the title Change Over Time? A Study of Culture, Structure, Time and Change in Secondary Schooling and codirected by Andy Hargreaves and Ivor Goodson. We have also drawn on two other projects: Change Frames, funded by the Ontario Minister of Education Transfer Grant in partnership with one of the province's largest school districts, and Succeeding Leaders, supported by the Ontario Principals Council.

We were privileged to have outstanding research support on all projects from colleagues who worked with us to collect, organize, and analyze the case study data on which we have drawn in this book. We are indebted to Michael Baker, Colin Biott, Carol Brayman, Martha Foote, Corrie Giles, Ivor Goodson, Shawn Moore, Paul Shaw, Robert White, and Sonia James Wilson. Outstanding administrative and research assistance was provided by Nancy Stahl, Paul Chung, and Kristin Kew in Boston and by Leo Santos in Toronto.

Our greatest professional thanks go to the teachers and administrators who worked openly with us, gave generously of their time, and responded with continual criticism to draft reports of our findings. We thank Lucy Hargreaves for providing insight and information on Education for Sustainable Development initiatives in particular.

Our greatest personal gratitude and love is reserved for our wives, Pauline and Ramona, who for over seventy years between them have sustained each of us beyond measure.

A.H.
D.F.

The Authors

Andy Hargreaves is the Thomas More Brennan Chair in Education at the Lynch School of Education in Boston College. The mission of the chair is to promote social justice and to connect theory and practice in education. Raised in a Northern English mill town, Hargreaves taught primary school and lectured at several English universities, including Oxford University, before moving in 1987 to the Ontario Institute for Studies in Education in Canada, where he later cofounded and directed the International Center for Educational Change. He took his current position at Boston College in 2002. Andy Hargreaves has authored and edited more than twenty-five books in education, which have been published in many languages. His previous book *Teaching in the Knowledge Society: Education in the Age of Insecurity* received outstanding book awards from the American Educational Research Association and the American Library Association.

Dean Fink is an independent consultant with extensive experience in over thirty countries. Born and raised in Hamilton, Ontario, Canada's largest manufacturing city, he spent thirty-four years in public education, thirty of which were in leadership roles as department head, assistant principal, principal, and superintendent. After taking early retirement in 1993 and completing his Ph.D., he wrote *Changing Our Schools* (with Louise Stoll), followed by *Good*

Schools/Real Schools: Why School Reform Doesn't Last, and *It's About Learning and It's About Time* (with Louise Stoll and Lorna Earl). His most recent book, published in 2005, is *Leadership for Mortals: Developing and Sustaining Leaders of Learning*.

Sustainable Leadership

Introduction: Sustainability
and Unsustainability
The Choices for Change

Recognizing that sustainable development, democracy and
peace are indivisible is an idea whose time has come.

*Wangari Maathai, Kenya's assistant minister for
environment, natural resources, and wildlife,
Nobel Peace Prize acceptance speech,
Oslo, December 10, 2004*

Leadership and Change

Change in education is easy to propose, hard to implement, and
extraordinarily difficult to sustain. Pilot projects show promise but
are rarely converted into successful systemwide change. Innovations
easily attract early enthusiasts, but it is harder to convince more
skeptical educators to commit to the hard work of implementation.
Beacon schools and lighthouse schools may shine brightly, but they
often draw outstanding teachers and sometimes even the best students from schools around them, leaving these other schools to
skulk in the shadows. Large-scale literacy reforms achieve early
results but soon reach a plateau. Extraordinary effort and extreme
pressure can pull underperforming schools out of the failure zone,
but they quickly fall back as soon as the effort is exhausted and the
pressure is off.

Sustainable improvement depends on successful leadership. But
making leadership sustainable is difficult, too. Charismatic leaders

may lift their schools to impressive heights, but the leaders' shoes are usually too big for successors to fill. When great leaders move to new challenges elsewhere, they are often tempted to take their best people with them, placing all they previously achieved in jeopardy. And while heroic leaders can achieve great things through investing vast amounts of their time and energy, as the years pass, this energy is rarely inexhaustible, and many of these leaders and the people who work for them ultimately burn out.

Better-quality education and leadership that will benefit all students and last over time require that we address their basic sustainability. If the first challenge of change is to ensure that it's desirable and the second challenge is to make it doable, then the biggest challenge of all is to make it durable and sustainable. What does sustainability mean? What does it demand of us? What strategic work do we need to do to bring it about? We address these fundamental issues of educational leadership and change in this book.

The Need for Sustainability

Our book on sustaining and sustainable leadership is being produced in the year that the United Nations is launching its Decade of Education for Sustainable Development (2005–2014). In the words of renowned naturalist and environmental activist Jane Goodall, it is a time to "curb the hunger to consume," to recognize that "our appetite is causing extinction," because not only are we depleting natural resources beyond the point where they can be renewed, but we are also undermining the very foundations of entire ecosystems and of biodiversity itself.[1]

The prominence and urgency of having to think about and commit to preserving sustainability in our environment highlights the necessity of promoting sustainability in many other areas of our lives. Foremost among these are leadership and education, where our consuming obsession with reaching higher and higher standards in literacy and mathematics within shorter and shorter time lines is exhausting our teachers and leaders, depleting and making it hard to renew the resource pool from which outstanding educators are drawn and turning vast tracts of the surrounding learning environment in humanities, health education, and the arts into barren wastelands as almost all people's achievement and improvement energies are channeled elsewhere.

When we take our heads out of the sand, the supermarket, or the SUV, we are beginning to grasp what the focus on sustainability means for the environment, the ecosystem, the world that gives us life. In factories, farming, and food consumption, *bigger* and *higher* more often actually mean *too much*—sometimes to the point where consumption seems obscene, more than enough by far.[2] *Faster, quicker, now* also rarely means *better*.[3] These words express the untempered, toddler-like demand for immediate gratification rather than the more moderated appetites of the mature adult. We cannot consume with impunity, without giving thought to the world we are leaving to our children. We cannot push for an endlessly greater gross national product (as most economists do) without factoring in the cost to all of us of cleaning up the air, the water, and the land.[4] And we cannot keep catching, growing, or producing more and more things to satisfy the cravings of our appetites without considering the lives and livelihoods of people who are imperiled by the chemical waste we dump in their rivers, the acid rain that falls in their lakes, and the labor conditions that rob children in developing countries of their basic human rights.

Rachel Carson, pioneering science journalist and iconic founder of the modern environmental movement, understood all this when she blew the lid on the widespread and long-lasting toxic effects of DDT pesticides in the early 1960s. She pointed to "the central problem of our age" as "the contamination of man's total environment with substances that accumulate in the tissues of plants and animals and even penetrate the germ cells to shatter or alter the very material of heredity upon which the shape of our future depends."[5]

Our push to produce more and to control, master, and standard-ize nature as we do so, she pointed out, is a problem of interrela-tionships and interdependence: "We poison the caddis flies in a stream and the salmon runs dwindle and die. We poison the gnats in a lake and the poison travels from link to link of the food chain and soon the birds of the lake margins become its victims. We spray our elms and the following springs are silent of robin song."[6] The coming of such "silent springs" in education, we will see, is also a looming danger as fast-paced, all-consuming standardized education reform leaves plagues of exhausted educators and joyless learning in its wake.

Although the warnings of modern environmentalists are grim and urgent, this state of affairs doesn't plunge them into abject de-spair but impels them into restorative action. Some of this takes the form of dramatic battles against logging companies or big polluters. But most of the energy invested in environmental sustainability, like most significant change in general, is expressed in the small efforts of the many rather than the heroic actions of the few: chang-ing how we behave, what we buy, whose products we consume. Like all change and leadership, the quest for environmental sustainabil-ity begins with ourselves.[7]

Environmental sustainability is a moral imperative on which the quality of our lives and the future of our planet depend. Dis-parate and internally differentiated as it is,[8] the environmental movement and its commitment to sustainability teach vital lessons for achieving sustainability in education organizations and other organizations, too: the value of rich diversity over soulless stan-dardization, the necessity of taking the long view, the wisdom of being prudent about conserving and renewing human and financial resources, the moral obligation to consider the effects of our im-provement efforts on others in the environment around us, the importance of acting urgently for change while waiting patiently for results, and the proof that each of us can be an activist and that all of us can make a difference.

Corporate Sustainability

Sustainability in the corporate world is as essential and desirable as it is in the natural environment that companies are so often criticized for degrading. Businesses that operate sustainably have a more durable record of profitability and success than those that do not. In their groundbreaking and best-selling study of eighteen prominent, long-lasting, and successful companies (which they systematically compare with a control group of eighteen less successful companies), Jim Collins and George Porras show how companies that are built to last

- Put purpose before profit
- Preserve long-standing purposes amid the pursuit of change
- Start slowly and advance persistently
- Do not depend on a single visionary leader
- Grow their own leadership instead of importing stars
- Learn from diverse experimentation[9]

Sustainable companies aren't just pipe dreams; they prosper in actual practice. Long-term investing in socially responsible companies that care about what they produce, how they treat their workers at home and abroad, and what impact they have on the environment and their community leads to higher yields in stock market investment compared with traditionally balanced portfolios. In *The Soul of Capitalism*, William Greider points out that the top 10 percent of profitable companies in the Dow-Jones sustainability index outperform those of the broader global index of all companies listed on the Dow-Jones by 2–3 percent. Likewise, a diversified portfolio of companies with high Eco-value ratings in terms of their attitudes toward workers and actual environmental impact scores

1.5–2.4 percent higher than comparable portfolios of companies with low Eco-value ratings.[10] Investing in socially responsible companies is one of the fastest-growing fund management strategies in the world.[11]

David Batstone combines the experience of companies seeking a morally defensible and sustainable path in eight principles for creating integrity and profitability:

1. *Responsibility* of directors and executives in ensuring the company's viability

2. *Transparency*, so that operations are visible and decisions can be scrutinized

3. *Community*, to which the company has obligations and commitments

4. *Honesty* in representation of products and handling of transactions

5. *Decency* in treatment of workers, including involvement of workers in the company's decision making

6. *Sustainability* in attitudes and approaches to the environment and to reducing negative impact on it

7. *Diversity* as well as balance and equality in the management of all relationships

8. *Humanity*, manifested in respect for workers' and citizens' rights in all global divisions and partners

Companies that are principled in this way, Batstone argues, "excel financially over the long haul."[12] Money and morality can mix. Profit with principles is being achieved in many ways. The pioneers of *natural capitalism* in agriculture and industry, for example, create networks of interdependence among manufacturers of different products in which the waste of each company provides the raw material for the next one, resulting in cascades of conservation and cost savings that reduce waste almost to zero.[13] In a few short years, these early experiments in green capitalism have moved into the mainstream of business practice, redefining corporate images and reducing business costs. The coalition of more than 150 companies that make up the World Business Council for Sustainable Development promotes what it calls *eco-efficiency:* "the delivery of competitively priced goods and services that satisfy human needs and bring quality of life, while progressively reducing ecological impact resource intensity throughout the life cycle, and at a level at least in line with Earth's estimated carrying capacity."[14]

Another significant environmental development is the *slow food movement.* From its beginnings in northern Italy, it has spread as far afield as Minneapolis and Portland, Oregon, stimulating business among local growers and distributors by promoting healthy eating of home-cooked food that is purchased locally and eaten in season. This practice reduces the environmental, financial, and labor costs involved in long-term storage and long-distance transportation and delivery of mass-produced, mass-consumed, and far less tasty fast-food alternatives.[15] The slow food, slow cities (greater use of public transit), and even slow sex movements are affirming that *better* doesn't always mean *faster, bigger,* or *more.*

While many companies have not always been so eager to embrace environmental responsibility, the pressures of the environmental movement are leading more and more of them to engage in adaptive change and thus become increasingly ecologically attentive.[16] For example, in response to Green Mountain Coffee Roasters' and Starbucks Coffee's highly successful initiatives in producing and marketing fair trade coffee, Kraft Foods announced in November 2004 that it would produce and market its own Sustainable Development coffee through its Kenco brand in an effort to provide more assistance to small producers and respond to its environmentally sensitive market.[17]

Strong though all these signs of success and sustainability might be, a great deal of corporate leadership still behaves very differently. Too many companies not only put profit before purpose but make profit their only purpose. Only the bottom line counts. Mergers, acquisitions, restructuring, and downsizing are pursued more out of personal greed than to advance people's good. Satisfying shareholders' insatiable hunger for increasing quarterly returns undermines long-term investment in the training, leadership development, and research infrastructure that produces long-lasting, sustainable growth.[18] Environmental resources are treated as endlessly consumable and utterly disposable and are insufficiently factored into corporate development plans.[19] Environmental costs are omitted from national economic calculations and strategies altogether.[20] Companies implement expedient downsizing of their staff, wasting all their prior investment in their employees' training and development.[21] They initiate and endure an accelerating succession of supposed miracle-working leaders who are given only months to turn the company's fortunes around, then are instantly replaced when they fail. And as we saw in the stock market collapse, or what Cassidy calls the *dot con* disaster, accountants and executives try to protect their competitive image and appease the overwhelming demand for instant results with creative accounting that spirals disgracefully downward into outright corporate fraud.[22] Micromanagement, standardization, short-term targets, staff burnout, endless processions of leadership turnover, and cynical or even fraudulent representations of results—these are the tainted legacies that unsustainable corporate management has left to the public sector in general and to public education in particular.

Far too much of the business world has become unsustainable and unaccountable.[23] According to change management expert Eric Abrahamson, this is evident in *repetitive change syndrome*, which has two components:

> *Initiative overload:* "the tendency of organizations to launch more change initiatives than anyone could ever reasonably handle"

Change-related chaos: "the continuous state of upheaval that results when so many waves of initiatives have worked through the organization that hardly anyone knows which change they're implementing, or why"—which leads, in turn, to a loss of organizational memory[24]

The challenge for educational leadership and change is not to be dismissive of practices in the business world but to learn from those that are most successful and sustainable. Public education should not be treated as a temporary business that is looking to produce quick returns and never-ending profits even if that requires creative accounting in regard to test results. Instead, as a near-universal process that shapes the generations of the future, education should be treated as one of the most long-lasting enterprises of all. It should learn from the environmental movement and from the principles and practices that the most successful, enduring companies employ to bring about and perpetuate sustainable improvement and leadership. Sustainability isn't just a metaphor borrowed from environmental science. It's a fundamental principle for enriching and preserving the richness and interconnectedness of all life, and learning lies at the very heart of high-quality life.

Unsustainable Educational Leadership and Change

The past decade and more has seen the educational reform and standards movement plummet to the depths of unsustainability, taking educational leadership down with it. The constructive and compelling idea of standards—that learning comes before teaching and that we should be able to know and demonstrate when learning has occurred—has degenerated into a compulsive obsession with standardization (one literacy or mathematics program for everyone, one way to teach it, one size fits all) and a ruthless pursuit of market competition ("our standards are going to be higher than your standards, whatever that takes").

The standards movement has become a standards bubble. Like the stock market and property bubbles, the standards bubble began with good intentions—improving all students' achievement and narrowing the gap between the richest and the poorest of them. But just as initial news of successful investment strategies can provoke ensuing frenzies of financial speculation, so can early or exceptional signs of success in raising educational standards rapidly escalate into collective assumptions and insistence that standards can and must rise for everyone, everywhere, all the time. Poor achievement results are not to be tolerated. Failure is not an option. If results do fall short, the answer is to tighten control of teachers and the curriculum, change the leader, or close the school. Fast change. Quick fixes. No limits.

Stock market bubbles, like the Internet bubble, reach their bursting point when companies create neither profits nor products; when workers and leaders are stretched beyond their limits; when corporate returns are inflated, payments are deferred, and figures are slid from one accounting column to the next. Although it may not look or feel like it, the education standards bubble is also about to burst. In fact, in a number of places—the United Kingdom, Australia, and many parts of Canada—it already has.

The signs are everywhere. In New York State and Ontario, Canada, we have been working with our colleagues to investigate the experiences of educational change and reform of almost 250 teachers and leaders in eight high schools over the last three decades of the twentieth century. Since the mid-1990s (and even before the impact of No Child Left Behind legislation in the United States), educators in both countries have reported how the rapid, relentless, and pervasive spread of standardization in educational reform has had the following effects:

- Brought about an *impending graduation crisis* among vocational and special education students because they will not be able to meet the unrealistic, content-loaded standards that have been set for them

- Narrowed the curriculum and *destroyed the classroom creativity* that is essential if all students are to learn to contribute to and compete in the sophisticated knowledge-driven economy that is being promoted across the world by the World Bank, the Organization for Economic Cooperation and Development, and others

- *Restricted innovative schools* in their distinctive capacity to connect learning to the lives of their diverse students, making them increasingly indistinguishable from conventional schools around them

- *Widened the learning gap* between elite and other schools because the subject-based and content-loaded standards are defined and designed in ways that favor the advantaged and penalize the rest

- *Encouraged cynical and calculated strategies for raising test scores,* from teaching only what will appear on the test to concentrating most teaching energy only on those students who fall just below the passing mark on pretests and who can be raised just above it with extra coaching and prepping

- *Undermined teacher confidence and competence* as the pace and priorities of reform have left teachers with no time or flexibility to respond to their students' needs or even mark their work in a timely manner

- *Eroded professional community* as teachers have kept their heads down and struggled alone to try and get through the overwhelming range of curriculum, testing, and reform requirements

- *Precipitated increased rates of stress, resignation, and nonretention,* even among younger teachers, as teachers have felt downtrodden, disillusioned, and disrespected by the reform process

- Instigated and *amplified resistance to change* among mid- to late-career teachers who have become weary of repetitive change syndrome and have reacted to their embittered sense of the present by taking defensive refuge in a nostalgic past

- *Created an accelerating carousel of leadership succession* as principals have been rotated in and out of schools with an increasing sense of desperation and panic, along with *early exits* of more and more disheartened principals from the profession altogether.[25]

In the United States, the National Association of Secondary School Principals has become all too aware of the impact of these trends on leadership recruitment. Based on study data, the association concludes that the failure to attract quality leaders has been due to "increased job stress, inadequate school funding, balancing school management with instructional leadership, new curriculum standards, educating an increasingly diverse student population, shouldering responsibility that once belonged at home or in the community, and then facing possible termination if . . . schools don't show instant results."[26]

In Ontario, 85 percent of teachers in six secondary schools with whom we worked on school improvement initiatives said that as a result of government reforms, they would be more hesitant to seek promotion to leadership positions.[27]

These results have been evident for many years in other parts of the world where standards-based, then standardized reforms were initiated long before they were in North America. For example, in England, the highly prescriptive and all-pervasive National Literacy and

Numeracy Strategy, which required one hour of scripted instruction in literacy and another in mathematics for every elementary student in England every day, did yield initial improvements in test scores, but the scores reached a plateau after four years and the improvements of the first two years are not easily attributable to the program. Even then, the improvements may not have been direct results of the strategy but could just as easily have resulted from lower scores in the first years as a consequence of teachers' being unfamiliar with and insufficiently prepared to teach the new program.[28]

Other issues in England emerging from the standardized literacy and numeracy strategy, from the culture of targets and testing, and from fifteen years of relentless inspection, administrative intervention, and imposed reform also surfaced in the spring of 2004:[29]

- The National Association of Headteachers reported that many middle-class parents were taking their children out of public education, not because standards were too low for their liking but because the standardization of curriculum that overemphasized the basics and heavy testing was taking the soul and the spirit out of their young children's experience of learning.

- Obesity rates escalated among young people after schools cut back time allocations for physical education to make room for more basics and testing.

- A report of England's national educational inspection agency, Ofsted, pointed to falling standards in arts and humanities, due, in part, to teachers being pressed to place endless emphasis on the basics.

- A survey of three thousand secondary schools showed that immediately after schools had undergone cyclical, intensive, and high-stakes external inspection by Ofsted, performance fell by an average of 2 percent as soon as the pressure was off.

...od, problems of recruitment and especially reten-
...leaders reached crisis proportions, as public edu-
...nd less attractive as a career for professionals.
...andardized educational reform had become the
... patient, gasping for air and sick to death.

Evidence of the effects of firmly imposed, tightly prescribed, and impatiently implemented educational reform in North America and around the world is consistent and compelling. Despite or perhaps even because of its apparent initial successes, *imposed short-term, target-driven standardization is ultimately unsustainable*. As we will see in the closing chapter of this book, this is the one place in which we diverge sharply from the improvement ideas of our colleague and friend Michael Fullan, who supports top-down impositions of short-term targets.[30]

Results reach a plateau when speed matters more than substance. Pressure is one way to turn failing schools around, but they rapidly regress once the pressure is off. Schools can't share their knowledge with other schools in a learning culture if bottom-line competitiveness forces them to fend for themselves. Excessive emphasis on the basics inflicts collateral damage on the surrounding environment of more creative, critical, and physically healthy learning. After early successes, the political pesticide of teacher-proof standardization only increases long-term resistance to repetitive change among the teachers it affects. And while the efforts of exceptional teachers and principals in raising standards among their disadvantaged students are admirable, all too often it demands so much of their energies in an uncongenial reform environment that they become depleted and burned out. Given all this evidence of unsustainability, it is time to build something more sustaining and sustainable instead, and many countries have already made a start.

Toward Sustainable Change

Outside the United States and sometimes within it, people are moving beyond standardization and beginning to understand and embrace the core components of sustainable improvement and leadership by taking some of the following actions:

- *Reducing the excesses of standardized testing.* Wales has abolished all external testing of students age fourteen or younger. In late 2004, England planned to allow seven-year-olds to take their tests at a time in the year when they are individually ready, in a context in which more weight is given to teacher-developed assessments, because the government's own research found that these practices lead to stronger improvements in student achievement.[31] For many years, the province of Manitoba in Canada has emphasized teacher-designed assessments.[32]

- *Becoming less punitive toward school underperformance.* For instance, Ontario, Canada, maintains clear and firm expectations that struggling schools will be turned around, but within a system of strong support and schools' voluntary acceptance of assistance rather than intrusive inspection and draconian sanctions.

- *Restoring educational diversity.* England has scaled back its national curriculum by over 30 percent of its original scope. Ontario, alongside its push for higher standards in literacy, is providing protected time for the arts. Finland, which tops most of the Organization for Economic Cooperation and Development's student achievement tables, attributes much of its success to employing highly qualified teachers (many with master's degrees) and providing a general curriculum outline that gives them a great deal of professional discretion, allowing them to adjust what they teach and how they teach it to the students, whom they know best.[33] The United Kingdom's Specialist Schools Trust is stimulating almost all English secondary schools to take on one of eleven specialist identities as a focus of their improvement efforts.[34]

- *Working harder to attract and retain high-quality teachers during a period of great demographic turnover in the profession.* Teachers Matter, the influential report of the Organization for Economic Cooperation and Development, draws attention to and advocates for a wide range of emerging policy strategies that provide greater recognition, respect, and rewards as well as learning support for teachers in twenty-two countries.[35] These strategies include developing and applying clear systems of *professional standards*; supporting strong school-based *professional learning communities* in which teachers improve together by examining data and evidence about successful practice; and creating *professional networks* in which schools learn from and support one another in their efforts to improve. Worldwide, more and more educational systems are starting to move from an age of standardization to an age of diversity and sustainability, raising new challenges for leadership at all levels as they do so.

• *Putting a premium on leadership in visible initiatives that support and give status to leadership and to all leaders in education throughout their careers.* For example, England has established the National College for School Leadership, which orchestrates all the leadership training and development throughout that nation. In the United States, the Wallace Foundation has made significant efforts to develop educational leaders and leadership.

Sustainable School Leadership

The term *sustainability* was first coined in the environmental field by Lester Brown, founder of the Worldwatch Institute, in the early 1980s. He defined a sustainable society as one that is able to satisfy its needs without diminishing the opportunities of future generations to meet theirs.[36] The key and most widely used definition of the slightly different but closely related idea of *sustainable development* appears in the Brundtland Report of the World Commission on Environment and Development in 1987: "Humankind has the ability to achieve sustainable development—to meet the needs of the present without compromising the ability of future generations to meet their own needs."[37] Agenda 21 from the United Nations Conference on Environment and Development in Rio de Janeiro in 1992 made repeated use of the idea of sustainable development, and the United Nations summit in Johannesburg in 2002 converted this agenda into a set of more practical goals.[38]

Despite many misconceptions about the concept of sustainability,[39] it is basically concerned with developing and preserving what matters, spreads, and lasts in ways that create positive connections and development among people and do no harm to others in the present or in the future.[40] In education, Michael Fullan defines educational sustainability as "the capacity of a system to engage in the complexities of continuous improvement consistent with deep values of human purpose."[41] Our own definition builds on the one we used when we started this work some years ago:

> Sustainable educational leadership and improvement preserves and develops deep learning for all that spreads and lasts, in ways that do no harm to and indeed create positive benefit for others around us, now and in the future.[42]

Unlike systems thinking or complexity theory, the idea of sustainability is inherently moral. One of us has a distant relative who used to be a bank robber. Over a period of months, he robbed banks within his own community, in sequence. After a few robberies, the police were waiting for him. Following a couple of years in jail, he returned to his community and also to robbing the banks where he had begun his criminal career—not a particularly smart move. By comparison, in the movie *The Planman*, a successful but disillusioned middle-aged Scottish lawyer, played by Robbie Coltrane, uses a book called *The Art of Systems Thinking* to plan the perfect bank robbery. Sitting with his criminal accomplice high in the stands of a Glasgow soccer stadium, he expounds the benefits of possessing a big-picture or helicopter view of the game—the same type of perspective that will create the perfect bank raid. The robbers in these two examples differ greatly in their capacity for using systems thinking, but at the end of the day, they are both still robbers! Advanced systems thinking is as useful in tobacco industries as it is in pollution control systems and as valuable for a totalitarian government as for a truly democratic one. It has no inherent moral purpose. In contrast, sustainability in its very substance addresses the value and interdependence of all life as both a means and an end. It is, by definition, a moral concept and a moral practice.

Our book draws directly on the corporate and environmental literatures of sustainability and sustainable development as well as on our detailed research, which examines educational change over long periods of time, to provide concrete strategies for realizing seven principles of sustainability in leadership and change in schools and school systems.[43]

Seven Principles of Sustainability

The seven principles of sustainability in educational change and leadership are depth, length, breadth, justice, diversity, resourcefulness, and conservation.

1. Depth

Sustainable leadership matters. We must preserve, protect, and promote in education what is itself sustaining as an enrichment of life: the fundamental moral purpose of deep and broad learning (rather than superficially tested and narrowly defined achievement) for all in commitments to and relationships of abiding care for others. The first principle of sustainable leadership is leadership for learning and leadership for caring for and among others.

2. Length

Sustainable leadership lasts. It preserves and advances the most valuable aspects of life over time, year upon year, from one leader to the next. As Collins and Porras remind us, "All leaders, no matter how charismatic or visionary, eventually die."[44] The challenges of leadership succession, of leading across and beyond individual leaders over time are at the heart of sustainable leadership and educational change.

3. Breadth

Sustainable leadership spreads. It sustains as well as depends on the leadership of others. In a complex world, no one leader, institution, or nation can or should control everything. Sustainable leadership is distributed leadership, which is both an accurate description of how much leadership is already exercised across a classroom, school, or school system and an ambition that encompasses what leadership can, more deliberately, become.

4. Justice

Sustainable leadership does no harm to and actively improves the surrounding environment. It does not raid the best resources of outstanding students and teachers from neighboring institutions. It does not prosper at other schools' expense. It does no harm to and actively finds ways to share knowledge and resources with neighboring schools and the local community. Sustainable leadership is not self-centered; it is socially just.

5. Diversity

Sustainable leadership promotes cohesive diversity. Strong ecosystems are biologically diverse. Strong organizations, too, promote diversity and avoid standardization. In sustainable communities, *alignment* is an ugly word. Alignment perpetuates hierarchical dependency in linear systems that are brittle and that break. Sustainable leadership, in contrast, fosters and learns from diversity in teaching and learning and moves things forward by creating cohesion and networking among its richly varied components.

6. Resourcefulness

Sustainable leadership develops and does not deplete material and human resources. Sustainable leadership recognizes and rewards the organization's leadership talent earlier rather than later in their career. It takes care of its leaders by making sure that they take care of themselves. It renews people's energy. It does not drain its leaders dry through innovation overload or unrealistic time lines for change. Sustainable leadership is prudent and resourceful leadership that wastes neither its money nor its people.

7. Conservation

Sustainable leadership honors and learns from the best of the past to create an even better future. Amid the chaos of change, sustainable leadership is steadfast about preserving and renewing its long-standing purposes. Most change theory and change practice has only a forward arrow; it is change without a past or a memory. Sustainable leadership revisits and revives organizational memories and honors the wisdom of memory bearers as a way to learn from, preserve, and then move beyond the best of the past.

A commitment to sustainable leadership must move us beyond the micromanagement of standardization, the crisis management of repetitive change syndrome, and the all-consuming obsession with higher and higher performance standards at any cost into a world where we can bring about authentic improvement and achievement for all children that matters, spreads, and lasts. Sustainable leadership acts urgently, learns from the past and from diversity, is resilient under pressure, waits patiently for results, and does not burn people out. Sustainable leadership is just and moral leadership that benefits all of us, now and in the future. Sustainability works in sound environmental management and in the best business practices; it's time to put it to work in education as well.

Studying Sustainability

Before we move on to the seven principles in detail, it's important to say a few words about the evidence base of our work. For us, sustainability isn't just a fashionable buzzword. If sustainability is just a way to "spin" randomly assorted ideas, it only adds to the problem of unsustainability. So in every chapter, our analysis is rooted in a solid understanding and exposition of the environmental and corporate literature, where the theory, practice, and evidence base of sustainability is to be found. We want educators to use the words *sustain, sustaining,* and *sustainable* not as glib synonyms for *maintain, maintaining,* and *maintainable* but with real depth and purpose, grasping what they truly mean. The origins and underpinnings of the idea of sustainability really matter; they give it its moral substance, conceptual precision, and strategic power.

Our understanding of sustainability comes from fifteen years of work together in which, with other colleagues, we have set out to investigate educational change over long periods of time and to work in partnership with schools and districts to bring about lasting improvement over periods of at least five years. We draw in particular on a large-scale study, funded by the Spencer Foundation in the United States, of educational change over three decades in eight high schools in New York State and Ontario, Canada, as seen through the eyes of teachers and leaders who worked there in the 1970s, 1980s, and 1990s. Codirected with Ivor Goodson and involving a team of professors and former graduate students from the University of Rochester and the University of Toronto, this study draws on more than 250 detailed interviews with present and past teachers and leaders in these varied schools, as well as on observational information and extensive archival and demographic evidence of how the schools have or have not changed over time.

Instead of providing a systematic discussion of our research findings, this book draws on evidence and examples from the schools and districts in our studies to present analysis, insight, and some practical guidance for practitioners and policymakers who live and work each day on the edge of sustainability, as well for researchers who want to delve more fully into it. For readers who want to engage with this research more deeply, a list of books, reports, and peer-reviewed articles documenting the design, methodology, and results is in the Research Sources section at the end of this book.

We have used pseudonyms for all the schools, districts, and individuals covered in our research and for one or two other sensitive examples. The original names have been retained for Noumea Primary School in Australia and its former principal, Jenny Lewis, as well as for Knowsley Education Authority in England and its former director, Steve Munby.

Conclusion

Sustainable educational change and leadership is three-dimensional—it has depth, breadth, and length. Our next three chapters set out and illustrate the fundamental three-dimensional character of sustainability and elaborate on four further principles that fill out the full meaning of sustainability and its challenges for leadership in schools. Our closing chapter addresses the essential interconnectedness of all seven principles and the necessity of treating them like a meal, not a menu. It also sets out some key action principles for bringing sustainability to life and making it real in three vital spheres of sustainable leadership: schools, localities, and nations or states.

1

Depth

Learning and Integrity

Seek truth, create, and live up to the title of teacher.
                    Motto of East China Normal University, Shanghai

❖ PRINCIPLE 1

Sustainable leadership matters. It preserves, protects, and promotes deep and broad learning for all in relationships of care for others.

A Sense of Purpose

For Winston Churchill, it was the defeat of Hitler and Nazi Germany; for Emmeline Pankhurst and Susan B. Anthony, it was votes for women; for Nelson Mandela, it was ending apartheid in South Africa; and for Martin Luther King, Jr., it was civil rights for all. Throughout history, leaders who made worthwhile and lasting contributions to society have been passionately, persistently, and courageously committed to compelling ideals and just causes that were meaningful in their time.

Sustainable leadership, like sustainable improvement, begins with a strong and unswerving sense of moral purpose. The core meaning of *sustain* is "to hold up; bear the weight of; be able to bear (strain, suffering, and the like) without collapse." Inner conviction, unshakable faith, and a driving, hopeful sense of purpose that stretches far beyond the self—these are the inalienable elements of moral character that truly sustain people during times of over-whelming difficulty and almost unbearable suffering. Reflecting on his long imprisonment on Robben Island, where he was deprived of company, exercise, and even food during long periods of solitary confinement, Nelson Mandela put it like this: "The human body has an enormous capacity for adjusting to trying circumstances. I have found that one can bear the unbearable if one can keep one's spirits strong even when one's body is being tested. Strong convic-tions are the secret of surviving deprivation: your spirit can be full even when your stomach is empty."[1]

In the corporate world, a strong and shared sense of purpose also sustains businesses, holds them together, and enables them to per-sist even in the face of apparently insurmountable odds. The most long-lasting and successful businesses are driven and defined by enduring purposes and timeless values, not quarterly profits.[2] In *Built to Last*, Collins and Porras reported that when they studied compa-nies that had maintained profitability over long periods of time, they "saw a core ideology that transcended pure economic consid-erations."[3] Jackson and Nelson's research in *Profits with Principles* confirms this finding: Explicitly linking profits with principles is a prerequisite for helping to restore trust and confidence while deliv-ering long-term value to shareholders."[4]

Developing and renewing a compelling sense of purpose is cen-tral to sustainable leadership. Yet a disturbing finding of Collins and Porras's foundational study of companies that are built to last was that the nature of that purpose didn't always matter! "The critical issue is not whether a company has the "right" core ideology or a "likable" core ideology but whether it *has* a core ideology—likable or not—that gives guidance and inspiration to people inside that company."[5] It makes no difference whether you produce titanium parts that give people new knees or tobacco products that corrupt their lungs; any purpose that motivates people internally seems to be enough to keep companies going. However, in the aftermath of widespread corporate scandals, more businesses are now pushing for a sense of purpose that is bigger and better than this, a moral purpose that is embedded in the essence of their products and that extends into the community and society beyond.

A growing number of companies are addressing the deeper purposes of sustainable corporate development by attending to the human value of what they produce, not just how they produce it. Product integrity matters; it is a qualifying criterion for companies included in responsible corporate development investment portfolios, for example.[6]

Gary Erickson is the founder and creator of the Clif Bar, a widely sold energy bar that began in his mother's kitchen and now has annual sales of $40 million. In *Raising the Bar: Integrity and Passion in Life and Business*, Erickson describes his quest to create a nutritious bar that would be more tasty and satisfying than existing alternatives, to defend and renew his private company in the face of tempting and lucrative buyout offers, and to extend his vision of sustainability in his personal life to sustainability in his business.

Clif Bar's philosophy of sustainability has five interconnected elements: "sustaining our brands, our company, our people, our community and our planet."[7] For Erickson, taking sustainability seriously means that "we want to be environmentally responsible and continually assess our business's impact on the environment . . . to minimize our ecological footprint on the earth."[8] Sustainability at Clif Bar also means wanting "to create and sustain a business where people can experience life, not just where they go to make a living."[9]

At the heart of Clif Bar's philosophy of sustainability is *product integrity*. Shareholder value isn't about getting the biggest possible quarterly returns. It is about "believing in the integrity of our products" and making a "tasty, healthy product." "That is our return, not increasing the profit margin at the expense of the ingredients."[10]

This purpose, embedded in the bar he named after his father, came from Erickson's own passions: his connection to and caring about the natural environment and the joys of baking in his mother's kitchen. Disappointed and disgusted by the tasteless, highly processed, and standardized ingredients of the only energy bar then available for his long cycle rides, Erickson set about creating a product whose brand vision would ultimately become "sustaining people in motion."[11]

Erickson discusses how the vision permeates the company: "At Clif Bar Inc., we delight in creating and savoring wholesome, delicious food. As bakers by trade and gourmet cooks on the side, we're energized by the joy people experience when they savor great food made with care. As athletes, we're committed to creating foods that sustain, nourish and support people through any endeavor. As concerned individuals, we want our business to contribute to a healthier, more sustainable planet. These ideals inspire and motivate our work."[12]

Product integrity is the core of sustainability. Sustenance is nourishment. And if our souls sustain our bodies, then learning sustains our souls. Nelson Mandela and his fellow political prisoners—the future leaders of South Africa—understood this very well in their darkest days on Robben Island when they agitated for the right to study, stole forbidden newspaper fragments from the sandwich wrappings discarded by their jailers, and conducted secret classes among the urine and feces of the Africans' toilets, where the white guards were too repelled to tread.[13]

If the moral purpose of what we produce is important for corporate sustainability, it is even more important in education and public life. Schools, school systems, and educational change advocates cannot be indifferent to or evasive about just what the moral purpose of education should be. From the standpoint of sustainability, the heart of that purpose ought to be learning—something that is itself sustaining—and not just any learning, but learning that matters, spreads, and lasts a lifetime.

Like an excellent meal, deep, sustaining learning requires wholesome ingredients, a rich and varied menu, caring preparation, and pleasing presentation. The primary responsibility of all educational leaders is to sustain this kind of learning. It is this, not delivering the curriculum, implementing the government's or district's mandates, or giving a gloss to how the institution appears, that is at the center of sustainable leadership.

Not anything or everything needs sustaining or maintaining. There is no point in sustaining learning that is trivial or that disappears once it has been tested. Sustainable leadership fully understands the nature and process of student learning, engages directly and regularly with learning and teaching in classrooms, and promotes learning among other adults in order to find continuing ways to improve and expand the learning of students.[14]

Sustainable leadership doesn't equivocate. It puts learning at the center of everything leaders do. Students' learning comes first, then everyone else's in support of it.[15] Michael Knapp and his associates explain that leadership for learning means "creating powerful, equitable learning opportunities for students, professionals and the system," in which leaders "persistently and publicly focus . . . their own attention and that of others on learning and teaching."[16] To this end, Knapp and his colleagues argue, educational leaders who practice sustainable leadership establish a focus on learning by doing the following:

- Making it central to their own work
- Consistently communicating that student learning is a shared mission of students, teachers, administrators, and the community
- Articulating core values that support a focus on powerful, equitable learning
- Paying public attention to teaching[17]

It is easy to advocate for more instructional leadership,[18] to insist that all educational leaders should become leaders of learning.[19] It is harder to make leadership for learning a practical reality. And it is hardest of all to do this in policy and reform climates that repeatedly pull the plug on leaders' efforts to achieve depth and breadth of learning in their systems and their schools. In his review of the present state of educational administration, Joe Murphy concludes that "we have responded to the challenges of purpose and development largely by ignoring them, or at least failing to grapple with them thoughtfully."[20] The courage to be a leader of learning is most called for in uncongenial conditions dominated by school rankings, test scores, and short-term achievement targets. Sustainable leadership demands firm convictions about and unwavering commitments to enhancing deep and broad learning, not merely tested achievement, for *all* students.

In 2001, the Canadian province of Ontario introduced a high-stakes literacy test in tenth grade for virtually all students, who were required to pass in order to graduate. High stakes, high pressure!

Ivor Megson was the new principal at Talisman Park Secondary School. Recently promoted from assistant principal at Talisman Park, Megson was dedicated to his work as a leader but didn't like to rock the boat too much. Most of his staff had

been at the school for a long time. They liked being innovative in their own academic subjects but were skeptical and
often cynical about larger-scale reform agendas. A coffee circle of embittered staff met every morning before school to
complain about the government's almost daily initiatives and
announcements. Like many principals, Megson saw it as his
responsibility to buffer his staff from the deluge of reforms that
descended on the school. This, he felt, was the best way he
could help them.

With his staff, Megson therefore figured out the most minimal and least disruptive school response to the tenth-grade
test, one that would produce the best results with the least
amount of effort. Quickly, he and his staff began identifying a
group of students who, pretests indicated, would fall just below
the passing mark. The school's English department then
coached these students intensively on literacy skills, so they
would perform acceptably when the real test came around.
From the staff's point of view, Megson's approach was appealing because most teachers could remain uninvolved in the literacy test.

Technically, the strategy worked; the school's results improved in comparison with the previous year. But teachers'
energies are finite, and as staff concentrated on the students
near the cutoff point, the ones who really needed help with
literacy, who had little chance of passing, were cast by the
wayside. In Talisman Park, authentic literacy and learning for
all, especially for the most needy, were sacrificed for short-term
results and the appearance of improvement.

Charmaine Watson was the principal of Wayvern High
School, just down the road from Talisman Park. Wayvern was
a culturally and ethnically diverse school and had a high number of students for whom English was a second language.

Wayvern had a lot to lose on the literacy test. Yet Watson's school made literacy, not passing the literacy test, one of their key improvement goals. Watson engaged all of her staff in inquiry about how to improve literacy skills to benefit all students in the long term instead of focusing on how to manipulate the short-term scores on the test. Working with large staff teams, across disciplines and with training support through workshops, Watson's school undertook an audit of existing literacy practices in classrooms, researched effective literacy strategies that might be helpful, and undertook a gap analysis to see what improvements were necessary. Teachers shared their literacy strategies across subjects, then dedicated a whole month to a high-profile focus on learning literacy skills in the school and with the community. They also continued a successful literacy initiative they had already implemented, in which everyone in the school read together for fifteen minutes a day. Watson harnessed her staff's learning in support of student learning.

The immediate results were not spectacular (as is usual with more sustainable change), but the staff and parents were confident that long-term improvement mattered most. Wayvern teachers were convinced that in future years, scores would increase and that they would reflect genuine learning and achievement rather than cynical manipulation of the testing process. The next year, Wayvern scored above the district mean, and in the third year, it was the second highest literacy performer among the twenty-two high schools in the district, far above leafy, suburban Talisman Park, which had gone for the quick fix.

One reform, two principals, two schools, different outcomes! Especially in the most adverse circumstances, the principals who are leaders of learning make the most lasting and inclusive improvements for students in their schools.

In the face of test-driven performance demands, Charmaine Watson and her colleagues refused to cave in, to trade their core values for unquestioning compliance, or to abandon authentic achievement for cynical attempts to boost test score gains. By building professional collaboration, creating opportunities for teacher leadership, and providing forums for teacher dialogue, Watson ensured that teachers never lost sight of their purpose of improving learning for all students. All teachers, not just those in the English Department, took responsibility for being teachers of literacy. Rather than treating the literacy test as a problem to be finessed with the least amount of upset for teachers, the principal and her staff used it as a catalyst to develop deep and sustainable learning for everyone, students and adults alike.

Sustainable leadership doesn't improve standards by thinking first about how to improve test scores. The price of overemphasizing the tested basics has become very evident in the United States, where social studies are increasingly being eclipsed by reading and mathematics.[21] Schools and systems that deal with the pressure to make annual literacy test gains (to meet, for example, the adequate yearly progress requirements of the United States' No Child Left Behind legislation or the yearly targets set by the United Kingdom's National Literacy and Numeracy Strategy) by pretesting students and then applying intensive coaching to a percentile of students that fall just below the passing mark are not creating sustainable improvement that matters. They are concentrating calculatively on the measured results instead of on the learning the results are supposed to measure. They are valuing what they measure, not measuring what they value. Sustainable leadership, however, improves literacy scores by focusing first on the deep need for literacy skills for all students, even those with little chance of getting above the passing mark in the first year.

For too long, a number of government reform strategies have put the cart before the horse, expending effort on testing, then achievement and achievement gaps, and leaving learning till last or omitting it altogether. This has led governments and educa-

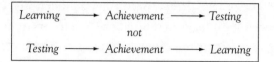

Figure 1.1. Standards and Sustainability

tional leaders to neglect or gloss over what exactly students are achieving. A more sustainable strategy is to focus on learning first, then achievement, then testing, so we never lose sight of the learning that truly matters as we strive to increase students' achievement in it (Figure 1.1.).

Sometimes the biggest impediment to understanding learning is not people's fixation with testing but their excitement about teaching. After spending time sitting in the classrooms of underperforming schools, Harvard professor Richard Elmore discovered that teachers are sometimes so excited about and committed to their teaching they don't really notice how or whether their students are learning. Teachers, he says, actually teach too hard! They give themselves no time or opportunity to step back, watch, and then respond to how their students are actually learning.[22]

The remainder of this chapter therefore looks more closely at two essential elements of leadership for learning:

- *Deep and broad learning* that satisfies our greater hunger for human growth and betterment

- *Slow knowing* that curbs our tendencies toward being fast school nations

Deep and Broad Learning

Learning is a preparation for life and also a part of life. The meaning of learning is embedded in the meaning of life. British management guru Charles Handy explains the connection between the two through the concepts of greater and lesser hunger. In Africa, he explains, "they say there are two hungers, the lesser hunger and the greater hunger. The lesser hunger is for the things that sustain life, the goods and services, and the money to pay for them, which we all need."[23] In contrast, "the greater hunger is the answer to the question 'why?' for some understanding of what life is for."[24] Deep and broad learning addresses our greater hunger. It engages the quest to know, to understand, to communicate, and to leave the world a better place. Deep and broad learning for all students—and for all the adults who work with them—is therefore learning for meaning, learning for understanding, learning for life. It is learning that engages students in every sense—intellectually, socially, emotionally, and spiritually.

These ideas about the basic purposes of learning have ancient roots. Five centuries before Christ, Confucius said, "Learning without thought is labor lost; thought without learning is perilous."[25] More than two millennia later, John Dewey connected education to the deep purposes of human renewal and sustainability: "The most notable distinction between living and inanimate things is that the former maintain themselves by renewal. . . . It is the very nature of life to strive to continue in being. Since this continuance can be secured only by constant renewal, life is a self-renewing process. What nutrition and reproduction are to physiological life, education is to social life."[26] For Dewey, the essence of education for renewal was learning for meaning and understanding—the ability "to grasp the meaning of a thing, an event or situation . . . in its relations to other things; to note how it operates or functions, what consequences follow from it; what causes it, what uses it can be put to."[27] Modern leadership scholars like Linda Lambert explain that "leadership is about learning together, and constructing meaning and knowledge collaboratively. It involves opportunities to surface and mediate perceptions, values, beliefs, information and assumptions through continuing conversations; to inquire about and generate ideas together; to seek to reflect upon and make sense of work in light of shared beliefs and new information; and to create actions that come out of these new understandings. Such is the core of leadership."[28]

In their work on leading learning, Bob Lingard and his colleagues, along with Queensland's department of education in Australia, address the characteristics of deep and broad learning in terms of what they call *productive pedagogies*. These are

- Intellectually *demanding*

- *Connected* to students' prior knowledge and to the world beyond them

- Provided within a *supportive* environment and learning process

- Prepared so as to engage students and their learning with cultural *differences*[29]

These principles are embedded in what Queensland policymakers call the *New Basics*, which, in addition to the old basics, they believe, are essential for students in new times. The New Basics comprise life pathways and social futures; multiliteracies (for example, print-based, oral, and visual literacy) and communications media; active citizenship; and environments and technologies.[30] This, the policymakers say, is not a "simplistic, paint-by-numbers system, and it doesn't buy into the argument that lots of tests will solve the complex problems we face."[31]

Despite or perhaps because of the galloping consumption that makes us into nations of shoppers and accumulators of gadgets, people still search for the greater hunger—"the answer to the question 'why' for some understanding of what life is for."[32] There is more to living than being a good consumer and producer, and there is more to education than the lesser hunger and human capital.

On December 26, 2004, one of our daughters was bathing on a beach in Thailand, alongside thousands of others seeking a brief respite from the cold northern winter. Inexplicably, the tide suddenly began to recede, like water draining from a bathtub. Exiting the ocean, she thought to glance over her shoulder for just a second. A terrifying sight met her eyes. Rushing toward her was a gigantic wave—part of the tsunami that devastated coastal communities across southern Asia. Taking no time to gather clothes or other belongings and begging others to flee, she sprinted for her life, escaping to higher ground with only seconds to spare.

Many others were much less fortunate. Parents, partners, children, and babies were swept to their death. Hundreds of thousands of poor fishermen and villagers across the region, whose flimsy homes afforded little protection, suffered similar tragic fates. Then, in the depths of despair, in the midst of this natural catastrophe and human tragedy, something remarkable happened. As news of the disaster spread and its appalling scale became apparent, and when governments at first appeared agonizingly slow to respond, there was a spontaneous eruption of human giving. The day after Christmas Day—the annual zenith of Western consumerism—with their bellies full and their presents strewn throughout their homes, people who had more than enough gave their money, their prayers, and their time to those who had lost everything. Public donations rapidly outstripped government contributions. Children handed over their weekly allowances. Homeless people went into banks and emptied their pockets. In less than a week, Britons alone raised 35 million pounds—one pound for every person in the country.[33]

Although capitalism may consume us and consumerism may distract us, moments like these remind us of the existence and the need for generosity of human spirit, for thinking about how we live together, for considering not just how we make a living but also how we live our lives.[34] Deep and broad learning that extends beyond the coverage of content, the basics of literacy, or the driving need for human capital is an essential part of the bigger and more hopeful narrative of what schools should do.

Just as the four food groups make up a broad and balanced nutritious diet, a sustaining program of learning must also address our greater as well as our lesser hunger. Toward the close of the twentieth century, the United Nations Educational, Scientific, and Cultural Organization (UNESCO), which promotes and supports sustainable development initiatives across the globe, produced a timeless and visionary document about the purposes of learning in a socially divided and conflict-ridden world. In *Learning: The Treasure Within*, the authors state, "Traditional responses to the demand for education that are essentially quantitative and knowledge-based are no longer appropriate. It is not enough to supply each child with a store of knowledge to be drawn on from then on. Each individual must be equipped to seize learning opportunities throughout life, both to broaden her and his knowledge, skills and attitudes, and to adapt to a changing, complex and interdependent world."[35]

The UNESCO commission proposed "four fundamental types of learning which, throughout a person's life, will be the pillars of knowledge":[36]

• *Learning to know* includes the acquisition of a broad general knowledge; intellectual curiosity; the instruments of understanding; independence of judgment; and the impetus and foundation for continuing to learn throughout life. In addition, learning to know "presupposes learning to learn, calling upon the power of concentration, memory and thought."[37]

• *Learning to do* involves the competence to put what one has learned into practice (even when it is unclear how future work will evolve), to deal with many situations, and to act creatively in and on one's environment. It includes teamwork, initiative, readiness to take risks, and the ability to process information and communicate with others and also to manage and resolve conflicts. Learning to do requires students to apply their learning within and beyond content areas. It calls for teaching, learning, and assessment that helps students understand the structures of academic disciplines, so they can apply them effectively in mathematics, science, the arts, and beyond.

• *Learning to be* addresses who we are and how we are with people. It incorporates our moral character, ethical judgment, and sense of personal responsibility, and it attends to all aspects of the self: mind and body, emotion and intellect, aesthetic sensitivity and spiritual values. People who have learned to be can understand themselves and their world and can solve their own problems. Learning to be means giving people the freedom of thought, judgment, feeling, and imagination they need in order to develop their talents and take control of their lives as much as possible.[38] In workshops that we conduct with educators, we often ask participants to give advice that will last a lifetime to "the child they used to be." People don't advise their younger selves to have better plans, produce or perform to higher standards, study more subjects, or spend more time at their desk. Instead, the most common answers include advice like "slow down," "live life to the fullest," "love God and love thy neighbor," "seize every opportunity," "go for it," "live each day like it is your last," and "feel good about yourself." What these adults, who are usually school leaders, find most important in their own lives is learning to be.

• *Learning to live together* calls on students and others to develop understanding of, respect for, and engagement with other people's cultures and spiritual values. It calls for empathy for others' points of view, understanding of diversity and similarities among people, appreciation of interdependence, and the ability to engage in dialogue and debate in order to improve relationships, cooperate with others, and reduce violence and conflict. Learning to live together is an essential element of deep and broad learning in an increasingly multicultural world where millions of families and their children have been mired in decades or even centuries of racial hatred, religious bigotry, or totalitarian control.

To these four pillars, we would add a fifth: learning to live sustainably.

• *Learning to live sustainably* is about learning to respect and protect the earth that gives us life; to work with diverse others to secure the long-term benefits of economic and ecological life in all communities; to adopt behaviors and practices that minimize our ecological footprint on the world around us without depriving us of opportunities for development and fulfillment; and to coexist and cooperate with nature and natural design, whenever possible, rather than always seeking to conquer and control them.[39] This emphasis, which UNESCO terms *education for sustainable development,* is

> a new vision of education, a vision that helps people of all ages better understand the world in which they live, addressing the complexity and interconnectedness of problems such as poverty, wasteful consumption, environmental degradation, urban decay, population growth, health, conflict and the violation of human rights that threaten our future. This vision of education emphasizes a holistic, interdisciplinary approach to developing the knowledge and skills needed for a sustainable future as well as changes in values, behavior and lifestyles. This requires us to reorient education systems, policies and practices in order to empower everyone, young and old, to make decisions and act in culturally appropriate and

locally relevant ways to redress the problems that threaten our common future.[40]

Because we live on an environmentally imperiled planet for which all of us have responsibility, this fifth pillar is as basic to learning today as are literacy and mathematics. If we cannot learn to live sustainably, we run the serious risk that we, as a species, may not be able to learn—or live—at all.

Learning to be, learning to live together, and learning to live sustainably are emotional, moral, and spiritual challenges, not merely cognitive and intellectual ones. All teaching and learning are emotional practices—in a good or a bad way, by intent or neglect.[41] Strong relationships with and emotional engagement among students provide essential prerequisites for civic responsibility, tolerance, and sustainability. When learners are diverse and demanding, caring means being responsive to students' varied cultures; inclusive of their own ideas when selecting curriculum content, defining learning targets, or sharing assessment criteria; and ready to involve their families and communities in lifting learning to higher levels. If learning isn't *personalized*—that is, customized to the meanings, prior knowledge, and life circumstances of each student experiencing it—then many students, especially the most disadvantaged, will scarcely learn at all.[42] The Bill and Melinda Gates Foundation, in its visionary initiative to transform high school behemoths into smaller learning communities, captures this spirit of deeper and broader learning, defining its quest as creating learning that is about rigor, relevance, and relationships.[43] It does not mean rigor first, then relevance, and relationships later, as an afterthought, but all three elements together.

These five pillars—learning to know, learning to do, learning to be, learning to live together, and learning to live sustainably—represent deep and broad learning goals for schools and suggest criteria by which they should be held accountable. Yet schools mainly emphasize only the first two—learning to know and learning to do.

Almost a half century ago, R. E. Callahan argued that public education was dominated by a business-driven cult of efficiency.[44] More recently, Canadian writer Janet Stein observed that "when we define efficiency as an end, divorced from its larger purpose, it becomes nothing less than a cult."[45] Elliott Eisner points out that efficiency is "largely a virtue for the tasks we don't like to do; few of us like to eat a great meal efficiently or to participate in a wonderful conversation efficiently, or indeed to make love efficiently. What we enjoy the most we linger over. A school system designed with an overriding commitment to efficiency may produce outcomes that have little enduring quality."[46]

It is incomprehensible, for example, why many parts of Canada should be putting the majority of reform energy and resources into improving the old basics of literacy, when Canada is already the world's second highest performer in literacy achievement at age fifteen and needs to be challenged more ambitiously to develop the new basics that will make it less dependent on the boom and bust economy of national resources and more able to thrive in a creative and culturally diverse knowledge economy in which its people will always be able to invent themselves out of trouble.[47] This strategy—importing plausible solutions from overseas for problems that one's own country mainly doesn't have—is a familiar one in policy.

Most of the public measures of what matters in schools—good test scores, inspection reports, short-term achievement results, over-subscribed schools, customer satisfaction, adequate yearly progress—answer the demands of a performance culture of learning to know and learning to do (at least the most trivial interpretations of it) rather than the larger questions of whether students are learning in a deeper and broader sense that has lasting relevance for their present and future lives. The modern-day equivalent of efficiency is this emphasis on cultures of measurable performance.[48]

Leaders of learning have to be much more than orchestrators of other people's performances. Being a leader of learning means more than poring over and perseverating on achievement results and finding quick ways to boost the figures or narrow the gaps. Rather, developing and preserving a sustaining product that matters means that leaders must

- *Be passionate advocates for and defenders of deep and broad learning* for all students with the public and among fellow professionals, against political and bureaucratic obsessions with prescribed basics, target-driven achievements, and school performance rankings

- *Commit to improving the old basics of literacy and math but not focusing on them to the exclusion of everything else, while also embracing the new basics* of creativity; communication in written, oral, and visual modes; engagement with new technologies; understanding and being able to work with social and cultural differences; and being aware of as well as committed to environmental sustainability

- *Put learning before testing* so that rising test scores reflect real improvements in authentic and productive learning, instead of narrowing the learning to get quick gains in testing

- *Make learning the paramount priority* in all leadership activity, so that in decisions about behavior, the budget, or the bus schedule, the first question is always "How will this help and not damage student learning?"

- *Become more knowledgeable about learning,* as is happening among female U.S. school superintendents who are much more likely than their male colleagues to come from instructional backgrounds[49]

- *Make learning transparent* among the educators in a school, through instituting peer-led walk-throughs and observations of classroom practice, reviews of examples of student work among colleagues, peer coaching and mentoring, and processes that allow teachers to study one another's lessons[50]

- *Become omnipresent witnesses to learning* by being visible in classrooms and by monitoring (but not micro-managing) teachers' curriculum plans and responses to student work[51]

- *Demonstrate evidence-informed leadership by promoting active inquiry into learning* through critical reviews of research on best learning practices in general and investigations of learning strategies and achievement results in teachers' own schools and classrooms in particular[52]

- *Promote assessment for learning*, so that diagnostic assessment stimulates discussion about and provides usable feedback on students' learning, instead of per-petuating *assessment of learning* that merely passes judgment on learning after it is over and done with[53]

- *Engage students in discussions and decisions about their own learning*, recognizing that students are often highly knowledgeable and articulate about how they learn best[54]

- *Involve parents more in their children's learning* by encour-aging shared homework assignments, interactive report cards, and three-way parent-teacher-student meetings, for example[55]

- *Model deep and broad adult learning* in their own leader-ship development and in the kinds of staff develop-ment they provide for others, so that deep engagement with educational change is never obstructed or obscured by the pressures for rapid implementation

of or in-service training on government or system
priorities

- *Create the emotional conditions for learning* by developing
  smaller schools or smaller learning communities within
  existing ones; by allowing teachers to migrate from one
  grade to the next in order to remain with the same
  group of students; by personalizing learning for every
  student through the provision of individual mentoring
  and other measures; and by actively cultivating greater
  emotional literacy among students and staff so that
  they can work more effectively with those around
  them[56]

Slow Knowing

Still waters run deep. Deep learning is rarely rapid or rushed. Have
you ever struggled to remember the name of a person or a book,
only to find that it comes to you much later, when you are thinking
about something else? Can you recall spending hours trying to solve
a complex problem, only to discover that the solution emerged easily after you had slept on it? Do creative and innovative ideas ever
come to you completely out of the blue? These are all examples of
what psychologist Guy Claxton, in his book *Hare Brain, Tortoise
Mind*, calls *slow knowing*.[57] Slow knowing, he says, is essential for
our learning and our lives. It gives depth to our experience and provokes the greatest breakthroughs in human understanding. Slow
knowing is vital in creative, knowledge-driven organizations and
societies in which profitability depends on how well corporations
and countries can draw on the creativity of all their citizens, not
just a few, to reinvent and reskill themselves as economic circumstances change around them.[58] Slow knowing is also essential in
addressing complex, interconnected problems such as global warming that will require increasing amounts of technical and social

ingenuity to resolve.[59] Yet slow knowing, which sows the seeds of creativity and ingenuity, is increasingly neglected in schools. Claxton makes the case for slow knowing: "The unconscious realms of the human mind will successfully accomplish a number of important tasks *if they are given the time*. They will learn patterns of a degree of subtlety which normal consciousness cannot even see; make sense out of situations that are too complex to analyze; and get to the bottom of certain difficult issues much more successfully than the questing intellect."[60] In other words, slow forms of knowing

- Are tolerant of the faint, fleeting, marginal and ambiguous
- Like to dwell on details that do not fit or immediately make sense
- Are relaxed, leisurely and playful
- Are willing to explore without knowing what they are looking for
- See ignorance and confusion as the ground from which understanding may spring
- Are receptive rather than proactive
- Are happy to relinquish the sense of control over the directions the mind spontaneously takes
- Treat seriously ideas that come out of the blue[61]

Deep learning is often slow learning. This sounds like a strange assertion after decades of associating slow learning with failure, disability, or backwardness. Slow learners are usually seen as people who should be helped, not admired. Yet learning that is not undertaken too fast or in a hurried way is at the heart of our capacity to incubate creative and innovative ideas; it is essential to our ability to walk around and ruminate on complex and difficult problems, then come up with unforeseen solutions; it is indispensable to a full appreciation of music, poetry, and the arts; and it is integral to learning and being able to apply new practices until we become confident and competent in their use. Drawing on Claxton's ideas, Michael Fullan argues that slow knowing enables us to "respect the complexities of situations that do not have easy answers."[62] Questioning assumptions, not rushing to judgment, and understanding emotionally and intuitively as well as rationally and deliberately— these are the hallmarks of slower knowing.

The call for slower knowing might sound irresponsible in a fast-moving knowledge society that places a premium on quick thinking, creative brainstorming, agile organizations, and people's capacity to think and learn their way quickly out of trouble as the economy or other aspects of the environment change rapidly around them.[63] In *The Rise of the Creative Class and How It Is Transforming Work, Leisure, Community and Everyday Life*, Richard Florida judges that in today's knowledge societies, human creativity is "the ultimate economic resource."[64] In the United States, for example, 50 percent of the national wealth is produced by 30 percent of the population—the nation's creative class.[65] Further prosperity depends on the capacity to extend beyond this 30 percent, Florida argues, to tap the latent creativity of the underclasses and channel it into creative work that adds to the economy instead of draining welfare resources. Singapore stakes its future on turning all its schools into learning organizations, so that despite whatever economic shifts or downturns the nation has to face, its future generations will be able to reskill quickly and learn their way out of trouble.[66]

Creativity and quick thinking are also crucial in other areas of our lives, outside the economy. Whether it is attending to the problems of global warming, the depletion of nonrenewable resources, the accelerating gap between rich and poor, or just the irritations of intrusive cell phones or e-mail spam, the problems we are creating seem to be outrunning our capacity to solve them. Thomas

Homer-Dixon calls this problem the *ingenuity gap*—the mismatch between the increasing complexity of our world and our inability to deal with the fallout from the unpredictability and pace of events. Homer-Dixon explains that "today, a disturbingly large proportion of people in rich countries seem to believe that our technical experts have all the authority and knowledge to deftly manage our ever more complex world. These beliefs and the complacency they produce are often completely unwarranted: in fact we only have superficial control over the complex systems we've made and critically depend upon."[67]

So if we need quick thinking, nimble judgment, and urgent action, won't slow knowing take us completely in the wrong direction? In *Blink*, Malcolm Gladwell illustrates how many of our most important decisions are made in the blink of an eye.[68] The firefighter who knows just when a building is about to collapse, the emergency room doctor whose intuition tells her to operate even though all the test results suggest otherwise, and the teacher who senses just when to intervene with the right question or who can instantly tell when a student is lying each appreciate and rely on the power of intuitive and instantaneous judgment.

But intuition isn't always right. Sometimes people make the wrong call. Gut feelings can be tragically wrong. The difference is what's behind the intuition. Sixth-year Harvard resident and medical writer Atul Gawande shows that effective intuition is based on years of slowly accumulated knowledge, experience, and wisdom that good doctors can draw on and interpret in a second.[69] The highest-performing cystic fibrosis treatment center in the United States, for example, distinguishes itself from other centers not by having more resources, better equipment, more rational approaches to diagnosis, or more stringent evidence-based procedures but by its highly experienced doctors, who use many intuitive judgments in interactions with and diagnoses of particular patients.[70]

So creative thinking is paradoxical. Some of the best creative thinking is actually slow. We have to make space for it. But sometimes, whether among comedy script writers or crisis response teams, creativity has to be fast. Yet being able to act in the moment and think on your feet depends on deep knowledge and understanding, accumulated slowly and carefully over many years. Quick thinking and slow knowing are alter egos, not alternate paths.

Mostly, our schools give us neither quick thinking nor slow knowing. Instead, they provide high doses of content or endless diets of memorization and testing. If we read a poem at home, we do it quietly, personally, reflectively, letting it affect our thoughts and emotions. If we study a poem at school, our teachers demand that we analyze it, pick it to pieces, read it aloud, discuss it with a partner, or write another poem ourselves. We are rushed to perform and produce, not to ruminate and reflect.[71] Learning hasn't really gotten much better; it's just gotten faster.

We live in fast school nations.[72] Grand goals are converted into short-term targets. Three-quarters of England's primary-age children will be up to standard in literacy within three years, it's proclaimed, or the secretary of state for education will resign! (Actually, he was transferred to crime and prisons before his disappointing numbers came up.) Seventy-five percent of twelve-year-olds in Ontario will read at the required level within three years, the province's premier boldly asserts soon after election! American public schools must demonstrate measurable "adequate yearly progress" for all categories of children, every year, all the time—or they will be labeled under-performers! In the age of instant information, parents desperately want to believe that their schools can and will deliver immediate results, and politicians, educational administrators, and school improvers are far too eager to feed their opinion-polled delusions.

So the curriculum is crammed with more content, testing occurs more often, concepts are downloaded to younger age groups, more time is devoted to the tested basics, teachers give students less time to answer questions in class, and questions and curiosity begin to dry up. The result of all this frenetic activity is what distinguished child psychologist David Elkind calls the *hurried child*. Elkind observes that "the factory model of schooling," with its increased emphasis on standardized testing as the sole measure of children's worth and "the progressive downward thrust of the curriculum" to ever-younger age groups is robbing children of their childhood.[73] The shrinking numbers of middle-class parents, who live in constant fear of losing their middle-class status, add to the problem by pushing their children too hard, pressing them into excessive amounts of scheduled activity, and leaving them little time for unstructured play.[74]

When children and their teachers are pushed for ever-improving performance, not only do teachers begin to deny and destroy the real depth of learning, but they are also tempted to do anything at all that will help them meet the short-term requirements of the targets and the tests. Schools and school districts start to treat targets in the same way that companies looking for a quick fix address quarterly returns. They turn into little Enrons of Educational Change. Many engage in creative accounting; a few even cheat.[75]

Don't get us wrong. High expectations for all students, especially the most disadvantaged, are essential. Having ways to monitor and measure progress toward meeting these expectations is vital. People can and sometimes should set targets together as part of a shared commitment, whether among congregation members launching a fundraising campaign for a new church steeple, among teachers and administrators setting achievement targets in a school district, or between a teacher and child agreeing to each do their part in helping the child master long division. Externally imposed targets are also sometimes necessary to make reluctant individuals or institutions comply with new policies—for example, pollution reduction targets for manufacturers.

But imposing short-term achievement targets on schools and students rather than agreeing on targets together raises two fundamental problems. First, when someone else sets targets for rather than with you, it communicates a lack of trust in your willingness to commit to or comply with them. While failure to achieve targets that were agreed on together leads to feelings of disappointment or guilt that can spur us to try even harder next time, failure to achieve unwanted high-stakes targets that were set by others leads to feelings of fear and a preparedness to do anything at all, however cynical or corrupt, to ensure that the targets are met.

In his research on distributed leadership, Jim Spillane has found that schools with highly qualified teachers and effective leadership can use targets and achievement results to push staff to work harder to make real improvements in teaching and learning. Schools in poorer communities, with less qualified teachers and a bigger achievement mountain to climb, however, act out of fear and will adopt any solution, however educationally superficial or morally bankrupt, to improve the scores and get the system off their back.[76]

Second, ambitious short-term achievement targets of three years or less are, for most people, inherently unachievable. These demands fly in the face of everything that is known in the change literature. Better learning requires better teaching. Learning to teach better isn't quick or easy. Our own research has shown that even the very best teachers need time to become aware of new reform requirements, to understand what these requirements mean and interpret their implications for their own practice, to see successful examples of other people putting the reforms into action, to learn from coaches and trainers who can help them develop the new practices themselves, to practice the changes over and over again until they become confident with them, to observe how these changes affect their children, and to be able to measure and monitor the effects on learning.[77]

The only way to turn results around in a shorter time than it takes to go through this process is by faking them. Put an end to the art of teaching, and turn it into a paint-by-numbers profession. Coach and prep the children in test taking. Teach only what is on the test. Abandon everything that isn't tested. Introduce the test clumsily, so the first year's scores will be artificially depressed and improvement will appear to be greater in subsequent years. Put all your efforts into coaching children who are just below the passing mark. Whisper or hint at the answers. Get children to chant out the right responses, long before they even see the questions. Arrange for the worst students to be absent. Transfer out those who will spoil the scores. Alter the entries, fiddle the books, exaggerate, cheat, lie. And if you can't make the numbers, then leave for another job before your numbers show up. These are just some of the ways that educators learn to meet other people's targets in low-trust systems that are rank with the odor of fear. Outright cheating—which is on the increase in the United Kingdom and in the United States—may be the outer limit of test-driven teaching, but in low-trust systems driven by imposed short-term targets, most teachers will find themselves somewhere on the continuum of creative accountancy that sacrifices depth of learning for the appearance of instant results.

Staff development trends merely replicate these tendencies. Deep and thoughtful professional learning is replaced by in-service training on political priorities. Time for inquiry is squeezed out by speed of implementation. Instructional practices are forced through via hurriedly constructed cascades of coaching, with each level of coaches having progressively less knowledge than the ones above them. Harried professionals beget hurried children.

In the face of all this stress, speed, and superficiality, a movement is growing for greater depth, slowness, and substance in our schools. This movement is modeled on the patient and purpose-driven practices of sustainable (and successful) corporate development. It takes its lead from the slow food and slow cities movements that were described in the Introduction.[78] As Maurice Holt, chief advocate of the slow schools movement, puts it, "You can't go on force-feeding pupils, and expect to get foie-gras."[79] "The slow school," says Holt, "is one which attends to philosophy, to tradition, to community, to moral choices. You have time not just to memorize, but to understand." Slow schools, he argues, must be like slow food—not standardized and homogeneous but grounded in understanding of and prepared to work with the community. Slow knowing is cooked, not microwaved, tasty instead of bland, grown and prepared locally rather than delivered from afar. Slow schools should "look critically at coverage," linking kindred subjects together in a world where "less is definitely more."[80] Slow schooling

- Starts formal learning later

- Reduces testing

- Increases curriculum flexibility

- Emphasizes enjoyment

- Doesn't hurry the child

- Rehabilitates play alongside purpose[81]

If this sounds fanciful, nostalgic, or even a bit precious, consider the following. Children in Finland, the highest-achieving nation in the world in high school literacy, don't start formal school until age seven—later than almost every other developed nation. Learning *does* take place before that—in families, communities, and day care—but in a much less deliberate, skill-driven, and structured way.[82] As we showed in the Introduction, after years of standardization, the United Kingdom and much of Australia are reducing rather than increasing the prevalence and impact of educational testing. Japan, Singapore, and China are introducing more flexibility and creativity into the curriculum because their economic futures as knowledge societies depend on it. At the beginning of the twenty-first century, one of the United Kingdom's most visionary policy documents for educational reform was titled *Excellence and Enjoyment*.[83] Queensland ensures that its curriculum engages fully with the new basics as well as the old ones.[84] Steiner, Waldorf, and Montessori schools for years have produced outstandingly successful learning while retaining pleasure and creativity in the curriculum.[85] In practice and not just in theory, slower schooling is begetting deeper learning. An overcrowded curriculum, scripted instruction, and standardized achievement testing only bedevil it.

Slow schooling doesn't mean relaxed expectations or comatose classrooms. Just as we sometimes have to microwave our food instead of cooking it conventionally, some teaching and learning also needs to remain fast-paced and snappy. But not all of it. Putting an end to fast schools means varying the speed, slowing things down from time to time. All learning, Claxton reminds us, should have its own pace.[86]

Slow knowing requires slow leading. Slow leading avoids rushing through the test score data looking for quick fixes and instant results. It doesn't hurry the curriculum through prescribed and scripted basics while ignoring learning in the rest. It doesn't make all learning earnest, productive, and testable, so that the school, its students, and its teachers begin to lose their soul and their spirit. Slow knowing and sustainable improvement don't move children and teachers along grindingly monotonous gradients of annual achievement increments to conform with short-term literacy targets or adequate yearly progress. Learning isn't instant or steady and doesn't always immediately show. Teachers sometimes need time to plateau and consolidate. Real learners have curves. What slow leading *does* require are leaders who

- Emphasize learning, then achievement, then testing, in that order, not the opposite

- Do not narrow the achievement gap in tested basics by widening the learning gap between children in wealthy suburbs, who get a rich and nourishing curriculum that flies far beyond the standards, and the urban and rural poor, who get only a staple diet of prescribed and standardized basics

- Resist the fast-paced karaoke curriculum and the compulsion to follow the bouncing ball of other people's scripts[87]

- Protect and promote deep learning in the arts, humanities, and health education
- Devise ways for children to take tests individually, when they are ready, instead of all at once
- Provide time for unstructured play and conversation with colleagues as well as children
- Act urgently for improvement; wait patiently for results
- Inquire into school problems, using an evidence-informed approach, before rushing toward solutions
- Understand and communicate that deep change takes time
- Retain depth in staff development, so there is time to think through and question changes before charging ahead to implement them

Conclusion

Change, improvement, and reform are, by themselves, indifferent to questions of moral purpose. Improvement can be narrow or superficial; reform can be wrong-headed or repressive; change may be not for the better but for the worse. Sustainability—in improvement and in leadership—however, is inherently and inalienably moral. The purpose of sustainability is to develop what matters and lasts for the benefit of all. What is sustained must count. In sustainable classrooms, as in sustainable corporations, the integrity of the product is paramount.

The central sustainable purpose of education is deep and broad learning; this is everyone's entitlement. Deep learning is often also slow learning—critical, penetrative, thoughtful, and ruminative. It is learning that engages people's feelings and connects with their lives. Deep learning is more like love than like lust. It isn't too preoccupied with performance. It cannot be hurried. Targets don't improve it. Tests rarely take its measure. And you can't do it just because someone else says you should. Mae West put it best: "Anything worth doing is worth doing slowly."

Sustainable school leadership defends depth of learning against the expediency of immediate results. It is not afraid to proclaim that an overriding preoccupation with short-term targets, like an obsession with quarterly returns, is immoral and unworkable. It is courageous enough to say out loud what most educators already murmur in private—that short-term targets and adequate yearly progress are not only nonsense, but nonsense on stilts. Sustainable leadership creates and protects a nourishing, sustaining, and balanced diet of well-prepared and tasty learning that contrasts with "fast school" reform policies that emphasize quantity more than quality, standardized product and efficient delivery, and a restricted diet of minimal sufficiency. Sustainable educational leadership, in other words, puts learning first. Address learning seriously, and, over time, even in the medium term, results will take care of themselves. All other principles of sustainability are subsidiary to this one.

2

Length

Endurance and Succession

It is a common defect in men not to consider in good
weather the possibility of a tempest.

Niccolo Machiavelli, The Prince, *1452*

❖ **PRINCIPLE 2**

**Sustainable leadership lasts. It preserves and advances the
most valuable aspects of learning and life over time, year
upon year, from one leader to the next.**

The Problem of Leadership Succession

The emperor Caligula murdered half his children. England's aging
queen will not cede the throne to her eldest child. The Greek god
Kronos ate his own son. What do all these people have in common?
They refuse to face the facts of leadership succession.

Leadership succession is the first and final challenge of leadership. None of us are immortal. We won't achieve or lead forever.
We can only influence how our achievements will live on and lay
a foundation for further improvement beyond us. This is the personal challenge of leadership succession, of leadership that leaves a
legacy and lasts beyond our own professional lifetime. It is also the
challenge of acknowledging and building on the legacies left before
us that will underpin (or undercut) our own efforts.

Taking responsibility for leadership succession is essential to ensure that improvement efforts endure over time. Adopting the long view and committing to the long haul is at the center of the philosophy of sustainability as expressed in the World Commission on Environment and Development's dedication to not "compromising the ability of future generations to meet their own needs."[1]

Beyond the implementation phase of change, in which new ideas and practices are tried for the first time, is an elusive institutionalization phase, in which these practices are integrated into teachers' repertoires and affect many teachers, not just a few.[2] This challenge of maintaining improvement over time, of persistence and endurance, is the second principle of sustainability.

Most externally imposed reforms never get implemented properly. Their designs are usually too inflexible to accommodate the varying needs and circumstances of different schools. They expose the folly of failing to secure teachers' ownership of the changes. They are implemented too fast for people to understand them properly, or, as has occurred in the case of the United States' No Child Left Behind legislation, the resources that were initially promised never fully materialize.

Innovative schools, each of which generally has a strong shared vision and a hand-picked staff, fare better at implementation. But these schools typically fail at the institutionalization stage; their innovativeness fades over time. A culture of continuous innovation burns many teachers out and leads the best ones to leave. Failure to include the community or neighboring institutions in the school's development foments feelings of envy and suspicion that eventually undermine it. And the school's sponsors in the district leave for other appointments or turn their attention to other agendas, leaving the school to flounder alone. But the most central challenge for maintaining improvement in innovative schools is leadership succession. Schools and school districts can't institutionalize their improvement efforts over time without a strong degree of leadership stability or continuity.[3]

One of the most significant events in the life of all schools is a change in leadership. Yet few things in education succeed less than leadership succession. We mismanage succession for many reasons, but mainly because our most basic assumptions about leadership are flawed. Most of us equate leadership with administratively senior individuals.[4] Heroic leaders who turn failing schools around stand out most in the public imagination. Transformational leaders rather than transformational leadership get the greatest attention in leadership research.[5] Yet leadership also exerts (or fails to exert) its influence *beyond* individuals, across many years, from one leader to the next and to others after that.

The impact of leaders on their schools is often profoundly affected by people they have never met—those who have died, moved on to other institutions, or not yet even arrived. These are the leaders' predecessors and successors—leaders of the school's past and leaders who have yet to come. Leaders are not islands in time. By design or default, leadership stands on the shoulders of those who went before and lays the groundwork for those who will follow. Sustainable improvement that matters and lasts depends on understanding and managing this process of leading over time.[6]

Reformers, change experts, and leaders themselves rarely grasp the long-term aspects of leadership. Quick-fix changes to turn around failing schools often exhaust the teachers or the principal, and improvement efforts aren't sustained over time. The principal's success in a turnaround school may lead to his or her rapid promotion but then result in regression among teachers who feel abandoned by their leader or relieved when the pressure is off.

Sustainable improvement and the contribution of principals to it must be measured over many years and several principalships, not just one or two. What legacy do principals and other leaders leave when they depart? What capacities have they created among students, community, and staff that will live beyond them? How can and should others build on what has been achieved? These are the central questions of leadership succession.

The coming years will see school systems awash with the demands—and opportunities—of leadership succession, due to the following factors:

- Rapid demographic turnover of leaders as the baby boom generation retires

- Early retirement of many leaders, precipitated by years of standardized reform

- Increasing demands on school districts to bring about rapid improvements in underperforming schools[7]

- Accelerating circulation of leaders as they make hasty exits from their schools or systems just before adverse performance figures are published[8]

- An insufficient pool of capable, qualified, and prepared replacements[9]

In the United States, while there seem to be enough qualified principals to cover the nation's needs, some states and districts face serious recruitment and retention problems.[10] For example, Kentucky and Texas have reported a low applicant pool; temporary principals have led many schools in New York City and Los Angeles,[11] and 48 percent of surveyed principals in New York State intended to retire by 2006.[12] Moreover, being qualified doesn't always translate into being available. One study in 2001 reported that of those qualified to apply for a position as a U.S. high school principal, only 30 percent intended to pursue the role in the following five years.[13]

Similar patterns exist in England. Severe shortages exist in some regions for some types of schools. A study of the frequency of newspaper advertisements for head teachers (principals) and deputies (assistant principals) concluded that the number of advertisements for head teachers was above the average for the past decade and the highest recorded for four years and that too many schools still failed to appoint a new head teacher after the first advertisement.[14]

In Ontario, Canada, it was predicted that close to 60 percent of public school principals and 30 percent of vice (assistant) principals in elementary and secondary schools in public school districts would retire by 2005. Yet while close to 8,000 teachers with principals' and vice principals' qualifications were likely to retire by 2005, only 715 teachers each year had acquired their principals' qualifications between 1997 and 2000.[15] The trends and forecasts are similar in Australia[16] and New Zealand,[17] leaving no doubt that leadership succession and sustainability will occupy the center of educational reform for the first two decades of the twenty-first century.[18]

Succession Outside Education

Succession issues fill a vast canvas. The Wars of the Spanish and Austrian Successions have shown that nations can fight to the death over succession. Succession can create dynasties like the Bushes and the Kennedys or lead to feuds and disinheritances, as in the families of Benjamin Franklin or the Borgias.[19] Leadership succession is always a high-stakes issue. Power and control, war and peace, change and continuity, life and death—all rest in the fateful hands of succession.

Corporate Succession

In their definitive review of the leadership succession literature, Kersner and Sebora document an explosion of interest in succession since the 1980s, which has set the agenda for understanding the dynamics of corporate succession.[20] Following are some of its lessons:

- All companies should have effective succession planning.[21] This process should be embedded in the company's strategic improvement plan. There should also be widespread involvement in succession planning so that top managers don't indulge the temptation to hire clones of themselves.[22]

- Amid conditions of rapid change and uncertainty, *succession planning* (identifying, selecting, training, grooming, and matching individuals for particular jobs) is being and should be replaced by *succession management* (creating a widespread culture of forward-looking talent and expertise from which successors can more easily be drawn).[23]

- Successions are affected by what triggers succession events: tragedy due to a death or serious illness; wrong-doing associated with incompetence or with unlawful or unethical conduct; unexpected departures arising from unanticipated promotions, transfers, or other career moves; or planned successions resulting from retirement or the end of a contract.[24]

- The rules for whether to choose insider or outsider successors are not straightforward.[25]

- Frequent successions usually lead to poorer performance results.[26]

- Successful succession depends on people's ability to face their own and others' mortality.[27]

- Successful succession depends on the capacity of leaders to accept and deal with their impending loss of power.[28]

Public Sector Succession

Although corporate insights into succession are important, schools and school districts are less like private businesses than like other public sector organizations, in which succession issues play out differently. The public sector is not immune from the passing of the baby boom generation, and recruitment and development of its leaders is also a major concern.[29] In 2001, it was thought that by 2005, 70 percent of the senior managers in the U.S. public service were eligible for retirement, "causing unique challenges for numerous agencies in maintaining leadership continuity, institutional memory and workforce experience."[30] Similar patterns have been reported in Canada and Australia.[31] Because of regulatory, budgetary, and collective agreement restrictions, the public sector has less flexibility to recruit and develop new leaders. Factor in criticism of the public sector by politicians, corporate leaders, and the media, and it's not surprising that many public servants feel disgruntled and marginalized.[32] As a result, the public sector finds it increasingly difficult to compete with business for people with leadership potential and thus has to approach succession planning quite differently and much less effectively (see Table 2.1).[33]

Table 2.1. Approaches to Succession in the Public Sector and the Private Sector

The public sector . . .	The private sector . . .
Passively lets candidates emerge	Actively recruits and encourages potential leaders
Focuses on the short term	Takes the long view
Handles succession informally formally	Manages succession more
Seeks replacement for existing roles	Defines future leadership skills and aptitudes
Selects in relation to current competencies	Emphasizes flexibility and lifelong learning in the face of changing needs
Views succession planning as a cost	Views succession planning as an asset

Source: Adapted from K. Jackson (2000), Building new teams: The next generation (presentation) (Perth: Government of Western Australia).

Drawing on the corporate and public sector literature, on the limited research on educational succession, and on our evidence of thirty years of leadership succession in eight schools, the rest of this chapter examines the four most critical aspects of leadership succession and sustainability:

- Succession planning

- Succession management

- Succession duration and frequency

- Succession and the self

Succession Planning

A central issue in all leadership succession is whether a transition in leadership establishes *continuity* or provokes *discontinuity* with past directions—and to what extent this is deliberately planned. Combining these possibilities creates four types of leadership succession (see Figure 2.1).

Planned Continuity

Planned continuity occurs when the assignment of a new principal to a school reflects a well-thought-out succession plan that is meant

	Continuity	*Discontinuity*
Planned	Planned continuity	Planned discontinuity
Unplanned	Unplanned continuity	Unplanned discontinuity

Figure 2.1. Succession Planning and Continuity

to build on the general directions and goals of his or her predecessor. Sustained school improvement over long periods and across multiple leaders depends on a great deal of carefully planned continuity.

The most successful instances of planned continuity that we encountered in the course of our research were in three purpose-built innovative schools, in which insiders were groomed to follow in their leaders' footsteps as they tried to embed achievements within the culture of the school.

Blue Mountain School was explicitly established as a learning organization in 1994. Its principal, Ben McMaster, realized that the first crisis for an innovative school may occur when the founding principal leaves.[34] McMaster therefore planned for his successor from the outset. He anticipated his own departure by working hard to create a school structure of professional learning teams and student councils that would perpetuate his devotion to the idea of a learning community when he eventually left the school. While McMaster's imprint was everywhere—in the school's philosophy, organization, design, and culture—he was very alert to the threats posed by the possibility of an ensuing principal importing a significantly different philosophy. He therefore canvassed the district to ensure that he could groom a successor who would understand and be committed to the school's distinctive mission and who would be able to maintain its momentum. After four years, the district did in fact move him to a larger, high-profile school and promoted his assistant principal, Linda White, to replace him. She remembers, "Before (McMaster) was moved to another school, we talked and we talked about how we could preserve the direction that this school was moving in. We were afraid that if a new administrator came in as a principal, that if he or she had a different philosophy, a different set of beliefs, then it would be quite easy to simply move things in that particular direction, and we didn't want that to happen."

White continued Blue Mountain's emphasis on relationships. While some staff had reservations, White and her leadership team were described by many of them as "wonderful," "supportive," "spectacular," and "amazing" people who were "still teachers at heart." She was highly valued as being "very caring" and as someone who recognized that "family comes first." White worked hard to be open and accessible as she dedicated herself to maintaining the originating philosophy of the school.

As principal, she stated, "I'm on the same road and any detours I take will only be for a few moments in the overall scheme of things before I come back onto the main road again." Unlike the founding principal, who had stressed the creation of the school's new values, she emphasized their continuation.

Choosing insiders who have been groomed as successors can work well in schools that are on a clear upward curve of improvement. Strong insider successors understand the school's or district's values, are accepted by the community, know what has been accomplished, and understand what has still to be achieved. Insiders need to be identified early rather than late, and be actively groomed for their future position through

- Early selection, based on demonstrated talent and potential

- Explicit signaling, so potential successors know what is planned for them and don't leave unexpectedly

- Exposure to all aspects of the position

- Shadowing, mentoring, and coaching

- Training

- Assignment of tasks and goals that stretch them

- Regular feedback[35]

However, insiders are not always advisable as successors of choice. First, their colleagues might view them as undeserving beneficiaries of favoritism or nepotism. This is especially true in family-run independent schools in which leadership is passed down to sons and daughters by their parents. In *In Praise of Nepotism*, Adam Bellow (son of famous father Saul) argues that "good nepotism" in a family business can "maintain an orderly system of reproduction and succession"[36] and be accepted by company employees if "able and justified" children have "carried on a proud family tradition"[37] and are at least as competent and hardworking as anyone else in the business. But "bad nepotism" has crept in if there is "preferential treatment for a relative who is grossly incompetent."[38] For parents and children, read *old boy's and new girl's clubs* when leaders are tempted to favor their own kind by passing on illegitimate power and unfair advantage to their professional protégés, who fulfill the role of surrogate children. This is not an argument against the role of families, networks, and relationships in mentoring and grooming strong successors. But it is vital that these informal processes be accompanied by clear and transparent performance criteria; otherwise, attributions of favoritism or even corruption will tarnish the successor's credibility forever.

Second, when leaders groom their own successors, they are often tempted to try to clone themselves. What Liebman and Bauer call "selecting in one's own image"[39] can present great barriers to diversity in the succession process. In their study of 370 cases of CEO succession, Smith and White found that CEOs tend to select successors with their own career specialization.[40]

Self-cloning can be bad for the organization as well as for individuals. Austin Powers–like "mini-me's" may seem less impressive or effective than their predecessors, as Blue Mountain's second principal, Linda White, seemed to some of her staff. And such "clones" may be so committed to leading the community as it is and as they like it that they don't differ enough from or even rebel a little against their mentor by moving the organization into its next needed stage of development. Instead of renewing the school's culture, they can end up repeating it. It is strongly advisable, therefore, to spread the responsibility for grooming a successor beyond the clutches of the existing leader.

Third, people are often drawn to appointing insiders or outsiders for the wrong reasons—for example, out of custom or habit, not because of the particular needs of their institution.[41] The worst-case scenario may occur in a school that is drifting or underperforming. Insiders are likely to stick with their staff and perpetuate the drift rather than push the school in another direction.[42] Ivor Megson, the insider appointment at Talisman Park Secondary School (described in the preceding chapter), is a classic example—a leader who conspired with his staff to raise literacy scores in a calculating attempt to maintain public relations and minimize disruption instead of engaging them in the more authentic and demanding struggle to improve literacy for all.

Planned Discontinuity

Planned continuity occurred only in our most innovative schools, and even then only for isolated transitions rather than all successions. More usually, leadership successions were designed to create *discontinuity*—to turn around a failing school, give a jolt to a cruising school, or implement a top-down reform agenda.[43]

> Bill Andrews was appointed as principal of Stewart Heights Secondary School in 1998. While once it had served a white, middle-class suburban and rural population, Stewart Heights

was now surrounded by urban development and reflected the increasing cultural diversity of the region. The students were changing, but the stable and long-serving staff stayed the same, pining nostalgically for the days when they had been a small "village" school.

Bill Andrews's predecessor, who had led the school for a decade since 1988, confessed, "One of the difficulties I found for my personal approach to leadership was that I didn't have a particular direction or goal for my school. I simply wanted to facilitate the relationship between teachers and students, and I thought my job was to take as much of the administrivia and annoyance and pressure from outside sources off the teachers as possible, so that they could work effectively with kids."

A policeman's son, Andrews was a tall, commanding, and self-confident figure. His wide experience and extensive knowledge of the larger school district through two former principalships and time in the district office allowed him to move confidently, quickly, and energetically to shake the school out of what he viewed as its historical lethargy.

Andrews articulated firm expectations for staff performance and student behavior and demonstrated that change was possible. When guidance personnel complained that student schedules could not be completed in time for the beginning of school, Andrews personally attended to the timetables of the more than eighty affected students and modeled that their problems were and from then on would be soluble. He aggressively addressed management and building issues, making public spaces more welcoming for students and the community, and gradually mobilized the staff behind a coherent set of school goals. He was not reluctant to initiate, preside over, and engage in the rough-and-tumble of difficult and lively staff room debate. For example, to heighten staff awareness of student needs, he presented teachers with survey data showing that 95 percent of staff were satisfied with the school even though only 35 percent of students and 25 percent of parents were. This created a common problem that staff had to solve together. An experienced teacher explained,

He's brought a willingness to think about kids, to do things for kids, and to make kids look good, as opposed to managing for the status quo. And I think for a long time, this school had a good reputation, and so it just went along. In the meantime, its reputation in the community kind of went away, but nobody within this building really realized it. I think with the principal's arrival, he knew the problems, and he set out to deal with them and to make changes, and I think, for the most part, it's been good.

Andrews ruffled quite a few feathers, however. "I think he has ideas of where he wants to go, and I think he's going to, but his overall style is almost an imposing kind of thing that will be—this is how it will be." "[He has been] insisting that there's certain things he has to do because this is his mandate from the district." "He's a change agent and an instigator, but it sometimes is decreed to be done."

Andrews pushed the school a long way forward during his brief tenure. Parent and student satisfaction levels soared. Plants and benches began to make the school feel less like a factory and more like a community. The School Improvement Team steamed ahead in its efforts to gain staff support for improving student learning.

In Stewart Heights and other schools like it, planned discontinuity can bring about much-needed change. People who appoint new leaders get excited by the prospect of discontinuity; they like the idea of rescuing a school, setting it off in a new direction, giving it a shake. It gives a feeling of urgency, a sense that in a single appointment, they can make a very real difference. And so they can, provided they watch out for two dangers.

First, the need for discontinuity must be diagnosed correctly. Susan Moore Johnson's classic study of American school superintendents shows that appointing panels of school boards sometimes get so fixated about an irritating fault of the previous superintendent that they concentrate all their attention on ensuring that the new appointee doesn't have that particular weakness.[44] The result of this tunnel vision is that they overlook the aspects of the previous leader's achievements that need to be continued. A need for discontinuity in one area doesn't mean there should be discontinuity in all or most of them.

Second, discontinuity needs to be pursued with steadfastness, over a long period of time, until it becomes the new continuity. While planned discontinuity can yield rapid results, its leadership needs time to consolidate the new culture, to embed it in the hearts and minds of everyone. Repeatedly, planned discontinuity was effective in shaking up the schools in our study but not at making changes stick. For example, because of his quick and visible success, Bill Andrews was lifted out of Stewart Heights too early, after less than three years, to take a promotion in the district office. Leaders of planned discontinuity in other schools were also transferred to struggling schools elsewhere long before their existing work had been completed. The result was a constant cycle of change throughout schools in the system but little lasting improvement in any one of them.

Unplanned Continuity and Discontinuity

In reality, most cases of succession in our research ended up being a paradoxical mix of *unplanned continuity and discontinuity:*

discontinuity with the achievements of a leader's immediate predecessor and continuity with (or regression to) the more mediocre state of affairs preceding that predecessor. In this carousel of leadership succession, successful leaders are lifted suddenly and prematurely out of the saddle of the school they are improving in order to mount a rescue act in a school system facing a crisis or a challenge elsewhere. Much less thought is given to the appointment of their lesser successors.

At Stewart Heights Secondary School, first-time principal Eric West was rapidly promoted in midterm to replace Andrews, who had been catapulted upward into district administration. Faced with a school that was experiencing its third principal in four and a half years and an escalating government reform agenda, West had no time to establish himself as a leader and little opportunity to acquire knowledge about the school or his new role from other sources. His response was to make no changes in his first semester and build relationships one at a time. Although this would have been understandable within an evolutionary climate of improvement, in a time of imposed and accelerating change, this strategy led to inertia and drifting. Departmental power structures reasserted themselves to fill the void, and staff on the school climate committee set about creating stricter codes for student behavior rather than continuing Andrews's commitment to whole-school change.

West's promotion occurred at the same time that the pressure to implement the government curriculum reform agenda was at its peak. He commented, "Sometimes the rules change, day by day in terms of what we can and can't do. As we were making our own changes, moving forward in the direction that we believed we need to go, other changes and outside pressures have been imposed on us as well. So things that you want to do have to take a back seat sometimes and that can be quite frustrating."

Staff said of West and his newly appointed administrative team: "Nice people! Can't cope!" Andrews, West's predecessor, had undoubtedly irritated and sometimes alienated a faction of the staff, but the force of his leadership and personality had kept pushing them forward. With more time and as the school achieved its goals, these cracks could have been filled and the school might have been pulled together. But Andrews's short tenure and premature replacement left his mission truncated, and the cracks he had opened widened into chasms when he left. Rapid rotation of leadership, poor succession planning, and the onset of an overwhelming reform agenda undermined two years of considerable improvement. After just three years, West himself was moved on to another school. Three days into his new principalship, he was taken to hospital with a suspected mental breakdown!

Successful planned continuity or discontinuity are the scarce commodities of educational leadership. Leadership succession is repeatedly spoiled by poor planning. Succession plans either go awry, or there is no real planning at all. Recent success is discontinued, improvement gains are eliminated, and continuity is reestablished with earlier, more mediocre patterns. Repeated and rushed successions don't push schools along an upward curve of improvement but around and around on a perpetual carousel in which all of them move up and down with depressing regularity.

The quest for enduring improvement can and must be significantly advanced through better succession planning. Good succession plans

- Are prepared long before the leader's anticipated departure or even from the outset of their appointment

- Give other people proper time to prepare

- Are incorporated in all school improvement plans

- Are the responsibility of many, rather than the prerogative of lone leaders who tend to want to clone themselves

- Are based on a clear diagnosis of the school's existing stage of development and future needs for improvement

- Are transparently linked to clearly defined leadership standards and competencies that are needed for the next phase of improvement

Succession Management

It is better to have a plan than not to have a plan. But succession plans alone are not enough. They rely too much on preparing just one individual to take over. A chosen individual might get impatient, prefer another opportunity, tail off in performance, or fall into disgrace. Then where would the organization be? Or if the organization suddenly changes, the successor may simply not be the right choice anymore. For all these reasons, the business succession literature now advocates *succession management*—creating a culture of leadership development throughout the organization from which chief executives can more easily be drawn[45]—rather than succession planning. It is easier to find successors when there are many to choose from and when human resource development has nurtured them and brought them along either on a schoolwide or districtwide basis.

Creating a culture of leadership development means putting less of the burden of improvement on the shoulders of heroes or stars.

Corporations who search for stars and commit large amounts of resources to securing them typically find that the stars shine less brilliantly than in their previous position—not because they have become complacent or are past their best but because their stardom depends on the people, networks, relationships, and other human capacity of all those who have worked with them over many years.[46]

Although the problem of finding a strong leadership successor is best solved by forming strong cultures in which leaders can come forward and flourish, this isn't easy to do, as the influential work of Etienne Wenger reveals. Wenger describes a number of trajectories that leaders can take as they move through their organization: peripheral, inbound, insider, and outbound.[47] Most leaders entering a new organization start from a *peripheral* trajectory—as outsiders. They then draw on different kinds of knowledge to try to exert their leadership and make an impact over time.

- *Inbound knowledge* is knowledge of leadership or of a particular school that is needed to change it, improve it, make one's mark on it, or turn it around.

- *Insider knowledge* is the knowledge gained from and exercised with other members of the community to improve the school after becoming known, trusted, and accepted by them.

- *Outbound knowledge* is what is needed to preserve past successes, keep improvement going, and leave a legacy after one has left.

Inbound Knowledge

Schools and school systems are mainly preoccupied with *inbound knowledge*, with initiating and imposing changes more than looking back and consolidating existing ones. This pattern is especially common among *charismatic leaders*. When Lord Byron Secondary School was established as one of the most innovative schools in

Canada in 1974, its charismatic principal, Ward Bond, was appointed to set its distinctive direction. Bond's adoring teachers acknowledged that he was a hard act to follow, and when he left after just three years, his successors could never quite live up to this legend, and the school began a long process of *attrition of change*—a gradual erosion of its innovative identity over time.[48] Mike Arness, a past principal of Talisman Park Secondary School, possessed some of Bond's charismatic qualities. When he left his school, he took not only his charisma with him but many of his key middle-level leaders as well. Staff members sometimes end up believing in the charismatic leader's mystical qualities rather than believing in themselves.[49] Charismatic leaders' inbound knowledge can generate significant change in a school but cannot sustain it after they have gone.

Inbound knowledge is also overemphasized in circumstances of planned discontinuity. Bill Andrews, inbound at Stewart Heights Secondary School, fulfilled his district's faith that he could turn his "cruising" school around. But his district didn't allow him to remain long enough to solidify a new culture and embed improvements in it. Those who try to sort out "failing" schools are especially prone to quick fix obsessions with inbound knowledge.

Sheldon High school, in New York State, faces designation as "in need of improvement" under No Child Left Behind rules. Once known as the jewel of its urban district, Sheldon went into decades of decline due to the impact of race riots in the 1970s, subsequent white and bright flight to the suburbs, the ensuing establishment of a magnet school that took away Sheldon's best students, and the loss of its connection to its local community when the magnet initiative resulted in closure of a school on the opposite side of the city and busing of some of its most difficult students into Sheldon.

Len Adomo, one of Sheldon's principals in the school's better days, was regarded as energetic but autocratic. His attitude
was "I'm the boss, and I'm going to decide how to do things."
Blocked from involvement in decisions that affected their
lives, teachers increasingly turned to their union as an outlet
for their frustrations and leadership impulses. The more frac-
tious the union became, the more Adomo dug in his heels. As
one teacher recalled, "Len Adomo likes to fight with the
union." Because he was unwilling to negotiate or compromise,
virtually every issue, large and small, became a bone of con-
tention. Over time, as the staff became more militant and the
school's students became more demanding, the district escalated the conflict by appointing principals they thought would
stand up to the union. A teacher described one of Adomo's
successors as a "vassal" of the school district, and the teaching
staff as "the serfs." Yet each successively more autocratic principal only reinforced the militancy of the teachers, so that
"Sheldonism" became a district synonym for unbridled union
resistance to change. This ongoing standoff, which diverted
teachers' energies to defending themselves, resulted in the
school's almost complete inability to address its changing student population. Instead of inspiring improvement, inbound,
top-down forcefulness only entrenched resistance to change.

In all of these dysfunctional scenarios of leadership succession,
the short-term inbound knowledge of school systems repeatedly
eclipses the long-term outbound knowledge that is needed to secure
sustainable improvement.

Outbound Knowledge

In the Change Over Time? project, outbound knowledge was only
evident in three innovative schools. Each groomed an assistant

principal as a likely successor to the incumbent principal who would continue promoting the leader's and the school's vision. The successful outbound trajectories of these principals were also due to their capacity to develop a large degree of distributed leadership among their teachers.[50] For instance, teachers at Durant Alternative School remembered its early days when "we were all administrators and we all shared the administration." One of them recalled how their founding leader was "the worst administrator . . ., because he never did his paperwork, he never submitted budgets, and he was always behind on everything. But since we were a community, we had no problems reminding him or helping him and in a sense bailing him out. I think we all admired David's intellect so much, we could grumble initially and say, 'Damn it David, why didn't you handle this? This is your job.' And then we would go ahead in the faculty meeting and work on it."

In this and other exceptional cases, it was the whole staff, not just one successor, who was able to move the school into its next phase of development. In the majority of schools, though, the sustainability of school improvement and reform initiatives is repeatedly undermined by excessive emphasis on the inbound knowledge of individual leadership at the expense of equally important and collectively shared and distributed outbound concerns.

Successful succession management requires giving serious attention to outbound as well as inbound knowledge:

- *Distribute leadership* effectively so that successful succession does not depend too much on the talents of particular individuals[51]

- Build strong and broad *professional cultures* with firmly held and courageously defended purposes that will inoculate schools against mediocre or indifferent successors[52]

- Develop deeper and wider *pools of leadership* talent in the school or district, so that succession issues are easier to resolve[53]

- Create *leadership development schools* in every district or region—outstanding schools that will grow new leadership that will influence, improve, and spread across the wider system

- In an environment in which demands are always changing, "prepare . . . future leadership, guided by *future leadership competencies* and an array of supporting development opportunities"[54]

- Commit to effective programs that identify, encourage and *support aspiring school leaders* in engaging and experimenting with outstanding leadership early in their educational careers—for example, in the aspiring and early leader programs supported by the National College for School Leadership and the Specialist Schools Trust in the United Kingdom and by the Wallace Foundation in the United States[55]

- Replace charismatic leadership that encourages followers to believe in their leaders with *inspirational leadership* that encourages people to believe in themselves

- Coach individual leaders and school communities to think about and *plan for the leader's exit* from the very first day of the leader's tenure

- Attend much more carefully to the *duration of leadership tenure* and *frequency of leadership succession* in terms of their impact on leaders' capacity to sustain improvement by becoming accepted insiders

Succession Duration and Frequency

Frequency isn't always an indicator of quality. In leadership succession, it almost never is. Indeed, corporate succession research shows that frequent succession is almost always associated with poor performance.

When leaders take on a new job and strive to become insiders whose improvements are championed by everyone, they move through a number of *succession phases*.[56] Reeves, Moos, and Forrest studied career stages in school leadership in Denmark, England, and Scotland.[57]

- In the first three stages—pre-entry, entry, and digging the foundations—leaders get their bearings and schools take their measure.

- In stage 4, taking action (nine months–two years), stage 5, getting above the floor level (eighteen months– three years), and stage 6, the crunch (two years–five years), the leader's engagement with change makes more substantial inroads into people's beliefs and values.

- As leaders enter stage 7, reaching the summit (four years–ten years) and stage 8, time for a change (five years–ten years or more), they begin to feel that their work is done and that it's time to move on.

Crucially, in this and other work on stages of succession, researchers find that leadership effects don't seem to become truly embedded in the wider culture until leaders have become accepted as insiders, which occurs when they have finally reached the summit, between four and ten years into the leader's tenure.

Patterns of successful leadership of schools in challenging circumstances carry a similar message. Leaders of these schools are wedded to, often come from, and sometimes still live in the community they serve.[58] Many are mavericks who courageously defend their school and its community against the onslaughts of external bureaucracies.[59] And their dedication shows in the fact that they stick around, resisting the temptation to take up bigger career prospects elsewhere.

Far too much leadership succession practice nowadays flies in the face of all this evidence. Demographically driven retirements, difficulties in retaining leaders in urban schools, the tendency for principals to seek new jobs just before their performance numbers are published, and the increasingly popular practice of moving principals around to plug the leaks in failing schools mean that principal turnover is accelerating dramatically. In our own study, while Talisman Park Secondary School had six principals in its first sixty-eight years, it had another five in a fifth of that time (fourteen years). From 1970, Stewart Heights Secondary School had just four principals in twenty-eight years, then three in quick succession in the next five. Lord Byron Secondary School had four principals in its first fourteen years after opening in 1970, then just as many in the past five. This revolving-door principalship breeds staff cynicism that subverts principals' credibility and their chances of securing long-term, sustainable improvement. A Talisman Park department head who had worked under five different principals spoke for many when he said that the school's principals in the 1970s and 1980s

> were totally committed to the overall program of the school. Their number one focus was the school. As time went on and principals changed, the principal was less interested in the school and more interested in his own personal growth. You could tell as some of these other principals came in; they spent more time outside the school than they did inside the school. I get to Bill Andrews [who was at Talisman Park two appointments prior to Stewart Heights] and his number one focus wasn't on Talisman Park. It was on the next step to be a superintendent, and that's what he is right now.

Meanwhile, at Stewart Heights, novice principal Eric West observed, "It's only been one-plus year [that he's been at the school], and people are already asking how long am I going to be here."

Robert MacMillan's research on regular administrative rotation of school principals in Canada shows how rapid rotations of less than three years harden teachers against any and all future leaders and their improvement efforts, no matter how worthy they are. Teachers learn to tolerate and accommodate each new leader on a temporary basis without actually committing to or complying with their change agendas. MacMillan concludes, "The policy of regularly rotating principals within a system is a flawed one, perhaps fatally so. When leadership succession is regular and routinized, teachers are likely to build resilient cultures which inoculate them against the effects of succession."[60]

Charmaine Watson was appointed as the first ever female principal of Talisman Park Secondary School in 1995 (which we saw under Ivor Megson's leadership in the previous chapter). Situated in an affluent, well-established neighborhood and with an eighty-year tradition, Talisman Park saw its mission as preparing students for postsecondary education. More than 70 percent of its graduates were accepted into universities and colleges. Over the previous decade, Talisman Park's student population, which had been largely middle-class, white, and Anglo-Saxon, had become more racially and ethnically diverse. Watson's predecessor, Bill Andrews (who later resurfaced at Stewart Heights after a spell in the district office) had already pushed Talisman Park's teachers to confront school change by advocating an inclusive approach to planning and problem solving and by involving students in the process. Just as at Stewart Heights, teachers either loved Andrews because of his unwavering dedication to students or resented him because he seemed to play favorites among the staff.

When Andrews had been suddenly transferred to the district office in 1995, Charmaine Watson was rushed in to replace him. Watson had had little opportunity to interact with Andrews or the staff before assuming her new role. Having taught at Talisman Park earlier in her career, Watson understood the school's history and culture. Although she was widely seen as caring and supportive by many of the staff, she didn't hesitate to try and change the culture so that it would benefit all students in the school.

Watson set out to democratize the school by taking major decisions to the staff as a whole, rather than depending on the previously powerful department heads. Distributing leadership beyond existing formal structures, she initiated a whole-school strategic plan that focused on improving assessment strategies for student work and engaging students in instructional technology. Watson participated with staff in professional development activities and encouraged teachers to diversify their teaching to meet the changing nature and needs of the school's students. She also initiated a strategic plan that involved parents and others in the Talisman Park community, and she engaged them in developing the purposes of the school.

After Watson had been at the school for four years, most staff members appeared to be supportive of her approach. In spite of her best efforts, however, a small but influential element of long-serving staff resisted her initiatives. Several were part of an embittered coffee circle of influential teachers who met every morning before school to cast scorn on the government's latest reform initiatives and to undermine cross-department improvement efforts in the school.

Thus, while Watson exerted a strong personal presence in the school, she was only partly successful in her attempt to instill her vision of an inclusive learning community. Even though she had the credibility of having taught at Talisman Park during its glory years and was seen by most staff as a caring and capable leader, dissenting teachers didn't want to share their difficulties with her because they didn't want to upset her. Watson had not yet become an insider.

Unfortunately, Watson would never get the chance to lead from the inside out. In 1998, in response to a number of unexpected retirements among its school leaders after schools had adjourned for the summer break, the district abruptly (and, from Watson's point of view, traumatically) transferred her to another school that was experiencing serious problems, Wayvern High School.

The district replaced Watson with Ivor Megson, a former assistant principal at the school. Megson's arrival coincided with significant government reforms that affected teachers with full force. Megson's style was more managerial than Watson's, and as we saw in the previous chapter, his more calculating approach to change allowed the department heads to assert their traditional academic priorities and pass up the opportunity to attend to all students' literacy in an inclusive way.

Watson's case brings together many of the key elements of leadership succession and sustainability over time: the district's *planning*, even in a time of urgency, which tried to follow the abrasive Andrews with the more collaborative Watson; the *inbound knowledge* of Watson and the system that began to distribute leadership and build shared commitment to improvement, along with the *outbound intention* to see the work through for at least five years so that its effects would become firmly embedded in the staff culture; then the *premature exit* and *rapid rotation* that prevented Watson from fulfilling her outbound intentions, inhibited her chances of being accepted as an insider, reinforced the power and cynicism of the entrenched staff even further, and reversed the progress toward achieving sustainable improvement for all students through more *distributed leadership*.

High succession frequency is a sure path to failed sustainability. The quest for successful and sustainable leadership must be defined less by how to remove school leaders from or rotate them between schools than by how to retain them in schools longer when they are doing well. This means that

- Leaders who are achieving significant success in a school must normally stay for at least five years if their improvements are to survive their departure.

- Outstanding leaders should anticipate fewer rather than more successions in any one period of their career so that leaders remain in particular schools long enough to ensure that the effects of their leadership will last.

- While leaders should be expected to change assignments over the course of their career, bureaucratic policies of frequent, regularized rotation of leaders between schools should be abandoned.

- Sustainable leadership that turns around underperforming schools must no longer depend on transient heroes or miracle workers but, where possible, on leaders who are attached to, grown from, and remain for longer periods in the community they serve.

Succession and the Self

Succession, we have seen, is about planning and management, preparation and rotation, culture and change. But at its core, leadership succession is also a matter of mortality. Throughout history, leadership succession has been about seizures of power and denials of death. Henry VIII's lord chancellor, Sir Thomas More, was beheaded because he refused to accede to the king's attempt to secure a male heir through the Act of Succession. Many of Shakespeare's greatest tragedies—Hamlet, King Lear, Henry IV, Macbeth—are dramas of power and greed, love and betrayal, played out through desperate life-and-death struggles over succession.

Leadership confers power. It makes you feel alive. You influence your own destiny and shape the destiny of others. Leaders like the limelight, and most are reluctant to give it up. Few want to face the facts of succession and confront their mortality by stepping aside for someone else. Many want to secure their immortality by building great monuments or naming their successor. Almost all want to see their leadership through, to have a chance to settle their affairs, to complete their work and feel it has been properly done.

At Talisman Park, Charmaine Watson had been transferred in to replace her predecessor, Bill Andrews. His unexpected exit reverberated through the school and undermined feelings of trust between teachers and the school's leadership. Although she had made steady strides in building collaboration and developing a common purpose that focused on all students, Watson still had considerable work to do when the district's unexpected glut of principal retirements led to her sudden transfer over the summer break to another school (Wayvern High School, in Chapter One) that needed outstanding leadership. The district seemed more concerned with placing a principal with considerable inbound knowledge in a challenging situation than to consolidating Watson's four years of attempted reform at Talisman Park. Watson herself was "devastated" by this ill-timed move. She had little opportunity to draw her tenure to a conclusion or even to say goodbye. In her own eyes, her work remained uncompleted, and the school's regression under her successor, Megson, merely vindicated her fears.

A test of the health of all organizations is their capacity to manage endings—to allow leaders to complete their work, to recognize their achievements, celebrate their promotion or retirement, and leave them feeling that their legacy is in capable hands.[61] Leaders who leave or are made to leave prematurely, like those who face an early death, may feel sad and frustrated that their work remains unfinished, business left undone, and these nagging feelings of disappointment or even bitterness can undermine their effectiveness as they move into their next leadership role.

Leadership succession, like leadership itself, is acutely emotional in nature. Yet as Brenda Beatty points out in her foundational work on the emotions of leadership, leaders' "emotional selves are anything but welcome in their work."[62] In their research on wounded leaders, Richard Ackerman and Pat Maslin-Ostrowski note that there is "no simple language or vocabulary in the workplace to speak of the feelings of leadership isolation, fear, vulnerability and loss."[63] Few situations cry out for such a language more than the moment of leadership succession—of leaving one's school and colleagues or of being the one who is left behind.[64]

In *The Inner Principal*, a prominent Australian principal, David Loader, eloquently reflects on his own emotional experience of the process of succession and the moment of exit in particular. In a room filled with 150 staff members and after three speeches of the governing council of his independent school, he recalls,

> I was invited to speak. I moved forward but only managed one or two words before I broke down in tears. I tried a couple of times to start again but it was hopeless. Suddenly I was overwhelmed by my grief. I was acutely

aware of the pain of parting but also the closeness and joy of present friendships. Suddenly it was obvious to me that these friendships would not be as rich in the future as they had been in the past. As well, it was clear that the College was already moving on confidently beyond me and I was left standing there.

As I reflected on this even later I thought how I had gone to that morning tea thinking about how the staff would take the news. I knew that some staff would think that I had abandoned them and their projects, and I was doing that by leaving. Others would be critical that I would now be responsible for a competitor school. I also knew that a lot of staff would be pleased for me. This was the reason for scanning the faces to read their emotions. Amazingly, . . . I had not thought about how I was feeling about leaving my friends and the school. I know that too much of my life is lived through the eyes of others. The good news is that I was in this instance saved from myself so that I could experience the moment. I had been able to get in touch with my emotions on such an important occasion. In my professional role I spend a lot of time thinking and caring about people and their emotions. Sometimes, maybe even often, this caring is at the expense of my own emotional life. How healthy is that either for the person cared for or for the carer?[65]

Paradoxically, it is precisely when leaders feel most isolated, vulnerable, or powerless, as well as when they feel valued and loved, that they most need to share these feelings with rather than hide them from their colleagues and their community. Otherwise, Ackerman and Maslin-Ostrowski warn, "Leaders who are insecure about their own emotional capacity and identity will create organizational settings which tend to deprive others of theirs."[66] Shakespeare's brilliant portrayal of the emotional dynamics of guilt in *Hamlet* applies equally well to all the other disturbing emotions of leadership and leadership succession.

> So full of artless jealousy is guilt.
> It spills itself in fearing to be spilt.[67]

There is a dark corner in the soul of many leaders that secretly wants their own brilliance never to be surpassed, that hopes their successors will be a little less excellent, a little less loved than themselves.[68] A few leaders even furtively hope that after they have gone, their organization will go to hell in a handbasket. Some even try to spoil things for their successors by blowing the entire budget or taking key colleagues with them. In his classic article, "The Dark Side of CEO Succession," Manfred Kets de Vries points out that stepping down involves

> the realization that one must give up power [which] threatens the deep-seated wish to believe in one's own immortality. . . . Relinquishing power is a kind of death for executives long accustomed to great power. So they avoid thinking of it, and senior subordinates and board members may oblige by avoiding the issue too. They may fear that the boss will interpret their talk of succession as a hostile act—evincing a none-too-subtle desire for the CEO's demise. Some CEOs even secretly nourish the hope that their successor will fail. Failure would be further proof of their own indispensability. They may even take steps, consciously or not, to set the successor up for failure.[69]

Moral leadership doesn't deny these feelings, but it rises above them for the good of others. Coming to grips with leadership succession means moving beyond a leader's darkest desires for and delusions of indispensability in order to help build success that will endure long after the individual leader has left.

To the teachers who experience processions of leaders coming through their school, leadership succession is also an emotionally intense process. It is surrounded with feelings of hope, expectation, apprehension, abandonment, loss, betrayal, relief, or even fear. People may grieve for well-loved leaders who have retired or died. They may feel abandoned or betrayed by leaders who are being promoted and moving on. Or they may be relieved when they are finally rid of leaders who are self-serving, controlling, or incompetent. Incoming leaders may be viewed as threats to a comfortable school culture or as saviors of ones that are toxic. Whatever the response, leadership succession events are rarely regarded with indifference.

When leaders leave suddenly and prematurely because of conflict, wrongdoing, or unexpected transfers or promotions, their organization and they themselves may be plunged into great emotional turmoil, with feelings of abandonment, betrayal, and confusion running rampant.[70] At these times, the endings that accompany succession events can be particularly hard to handle.

Henry Warner was CEO of one of England's largest and most disadvantaged urban school districts. The district was very near the bottom of the national rankings of district performance in student achievement. Warner came to the district with a reputation as a successful and charismatic leader. Appointing a world-class international consultant in school improvement to assist him, Warner embarked on an ambitious plan to reculture the schools in his new district, building team leadership, developing learning networks, and focusing on improving student learning. Staff became excited by his visionary and energetic approach to turning their schools and their city around. He promised them faithfully that he would stay at least five years to see the improvement efforts through.

In 2004, one of us (Andy) was asked to undertake a day of staff development for all the school leadership teams in the district. Arriving the evening before, he was greeted by senior staff with ashen faces—including the CEO himself. Most of the district's staff had just learned that after only eighteen months, their CEO was going to leave them for a highly paid national position in the private educational sector. Staff were furious, rumors ran riot, and embittered, caustic remarks were uttered everywhere.

Over dinner, Warner, Andy, and the district staff discussed how to approach the day in light of the nature of this crisis. Acknowledging that he had walked into a tense situation, Andy proposed to begin by showing a video clip from the award-winning British comedy series *The Office*.

In this clip, David Brent, the superficially collaborative but loathsomely self-serving office boss, is pressed by his employees to disclose details of the company's upcoming restructuring. Emerging from hiding in his office, Brent gathers his employees around him.

"Well," he announces, "there's good news and bad news.

"The bad news is Neil will be taking over both branches, and some of you will lose your jobs. Those of you who are kept on will have to relocate to Swindon [an undesirable location more than an hour's drive away], if you want."

Staff groan and look at their shoes while Brent utters the fake empathy of "Gutting, . . . phew!"

"On a more positive note," Brent continues, "the good news is I've been promoted!" Silence and disbelief sweep the room. "So every cloud . . . has . . . a . . . "

More silence. "You're still thinking about the bad news, aren't you?"

At the close of the video clip, which the district's senior staff had initially hesitated to show, the hall of several hundred school leaders erupted in applause. The elephant in the room had been acknowledged; the tension had been broken.

The leadership teams were then given a thirty-minute presentation on the emotional aspects of leadership succession—the intense and confused emotions that people feel when they undergo succession events. Andy explained that in difficult succession situations, it was necessary for the CEO to communicate as clearly as possible his or her own reasons for leaving, however emotionally or politically difficult that might be, to scotch any gossip or rumors that might otherwise paralyze the organization and prevent it moving forward. He exhorted the staff to listen to these explanations, trust the sincerity behind them, wish their CEO well, and then move on.

After the break, the next hour focused on the original plan to analyze issues of trust and betrayal in the workplace. Working together but not in relation to the current experience of succession, school teams explored what factors helped build or breach trust in an organization.[71] The greatest source of trust in an organization, they learned, is *communication trust*, meaning that there is clear, frequent, open, high-level, and reciprocal communication. Without communication trust, it was noted, feelings and attributions of suspicion and betrayal infect the organization like a plague.

At the end of a long day, Henry Warner stood up, ostensibly to thank Andy. With no forewarning, this proud and charismatic leader then made a stumbling, inarticulate, and compellingly authentic explanation of his reasons for leaving the district. As a result of the day's staff development, he had realized that he hadn't been trusting his staff. He wasn't leaving them, he explained, for greener pastures or greater reward. Rather, he had come into conflict with the district's education committee (the equivalent of the school board), whose demands were turning him into the kind of person he didn't want to be. He understood that many senior colleagues felt the same but had decided to stay and stick things out. He congratulated them for that and apologized for not being as strong as them. Choking back a tear or two, he complimented them on what they had achieved and wished them well in the future.

The room burst into thunderous applause. Where before the staff had had an air of suspicion and betrayal, the leaders in the system now exuded only warmth and well-wishing. The ending had been properly completed; the district could and did move on.

This case speaks volumes about the emotional aspects of succession. Premature exits, confused emotions, miscommunications and misattributions are often accompaniments to emotionally mismanaged succession events. Emotional honesty, moral maturity, and communicative transparency are their antidotes. More specifically, an emotionally successful succession process:

- Makes counseling and coaching services available to all senior educational leaders, including at times of succession entry and exit—so leaders can acknowledge and understand their own conflicting emotions and be more able to manage the turbulent feelings of others

- Communicates quickly, clearly, and openly the reasons for a leader's departure

- Properly honors and celebrates the leader's contributions to the organization through appropriate rituals and ceremonies[72]

- Recognizes that leadership succession and secession processes closely follow Kübler-Ross's predictable stages of grief: *denial* (the leader's belief in their own immortality), *awakening* (a crisis-invoked awareness of the need to step aside), *reflection* (taking time to reflect on past successes and prepare for the future), and *execution* (actively identifying and choosing successors)[73]

- Confronts the two most common and unhelpful myths of succession: the Messiah myth (that the coming successor will save everyone)[74] and the Rebecca myth (from Daphne du Maurier's novel *Rebecca*, that the predecessor was an irreplaceable paragon of virtue)[75]

- Treats leadership exit, like eventual retirement, as something to be planned for from the outset, not as an afterthought, when it is too late

Conclusion

Successful succession doesn't guarantee enduring improvement—the second principle of sustainability—but it goes a long way toward doing so. Effective succession means having a plan and making plans to create the positive and coordinated flows of leadership, across many years and numerous people, that will secure improvement over time. It puts a premium on outbound as well as inbound knowledge. Successful succession also means acknowledging, confronting, and managing the emotional turbulence that succession events create. It means avoiding treating leaders as if they will last forever, on the one hand, or as if they are interchangeable and can be rotated with impunity, on the other. Successful succession demands that we set aside our yearning for heroic and everlasting leadership and that we treat leadership instead as something that stretches far beyond any one leader's professional and even physical lifetime. Successful succession challenges leaders to think hard about whether they should start any initiatives that uniquely depend on them and will not survive their departure. One of the best ways to secure successful succession is to stretch and spread leadership across people now, not just in the future, to distribute and develop leadership so that successors will emerge more readily and take over more easily. Distributed leadership develops capacity in others, so they can become as gifted as those who lead them and can build on their achievements. This dimension of leadership brings us to our third principle of sustainable leadership: breadth.

Br

Distribution, Not Delegation

I not only use all the brains I have, but all I can borrow.
Woodrow Wilson, 1912

❖ **PRINCIPLE 3**

Sustainable leadership spreads. It sustains as well as depends on the leadership of others.

Lone Leaders

In a complex, fast-paced world, leadership cannot rest on the shoulders of the few. As one Australian principal puts it, principals "can't know everything about everything."[1] The burden is too great. No one leader, institution, or nation can control everything without help. Historians generally agree that Ronald Reagan was a more successful president than Jimmy Carter because Reagan chose strong subordinates and distributed authority widely, whereas Carter, the former engineer, tried to do it all himself, with limited success.[2] The third principle of sustainable leadership, therefore, is *breadth*; it is leadership that spreads, that is a distributed and shared responsibility that is taken as well as given. Sustainable and distributed leadership inspires staff members, students, and parents to seek, create, and exploit leadership opportunities that contribute to deep and broad learning for all students.

The protagonist of Witi Ihimaera's acclaimed novel *The Whale Rider* is an adolescent Maori girl who becomes the unexpected daughter, not the anticipated son, who will lead her people out of the darkness. As she gathers her community to turn beached whales back to the ocean, she challenges her patriarchal elders to understand that one lone leader cannot do it all, that the leader just gets too tired if he takes everything on himself.[3]

The educational leadership literature has its own blind spots about the nature and necessity of distributed leadership.[4] Its preoccupation with the leadership of principals has reinforced the assumption that school leadership is synonymous with the principal. Other sources of school leadership have largely been ignored. This perpetuates the myth that the answer to complex educational problems "is tightly wrapped up in finding the right persons to fill those formal roles at or near the top of the education hierarchy."[5]

There will always be a few maverick or heroic principals who can turn around "failing" schools, and we should always be grateful for their efforts and achievements. But for the most part, the heroic leadership paradigm is a flawed and fading one. We can't base entire systems on it. In England, for example, when the government assigned a group of "super heads" to run "Fresh Start" schools, many of them resigned because the challenge of change proved too great and the expectations too high for one person.[6]

The problems of heroic, or gallant, leadership don't just apply to education.[7] In *Complications*, medical doctor and writer Atul Gawande describes a Harvard Business School study of surgeons learning to master the microtechnology of new heart surgery.[8] The Harvard researchers identified the highest- and lowest-performing teams undergoing this vast learning curve, then went to observe them. The lowest-performing team had one of the technically most well-qualified doctors as its leader, but he couldn't share his uncertainties or discuss mistakes with his colleagues, the composition of his team changed considerably between operations, and the operations were often spaced at wide intervals, so that the surgeons forgot what they had learned. The highest-performing team, meanwhile, had a younger doctor as its leader who secured shared commitment to open discussions about the surgeries, kept his team together for the first thirteen operations, and ensured that only short intervals separated each operation. In medicine, successful teamwork, open discussion, and distributed leadership are literally matters of life and death. In education, people are now looking to similar kinds of distributed leadership for answers to the long-standing problem of how leaders can sustain the conditions in schools that foster successful results for students.[9]

Toward Distributed Leadership

Distributing leadership across schools and other organizations isn't just common sense; it is the morally responsible thing to do. More than a century ago, John Dewey argued that public education should be organized so that "every teacher had some regular and representative way to register judgment upon matters of educational importance, with assurance that this judgment would somehow affect the school system."[10]

The basic idea of distributed leadership has, in different guises, been a central part of organizational theory and the field of educational administration since the 1960s. Chester Barnard pointed out that leadership was not limited to executive positions and might be carried out by any member of an organization.[11] James Thompson was among the first to argue that leadership doesn't just exert influence in a downward direction but flows throughout an organization, spanning levels and circulating up and down hierarchies.[12]

Those who embrace or promote distributed leadership have historically done so for reasons of theoretical preference or ideological inclination, more than out of any respect for evidence about the impact of distributed leadership on performance or success.

These preferences and inclinations are best set out in the classic distinction between Theory X and Theory Y assumptions about human motivation.[13]

Theory X leaders consider people to be inherently lazy and untrustworthy. People must therefore be motivated to work through tight controls, heavy supervision, and exclusion from organizational decisions. Subscribers to Theory X assume that people come to the organization in a state of original sin. People need to be constantly watched, supervised, regulated, and held to account to ensure that they do not deviate or transgress. The legacies of Theory X are strongly present today among advocates of strict performance standards, sanctions for underperformance, transparent school rankings that shame the wayward, and extensive records of accountability that draw attention to mistakes and misdeeds.

Theory Y leaders regard people as basically honest, industrious, and capable of sharing responsibility for organizational decisions. To advocates of Theory Y, people in organizations need only the conditions, opportunities, and encouragement to bring their goodness out. Theory Y proponents believe that developing cultures and understanding rather than imposing contracts and mandates provide the best path to improvement. The leadership legacies of Theory Y are also still with us today—in individual professional development plans, emotional intelligence training, commitment to collaborative decision making, team building, partnerships, mentoring, and so on.

The intellectual distinctions between Theory X and Theory Y, and their many counterparts, help us understand why leaders approach the world the way they do. But in an age of appalling achievement gaps and widespread waste of young people's potential, we can no longer let educational leadership styles and strategies rest only on leaders' personal beliefs or ideological inclinations. Educational leadership, including distributed leadership, must be judged by the evidence of its impact on student learning and of its overall sustainability.

Some of the most thorough, large-scale studies of leadership effects on student learning point to the benefits for student achievement of at least some degree of distribution of leadership. These effects have been evident ever since the earliest days of school effectiveness research, which showed clear correlations between teacher involvement in school decision making and positive student outcomes.[14] Two of the most thorough examinations of what is behind these correlations and leadership effects have been conducted by Ken Leithwood and his associates in Canada and by Bill Mulford and Halia Silins in Australia.

Leithwood and his associates have undertaken more than a decade of quantitative and qualitative research on the nature and effects of *transformational leadership* in schools. Outside education, the foundational work on transformational leadership had already been conducted by Douglas McGregor and James Burns.[15] They maintained that individual leaders could inspire followers to greater commitment through shared purpose rather than bureaucratic mandates. Burns, for instance, asserted that "leaders and followers raise one another to higher levels of morality and motivation."[16] Adapting these ideas to education, Leithwood and his colleagues argued that transformational leadership moves schools beyond first-order, surface changes to second-order, deeper transformations that alter the "core technologies" of schooling, such as pedagogy, curriculum, and assessment.[17] Transformational leadership achieves these ends through the pursuit of common goals, empowerment of people in the organization, development and maintenance of a collaborative culture, promoting processes of teacher development, and engaging people in collaborative problem-solving strategies.[18] These qualities are reflected in such strategies as teacher-led professional development committees, mentorship programs, teacher-initiated curriculum innovation, and staff-led school planning teams.

Among the findings and claims of Leithwood's transformational leadership research, the ones that have most significance for distributed leadership are the following:

- The effects of leadership on student learning are small but educationally significant.[19]

- Schools in which teachers provide more influential leadership are seen by teachers as more effective and innovative.[20]

- Distributing a larger portion of leadership activity to teachers has a positive influence on teacher effectiveness and student engagement.[21]

- Transformational leadership practices are useful in almost all organizational circumstances.[22]

- Transformational leadership "depends on recognizing and responding to the unique challenges and features presented by particular types of organizational contexts."[23]

- Teacher leadership has a significant effect on student engagement that far outweighs principal leadership effects after taking into account students' family background.[24]

In Australia, Halia Silins and Bill Mulford's comprehensive study of leadership effects on student learning has provided some cumulative confirmation of the key processes through which more distributed kinds of leadership seem to influence student learning and achievement.[25] The Leadership for Organizational Learning and Student Outcomes (LOLSO) project investigated the effects of leadership and organizational learning on secondary school student outcomes. Researchers collected survey data from over 2,500 teachers and their principals, who were drawn from almost one hundred secondary schools in two Australian states. The LOLSO project used model-building techniques to investigate the relative influence of external and internal school factors on student outcomes. Among Silins and Mulford's research results are the following:

- School-level factors have a stronger influence on students' academic achievement than do students' socioeconomic status or home background.

- Leadership characteristics of a school are important factors in promoting systems and structures that enable it to operate as a learning organization.

- Student outcomes are more likely to improve when leadership sources are distributed throughout the school community and when teachers are empowered in areas of importance to them.

- School-level factors such as leadership, organizational learning, and teachers' work have a significant impact on nonacademic student outcomes such as participation in school, academic self-concept, and engagement with the school.

These large-scale studies of educational leadership effects provide clear indications that some element of shared, collaborative, or distributed leadership is strongly associated with effective leadership in schools. This work shows that the effects of principals' leadership are largely indirect. Principals improve student learning by influencing the adults who affect that learning more directly. And adults seem to achieve and improve more if they are involved in shaping the processes and practices for which they are responsible.

Yet this impressive and wide-ranging body of research on leadership effects begs as many questions as it answers.

1. The research still ultimately equates leadership with principalship. Leadership starts in the principal's office. The principal does the distributing of leadership or creates the culture in which distribution emerges. The primacy of the principal is assumed, not investigated. Because the focus is restricted to the principal, other sources of distributed leadership are not accessed for inquiry or analysis.

2. The idea of transformational leadership has its origins in Max Weber's concept of charismatic authority, in which leaders receive legitimacy from the mystical, ineffable properties of their individual personality and their ability to motivate others to follow them.[26] While the origins of transformational leadership can be traced to dramatic demonstrations of ultimately hierarchical authority among charismatic leaders, Leithwood and his colleagues argue that in education, many transformational school principals create powerful cultures of change by avoiding the limelight and leading quietly from behind. In either case, charismatic or not, it is still the principal who, quietly or dramatically, inspires and motivates others to follow and also to lead. It is the principal who manages and even manipulates others' emotions so that their leadership will, within the principal's parameters, eventually come forward.

3. Distributed leadership may not always be good leadership that advances worthwhile causes. Hitler and Mussolini were exceptional charismatic leaders who did not serve the greater good. While transformational leadership might tend to be associated with genuinely improved student outcomes, the shared leadership and collaboration it creates can just as easily support cynical targeting of gains in narrowly construed achievement scores as bringing about authentic improvement of deep and broad learning for all students. Distributed patterns of leadership don't always serve the greater good. Distributed leadership is sometimes bad leadership.[27]

4. Overall patterns of distributed leadership and its effects in large-scale samples may hide significant variations and discrepancies in which distributed leadership is less useful. If teachers are not well qualified and their knowledge base is weak, for instance, distributed leadership produces only pooled ignorance and prejudice rather than shared knowledge and professionalism. Distributed leadership can sometimes incite conflict and chaos among a divided staff that has been bequeathed to an incoming principal by his or

her predecessor. Dysfunctional schools with widespread disorder may also need a firm hand to establish a climate of safety and security before more distributed decision making can evolve.

In summary, distributed leadership can be effective or ineffective; it can be used for good purposes or bad ones; and it can emerge from the school community or be imposed or orchestrated by the principal. Distributed leadership is not automatically sustainable leadership. Who distributes leadership? Where and when is it best for leadership to be distributed? How is leadership distributed? These are the crucial questions behind the principle of breadth and spread in sustainable leadership. To address them, we first look at one of the great debates in distributed leadership— whether distributed leadership is a property of all leadership, and thus is simply a way of looking at how most leadership practice already engages many people in its execution, or whether distributed leadership is something we need more of in order to improve what schools do.

We will then set out a continuum of different kinds of distributed leadership that are evident in our own research and experience and comment on the contribution of each of them to the goal of educational sustainability.

Aspiration or Actuality?

Is distributed leadership an aspirational future state that we should strive to achieve or an existing and unavoidable reality that we need to acknowledge?

Aspiration

Most of the literature on teacher leadership is one of advocacy. It bemoans the lack of leadership opportunities for teachers and the silencing of teachers' voices. More teacher leadership, it suggests, is better leadership that will lead to better schools.

Visitors to Lord Byron High School probably wouldn't notice the quiet, informal leadership of Greg Allan, but his colleagues certainly recognized it. Allan joined the school in its second year and retired after thirty-two years there. While a number of his principals encouraged him to pursue formal leadership roles, he preferred to stay close to his first love, the classroom. At the same time, he provided enduring and pervasive leadership throughout the school for his entire career. He recalled how another staff member contributed to his development: "My colleague took me under her wing, and we worked together to develop courses and work on objectives and student activities. She had a great influence on me in terms of teaching style. She was so full of energy with the kids, and she established such strong bonds with them. In the early years, there was such an awful lot of this role modeling that occurred."

As an informal leader, Allan saw it as his responsibility to carry on this mentoring tradition and contribute to the induction and development of teachers who were new to the school, in order to preserve and extend the student-centered learning culture that he valued so deeply. "One of the aspects of my career that really gives me a sense of satisfaction is mentorship," he said.

In 2000, the school hired eleven new teachers. Six of them spontaneously mentioned Allan as a positive force in their career. Not only did he mentor his colleagues, but he also modeled his commitment to the school and his willingness to be a learner by actively seeking an assignment to teach severely learning-disabled students in the school's satellite unit. In addition, any time he became involved with a school committee, it gained instant credibility with other teachers. Through mentoring younger staff, modeling good professional practice, and being involved in schoolwide functions and improvement work,

> Allan epitomized the humble and essential work of everyday teacher leadership that holds so many schools together.

The contributions of the Greg Allans of this world to their colleagues and schools are extolled in a burgeoning literature of teacher leadership. In the guise of shared, democratic, moral, parallel, participative, and productive leadership, this literature explains and advocates for greater teacher involvement in school decision making and for collective and collaborative processes that enhance teacher learning and contribute to school improvement.[28] This confidence in teacher leadership stems from a belief that teachers are closest to the students and better placed than other leaders such as principals to make changes that benefit students' learning. In Ann Lieberman and Lynne Miller's words, teacher leadership is about "the development, support, and nurturance of teachers who assume leadership in their schools. Teachers who formally or informally acquire leadership positions can make change happen."[29] Altogether, the teacher leadership literature presents evidence that teacher leaders

- Contribute to school development and classroom change[30]

- Promote teacher collaboration within and across schools that leads to school effectiveness, improvement, and development[31]

- Improve schools' decision-making processes[32]

- Enhance teacher self-efficacy as well as morale and retention in the profession[33]

- Treat leadership as an emergent property of a group rather than as a function of an individual[34]

- Improve the achievements of students in disadvantaged schools[35]

Yet despite the enthusiastic advocacy of the teacher leadership literature, not all teacher leadership is better leadership. There is bad leadership in some corporate and government offices, and there is sometimes bad leadership among teachers, too.[36]

The "Circle" group at Talisman Park Secondary School met every morning in the staff room for coffee. Its membership included mostly experienced teachers from the large departments like math, science, and English. Young teachers and teachers of the arts, special education teachers, and guidance counselors were subtly excluded. A teacher who was new to the school explained, "The school is a little bit cliquey. There is a group that always hangs out in the staff room. There is a lot of self-importance there." As teachers who taught compulsory subjects to middle-class, university-bound, academic students, the Circle group believed that the school was in no need of change. Their morning sessions provided a forum for complaints about changes initiated by the government, the school district, and the principal and for developing strategies that would maintain the status quo. Plans hatched in the morning and revealed at staff meetings undermined the principal's efforts to move the school out of its complacency. One of the assistant principals commented, "You always hear from the coffee circle, you always hear from the most vocal. And is that really representing your school?" Teacher leaders in the Circle group were convinced that keeping the school as it was served the best interests of the academic students who they felt counted most.

When Charmaine Watson took over the school, she created opportunities for greater staff involvement in leadership through inclusive committees, professional development opportunities, and more democratic staff meetings. These diminished the Circle group's influence. But after Watson's sudden transfer to another school, her successor, Ivor Megson, had to rely almost exclusively on traditional delegation through his department heads—a number of whom were in the Circle group—to implement the government's subject-centered curriculum reforms. Most of Watson's efforts to re-culture her school were reversed overnight as the Circle group experienced a resurgence and as traditional structures re-asserted themselves.

Teacher leadership goes bad when it leads teachers to protect their own interests at the expense of students' learning, as the Circle group did. High school teachers often defend classes grouped by ability in the early years of high school because elite parents support them and because they are easier to teach, even though they are less effective for students.[37] At Stewart Heights Secondary School, for example, teachers who had become embittered by the imposed reform agenda exploited the seeming indecisiveness of the incoming principal and his leadership team and rewrote the school's code of student conduct in more punitive terms. Teachers' voices can exclude other voices, such as those of students or parents. There is more to distributed leadership than giving more leadership to teachers.

Teacher leadership can also be double-edged: a method to contain and co-opt teachers as much as a way to give them more control. Ironically, as Mark Smylie and his colleagues have observed, "We look to teachers and their leadership to help to solve today's educational problems, yet we consider teachers a primary cause of the problems that we call on leadership to solve."[38] Teacher leadership initiatives, therefore, are often compromised; they give some power to teachers but also allow administrators to hedge their bets. In that spirit, early teacher leadership programs such as merit pay, career ladders, mentorships, professional development schools, and advanced skills teachers programs in Australia and the United Kingdom gave formal leadership roles and quasi-administrative positions to some teachers, but no official leadership to the rest.[39]

This strategy of *appointment and anointment* had mixed outcomes.[40] A few teacher leaders welcomed the extra money and responsibility, as well as the chance to improve their leadership capabilities. Others found their new roles problematic. The roles were often poorly defined. They came into conflict with other leadership positions, such as department headships. It was hard to take on new leadership functions and still fulfill classroom responsibilities. Relationships with colleagues who hadn't been anointed sometimes turned sour. And when unwanted reforms made teachers feel overloaded, they sometimes turned to or even turned on their newly anointed colleagues, proclaiming, "You're the new teacher leader, you do it!"

The failure of the appoint-and-anoint approach has resulted in a wider quest to involve teachers in leadership activities, without simply adding on more formal roles. Linda Darling-Hammond and her colleagues suggest that teacher leadership doesn't have to be restricted to formally defined positions but can be "embedded in tasks and roles that do not create artificial, imposed, formal hierarchies and positions."[41] All teachers, they say, should get a chance to grow toward greater professionalism—for example, by

- Working with students and teachers as facilitators, coaches, or mentors

- Performing administrative tasks as action researchers or task force members

- Participating in school improvement teams, committees, or business-school partnerships[42]

Jim Spillane has undertaken an intensive investigation of distributed leadership. He calls the assignment to teachers of additional roles and tasks the *leadership-plus* perspective.[43] This leadership-plus approach to distributed leadership is a limited one, he says, because it overlooks the less glamorous and more mundane daily leadership work that teachers undertake on their own initiative to keep a school running smoothly. The quiet advice from an experienced teacher to a new colleague on a difficult discipline issue, the sharing of materials among colleagues, or the phone call to a parent to head off a potential student problem—these more ordinary acts of teacher leadership often go unnoticed and unheralded. There is a lot more to distributed leadership than leadership plus.

Actuality

Like it or not, good or bad, leadership is always distributed. Whether formally recognized or not, rewarded or not, leadership is not just a bunch of roles or a set of styles. It is "fluid and emergent rather than a fixed phenomenon."[44] Drawing on theories of distributed cognition, Spillane argues that leadership is an activity, a social practice that stretches across many people and includes the situation in which leadership activity takes place. "School leadership is best understood as a distributed practice, stretched over the schools' social and situational contexts," he says.[45]

Spillane uses the metaphor of two people performing a dance—the Texas two-step. The actions of the individuals in the dance are important, but it is the interaction between individuals that is the practice or activity of the dance. The music is an important part of the situation, and therefore the dancers' interaction with the music becomes part of the activity. If the music changes, so does the dance.

Spillane illustrates his point by describing the leadership practices of an elementary school's literacy committee and a meeting of its mathematics teachers. All the members of the literacy committee, including the school's principal, a literacy coordinator, the African American heritage coordinator, and approximately twenty teachers, participate actively and enthusiastically in an analysis of the school's standards data. They share new information and develop plans for future instructional activities. Program coordination in literacy is spread across a number of key players, including the principal.

In the case of mathematics, only the four teachers directly involved show up for the meeting. The two formal teacher leaders do most of the talking as they review the appropriate mathematics standards, introduce new resources, and suggest alternative pedagogical approaches. The other teachers ask a few questions for clarification, and then the meeting breaks up. It is quick, efficient, and clinical.

School subjects aren't just bodies of knowledge. They are small worlds. People in them think and act differently.[46] Literacy attracts those who are strong in language and like to talk. Conversation tends to be extensive and inclusive. Mathematics teachers are typically more focused and precise, and because many elementary teachers are less comfortable with mathematics than with literacy, fewer colleagues get involved.

The strength of Spillane's research is not only that it demonstrates the ubiquitous nature of distributed leadership but also that it highlights how patterns of distribution vary from one teacher community to another. Distributed leadership, in other words, doesn't always have to look the same. Long meetings or short ones, many participants or a few, wordy exchanges or clipped remarks—all of them count as distributed leadership.

Summary

There are two ways to look at distributed leadership, then. The first is *normative*. The more distributed leadership we have, the better. Leadership that is distributed should extend beyond teachers to students and parents; should avoid becoming self-serving and remain focused on students; and shouldn't deteriorate into co-opted leadership, like the puppet governments of wartime collaboration. Despite these cautions, the current problem is not that there is too much teacher leadership and that we need to rein it in, but that self-conscious and deliberate leadership activity in schools is still too scarce.

The second view of distributed leadership is *descriptive*. Looking at leadership as leadership activity points to all the leadership that is already there. As Frank Crowther and his colleagues put it, "By any standards for judging, teacher leadership exists, it is real."[47] Leadership is always distributed in some way or other. The point is to show how the distribution occurs. Proponents of this second view, especially Spillane, are agnostic about whether distributing leadership more—or adopting the leadership-plus position—is generally a good thing.

If Spillane's view seems intellectually self-indulgent, there are, we believe, significant strategic implications to his work. His activity-based approach is a good way to audit existing leadership practices. It draws attention to leadership contributions that might otherwise go unrecognized.[48] It can highlight emerging leadership talent. And it validates the leadership achievements of the group, beyond the gallant individuals who usually get the credit. While these implications are not necessarily ones that Spillane himself would draw, they do provide a way for his more descriptive framework to be put to good use.

The Distributed Leadership Continuum

Sustainable leadership is distributed leadership. But not all distributed leadership is sustainable leadership. It depends on how the leadership is distributed and for what purpose. In a research report and position paper on distributed leadership for England's National College for School Leadership, Hay Group Education sketches out the risks of adopting a naively optimistic view of distributed leadership: "If they are not bound together by a clear vision, tight processes and clear accountability, multiple sources of leadership can pull a school apart. The consequences of not distributing leadership are staleness and stagnation. The risks of distributing leadership are anarchy and confusion."[49]

Hay Group Education proposes five dimensions of distributed leadership that it arranges on a continuum from highly concentrated to highly distributed leadership, until a point of excess is reached when, like ripe fruit turning rotten, distribution becomes too much for its own good. The points on the Hay Group's continuum are as follows:

- *Instruct*: Initiatives and ideas come only from the top and can seem arbitrary and unexpected.

- *Consult*: Staff are given opportunities for input, even though decisions are still largely made higher up.

- *Delegate*: Staff make decisions and exercise initiative within clear areas of responsibility and accountability.

- *Facilitate*: Ideas are solicited, taken up, and championed at every level.

- *Neglect*: People are forced to take initiative and responsibility because there is a lack of interest or direction at the top.[50]

Our own evidence suggests a continuum of distributed leadership that overlaps with Hay Group Education's but diverges from it in two respects. First, in line with Spillane's position on distributed leadership, even autocracy, or Hay Group Education's Instruct mode, contains distributed leadership. Distributed leadership isn't absent here, as Hay Group Education claims. It may not be intended or wanted, but it still surfaces in ways that undermine and obstruct the autocrat's wishes. Even Huxley's *Brave New World* created rebellious outsiders. So do autocratic leaders in schools.[51]

Autocratic principals, districts, and governments can never eliminate distributed leadership!

Second, the category that Hay Group Education terms *Facilitate*
is, in fact, a much bigger box of different possibilities and styles.
There are many ways to facilitate. Some can be quite controlling,
manipulative, and even cult-like, giving teachers no opportunity to
question what their leaders are asking them to do.[52] Others can be
more empowering and inclusive, stimulating vigorous and challenging inquiry and debate.[53] The overall term *Facilitate* masks a
multitude of virtues and sins as well as the difficult choices to be
made between them. Facilitative leadership is not a facile thing, as
our "thermometer" of distributed leadership shows (see Figure 3.1).

As the mercury ascends the thermometer, distributed leadership
occurs primarily through structural means such as roles, committees, and formal procedures at the bottom; then factors in cultural
forms of distribution through communication, relationships, and
group life in the middle; and adds in political elements and assertiveness toward the top.

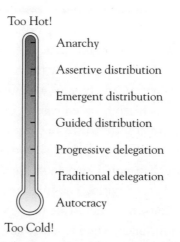

Figure 3.1. Raising the Temperature of Distributed Leadership
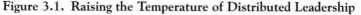

Autocracy

Len Adomo and his successors at Sheldon High School, whom we met in Chapter Two, kept very tight control of leadership tasks within the formal structures of the school.[54] They actively squelched any signs of emergent leadership. In their desire to control all aspects of the school, they entertained very little involvement of teachers or other stakeholders in decision making and suppressed individuals or groups who deviated from the predetermined directions that each principal had established. This deliberate failure to distribute leadership galvanized the teaching staff into a powerful adversarial community that came together to oppose the school's leadership and support their teachers' union. The result was a conflict between old-style principalship and old-style unionism. The real losers were the students, since autocratic leadership and defensive opposition undermined the school's ability to develop quality programs for its changing body of students.[55]

Schools like Sheldon in which the principal, sometimes assisted by a small group of formal leaders such as department heads, makes all the important decisions not only fail to engage the leadership abilities of others within the official structures of the organization but also invite a backlash from emergent groups that need outlets for their leadership abilities. If leadership is not deliberately distributed in ways that engage teachers with the goals of the school, it will end up being distributed by default. Leadership will emerge to subvert and sabotage the principal's plans at every step. There are times when autocratic approaches are necessary and must be used as a last resort—for instance, when teachers abdicate responsibility for poor performance.[56] But in general, autocratic leadership doesn't just fail to sustain important changes; it leaves them stillborn.

Traditional Delegation

Mark Warne was the principal of North Ridge High School. Three years from retirement, Warne had a keen intellect and a deep knowledge about imposed change and its effects. He valued and was skilled at seeing the big picture of reform. When legislated reforms were announced, Warne produced detailed and thoughtful written statements and projected time lines for implementation responses, which he circulated to the staff for comment. The response was disappointing, though, and Warne confided that his staff was generally apathetic about getting involved with change. His strength was that he possessed great intellectual clarity, but he couldn't develop the capacity among his teachers to share it with him.

Warne controlled the school's directions through the line management of the department heads. These subject leaders were quite autonomous in their areas, and staff involvement depended on the leadership style of each head. One of Warne's assistant principals, who was close to retirement, performed traditional disciplinary and administrative roles. The other was battling with what turned out, sadly, to be a terminal illness. Warne delegated work to his subordinate department heads and accepted their advice in areas in which they had more expertise than he. The department heads generally described him as "supportive," "compassionate," and "well-intentioned." Yet the wider staff felt excluded from decisions and ill-informed on important issues. They considered him to be "indecisive," "inconsistent," and "lacking a personal vision." At a school improvement workshop in which the majority of teachers identified their community as a "cruising school," the improvement priority the staff chose to address was "communications with the administration."[57]

Like most secondary school principals of his generation, Mark Warne's idea of distributed leadership meant delegating specific tasks to particular people. Warne worked closely with his department heads, distributed leadership to them within their subject areas, and worked with them to develop broad school policies, manage day-to-day operations, and react to outside reform initiatives. Warne seldom interfered in departmental affairs. Innovations occurred within some departments but not others. For the most part, he kept the school on an even keel by avoiding controversy and creating the illusion of movement on government reforms with a blizzard of papers and plans that resulted in little concrete action.

Leaders like Warne, who distribute by delegating within their designed structures, manage their schools efficiently and maintain stability and continuity with the past without also moving beyond it. Rather than actively suppressing emergent leadership, like autocrats such as Adomo at Sheldon, leaders like Warne frustrate it.

Distributed leadership means more than delegated leadership. At its worst, delegated leadership amounts to assigning to subordinates tasks that are menial, uninteresting, or unpleasant. Student discipline, routine committee work, and unimaginative and unpopular teacher evaluation procedures are the stuff of traditional delegation. They get the existing work of the school done but don't really change or challenge it. At its best, delegates like Warne's department heads might enjoy opportunities for prestige and power. But staff members who feel ignored and out of the loop are likely to express their dissatisfaction and alienation by withdrawing into their classrooms, disengaging from school activities, or quietly subverting schoolwide change.

Progressive Delegation

Soon after the school improvement workshop, North Ridge began to change, but not through a change of principal. Two new assistant principals were appointed. Together, they infused the school's administration with renewed enthusiasm, optimism, and focus. Diane Grant's infectiously energetic style brought her sophisticated knowledge of curriculum and classroom assessment to the challenge of reform. Before long, she was skillfully leading the staff in curriculum gap analyses or having them share successful experiences in classroom assessment by seating them in cross-disciplinary tables at the staff picnic, where they scribbled their ideas as graffiti on paper tablecloths. Meanwhile, Bill Johnson, the other assistant principal, drew on his counseling skills to develop effective communication and relationships with and among the staff. As a team, they were able to set a common vision for the school and a more open style of communication. Through this fresh approach, the staff focused on collaborative learning, inquiry, and problem solving. Warne's strength was in having the good sense to distribute the leadership of important classroom-related changes to his assistant principals. They, in turn, redistributed much of the leadership among the staff, who learned to be critical filters for government mandates rather than mere pipelines for implementing them.

Warne took advantage of the strengths of his two new assistant principals to distribute leadership more widely, which was a significant shift in his self-understanding about and approach to his own leadership. But teachers were never allowed to deviate too far from his organizational framework.[58] Diane Grant did distribute leadership beyond the formal department head structure by initiating and facilitating committees for assessment and literacy. As a result, a larger percentage of the staff became involved in reworking government initiatives to meet the needs of North Ridge students—a giant step forward. Yet all of the improvements still fell within the limits of the school's formal structures.

The more progressive patterns of delegation in schools like North Ridge redirect their schools' structures toward supporting improvement. However, they succeed only as long as the formal leaders are around to guide them and the teachers involved remain committed and supportive. Progressive delegation shares most of the shortcomings of traditional delegation, with one twist. In traditional delegation, teachers don't expect or get much significant involvement, so they become frustrated. In progressive delegation, people's hopes are raised, only to see them dashed when their administrative champions move on.

Guided Distribution

Noumea Primary School (actual name) is part of a post–World War II planned community near Sydney, Australia.[59] Over time, the community has deteriorated into a lower-class, multiethnic neighborhood of intergenerational unemployment and endemic poverty. In spite of its challenging community and a student turnover rate of over 40 percent, this school of 530 students has won national awards and international recognition for its high standards, innovative approaches to literacy and mathematics, and ingenious uses of technology. All this has been accomplished despite state staffing practices that promote high teacher turnover and leave challenging schools like Noumea to be run by young and inexperienced teachers.

Principal Jenny Lewis is a five-foot dynamo of energy and enthusiasm. She handles her youthful staff and demanding community with skill, tenacity, and charm. Over ten years, she has created a professional learning community that ensures that teachers have the time, resources, and encouragement to develop, share, and use their knowledge in support of teaching, learning, and caring for every child in the school. Nor is the organizational learning confined to the teachers. Parents and students also have a meaningful voice in school directions and day-to-day operations.

Lewis and her colleagues promote community learning through ongoing visioning activities, development of a shared language, and collection and analysis of information about the school and its mission. Through shared self-reflection and with more-than-satisfactory results as their ally, Noumea's staff decided that state-sponsored standardized tests interfered with their focus on student outcomes. Through mobilizing community support and some expert politicking with the state government, Lewis and her colleagues received permission to use daily teacher assessments of student learning and achievement to inform lessons and communicate with parents. Grade-related teacher teams monitor this process at weekly staff meetings and use their three hours per week of out-of-class time to analyze student data and samples of student work together. Results of these data-driven sectional meetings are shared at monthly staff meetings to determine trends and patterns for the entire school and to strive for continual improvement. Lewis provides an example of how her learning community works. When behavioral problems in the school increased, she explains, "There was a strong belief . . . that Samoan and Tongan boys were the most violent and were not performing well in their schoolwork, as they seemed to arrive at irregular times to school. Yet, when data were reviewed collectively, it was found that it was the white, Anglo-Saxon boys that were the most violent and the most at-risk learners. Many of our white Anglo-Saxon families were isolated, single-parent, and on third- and fourth-generation welfare benefit."[60]

Collegial interaction at Noumea is always connected to classroom learning. Technologically, this is made possible by teachers' having laptop computers in every classroom, so class tests, marks, and comments on student work and other information can all be entered (and accessed) in real time, as needed. The school's computer program, Schoolmate, which was invented at the school, enables staff to access and use data on an individual, team, or whole-school basis to guide decision making.

Noumea has created an evidence-informed environment that can challenge or confirm intuition in a practical way. This environment is not an antiseptic world of data management teams but a living professional community in which leadership is distributed widely throughout the staff and evidence is taken seriously within a clear and shared vision of student success. These integrated efforts have lifted the school from being at significant risk of failure to ranking among the top twenty-five schools in New South Wales.

Leadership at Noumea spreads across the school. It also stretches through its various layers, achieving what Peter Gronn calls *leadership density*—proportionately large amounts of leadership within the community.[61] Noumea distributes leadership through coordination between the principal and her assistants, through the various grade teams that work together in the weekly and monthly review meetings, and through the staff visioning process. Teachers also meet in collaborative grade teams to examine students' work folders and interact with the school's database to plot directions for student learning. Furthermore, the school demonstrates collective distribution of leadership between the principal and her assistants, who work separately but interdependently with grade teams to prepare for the school's monthly gathering, which decides the school's short-term and long-term directions.[62]

At Noumea, distribution of leadership means more than downward delegation. But the distribution is still very directed, or guided.

It is distribution by design. In a school with a very high annual turnover of staff, it could scarcely be anything else. Lewis purposefully and skillfully designed a structure and developed a culture that really engaged teachers in improving teaching and learning. Facing substantial annual changes of personnel, Noumea worked hard and successfully to revision itself and renew its culture every year. Teachers were energetically engaged in all aspects of the school and its development, but Lewis's firm and guiding hand was also undeniably everywhere.

Guided distribution can create strong professional learning communities. It can also sustain them—as long as the principal lasts. Jenny Lewis stayed with her community for ten years and used guided distribution to create real improvement that endured for a long time. But now that she has finally gone, will the firmness of her guidance combined with the instability of the school's staff enable her legacy to survive, or stretch, to the next principal, then the next?

Two of our secondary schools—Talisman Park Secondary School under Charmaine Watson and Stewart Heights Secondary School under Bill Andrews—illustrated the same potential and pitfalls of guided distribution. These leaders extended and expanded their schools' formal structures by creating schoolwide committees, task forces, representative groups, and open staff meetings. They began to build stronger staff cultures, though these were still heavily dependent on their presence and direction. Andrews started to develop a critical mass for improvement but was still too forthright for many of his female staff. Watson worked with her very broad school improvement team to place a priority on technology, but as soon as her back was turned, staff bickered about really wanting to concentrate on student behavior—and didn't want to disclose their disagreements in case they might upset her.

When Watson and Andrews each departed after less than three years, their influence quickly evaporated and the informal leaders in their schools reasserted their power and influence and returned to the old status quo. Guided distribution and firm facilitation are one and the same. They can create professional learning communities but are unlikely to sustain them over time. Guided distribution is so dependent on the senior leader (in these cases, the principal) that the sustainability of significant change is confined to the period of that person's tenure.

Emergent Distribution

Distributed leadership doesn't occur by design only. Leadership also emerges from individuals and groups who seize the initiative to inspire and influence their colleagues to take up opportunities, move in new directions, or attend to external pressures—with or without the principal's blessing. Leadership from this perspective is everywhere—in the principal's office, the science labs, the literacy team, teachers' workrooms, and anywhere that staff members join together to focus on learning, teaching, or change.

Emergent leadership doesn't happen at the immediate instigation of senior leadership. It can't be delegated or directed. Instead, it comes forward from the staff in ways that are unanticipated and even surprising. But if emergent leadership isn't directly dependent on the principal, this doesn't mean that principals are indifferent to it or that they don't and shouldn't influence it. Mysterious and surprising as it is, emergent distribution is still at least partly attributable to the influence of the principal or other senior leaders.

In *Developing Teacher Leaders*, Frank Crowther and his colleagues describe compelling cases of what we call *emergent distributed leadership* in Australian primary and middle schools.[63] In one instance, when a classroom teacher with no formal authority returned from a professional development day "buoyed by new ideas and possibilities" about teaching literacy, her "boundless enthusiasm" and determination gave her the courage to approach her principal and suggest a new schoolwide approach for literacy.[64] Fueled by her own passion for "getting a better deal for public schools," buttressed by her reputation as a thoughtful educator, and emboldened by a more seasoned colleague who helped her secure funds, build a team, and develop an implementation and communication plan, the teacher was able to secure the principal's support.

Building on foundations of wisdom, expertise, and willingness to learn, the passion, political savvy, and sheer pluckiness of teachers like this are what propel teacher leadership and school improvement forward in many schools. The leadership may emerge across a whole school or in a department, grade level, or small teacher team, but its effects are real and potent. In these circumstances, when initiatives evolve in ways that truly benefit students, it is to be hoped that the principal at least knows to get out of the way! But more usually, as Crowther and his colleagues note, "the strong facilitative support" of the principal in listening, advising, and helping to take things forward is essential.[65] Pride in the community and humility about one's own educational gifts are essential attributes in this kind of leadership. As the principal in this case reflected, "I personally couldn't do what these teachers do!"[66]

The most important contribution that senior leaders can make to the development of emergent distributed leadership is to create an inclusive, purposeful, and optimistic culture in which initiatives can easily come forward.[67] Indeed, for Lieberman and Miller, as well as others, the heart of teacher leadership is "groups of teachers intentionally working together to transform the very cultures in which they work and lead."[68] The best facilitative principals can work with others, supporting and inspiring them to reculture their schools and districts so that they become strong professional learning communities.[69]

Blue Mountain School opened in 1994 and enrolled 1,250 students by 2000. Established with a charismatic principal and carefully selected staff, many of whom had former connections with him, and with the advantage of a full year's advance planning, the school established great technological, structural, and curriculum innovations compared with the standard "grammar of secondary schooling."[70] The initial leadership team comprised eight "process leaders" in cross-curricular areas like technology or assessment and evaluation rather than the customary group of subject department heads. In addition to their own subject area, all teachers belonged to at least one process team that met regularly.

The school is self-consciously a learning organization and, more recently, a professional learning community. The ideas of organizational learning and systems thinking permeated almost everything the founding principal did. Inspired and informed by his doctorate on schools as learning organizations, he set up monthly meetings with the community, leading to the creation of a school advisory council long before school councils became official policy within the province of Ontario. Parents, administrators, and founding faculty members collaborated on defining the school mission and graduating outcomes, openly shared information and data on the progress of the school, and determined how to undertake an annual assessment of the organization and its effectiveness.

In the early years, the principal worked with teachers and other staff to build a vision of a student-centered community that focused on learning, teaching, and caring, based on strong relationships, mutual respect, the importance of family, and achieving balanced personal and professional lives. As one teacher commented, "I'd never been in a place where the priority was so much the student, and for me, that's it—all that matters is the student." Virtually all of the highly dedicated and enthusiastic staff participated in personal and professional learning outside school as well as within it. Many teachers felt they had experienced accelerated professional growth through belonging to a community of learners in which new ways of working and thinking were internalized and rapidly became recognizable as their philosophy in practice. For example, systems thinking was explicitly taught to staff and to students.

Blue Mountain faced great challenges during the era of standardized reform. Its school district rotated the school's principal twice between 1998 and 2004, and the time constraints and budget cuts resulting from reform measures undermined the school's unique departmental structure and forced the senior leadership to be somewhat more directive. In spite of this adversity, the formal and informal leaders who remained at the school succeeded in salvaging much of the student-centered nature of the school's program and continued to renew the school's distributed leadership culture as new teachers joined it and the reform climate improved again. As one of the school's original teacher leaders explained, "Blue Mountain had a real period of low cloud cover that hid the peaks for a while, but (with a new government in power), we have now been released so that the vision of its peak is still evident, clear, and desirable."

The ultimate goal for sustainable leadership in a complex, knowledge-sharing society is for schools to become *professional learning communities*.[71] Shirley Hord, the first person to distill this idea and bring its three subcomponents together, described these kinds of communities as ones "in which the teachers in a school and its administrators continuously seek and share learning and act on that learning. The goal of their actions is to enhance their effectiveness as professionals for the students' benefit; thus, this arrangement may also be termed *communities of continuous inquiry and improvement*."[72]

Professional learning communities are exactly what the name implies. They are

- *Communities* where diverse people have a shared commitment to a common purpose, to each other as people in pursuing that purpose, and to acknowledgment and inclusion of minority views in collective decision making.[73] These communities include not only teachers but also students, parents, and the growing number of other adults and assistants who work alongside teachers in their classrooms and schools.[74] The communities focus on . . .

- *Learning* of the students, the adults, and the organization more generally. The learning is deep and not superficial, and the community's first response to problems and challenges is "What do we know about this?" These learning communities are . . .

- *Professional* in how they value grown-up norms of difference, disagreement, and debate about the best ways to identify and implement needed improvements and in how they promote, value, and bring together formal evidence (including both achievement data and other data, as at Noumea Primary School) and experiential knowledge and intuition as a basis for decision making.[75]

One of the keys to achieving the cohesion and dynamism of a strong professional learning community is in how leadership is stretched over the school. Leadership certainly flows through formal roles and structures, though many of these are explicitly innovative and improvement-oriented. But if a professional learning community works well, leadership is also creative, spontaneous, and emergent, leading to temporary structures and committees, unexpected and inspirational initiatives, and adaptive changes that strengthen all students' learning, as well as the school's ability to help them learn.[76] As we have seen in the case of Blue Mountain School, professional learning communities do more than exemplify the cliché that everyone is a leader; they create the conditions and encouragement that allow everyone to lead with purpose and positive intent.

At their best, professional learning communities embody and include the strong principles of emergence and self-organization that we will discuss in more detail in Chapter Five. They also have clear design elements that make their own emergence possible, especially in the early stages. The principal is not made irrelevant by the positively distributed leadership that professional learning communities represent. As Rick Dufour and Robert Eaker argue in their prominent advocacy for professional learning communities, "Strong principals are crucial to the creation of learning communities."[77] But, they continue, "the image of how a strong principal operates needs to be reconsidered."[78] In the context of professional learning communities, strong leaders are not strident and forceful. Although their commitment to all students' learning needs to be insistently and clearly voiced, their true strengths may lie in

- Modeling and building strong and rewarding relationships by paying attention to the human side of school change[79]

- Establishing a high-trust environment[80]

- Developing and renewing a culture of learning and improvement at all levels through problem solving, inquiry, and intelligent, evidence-informed decision making[81]

- Helping the school community develop and commit to a cohesive and compelling purpose that also prevents dissipation of initiative and effort

- Stimulating a culture of professional entrepreneurship in regard to innovations and ideas that benefit student learning

- Establishing and enforcing grown-up professional norms of civil argument and productive debate[82]

- Ensuring that the voices of minority members of the culture always receive a proper hearing[83]

- Doing all this within an unswerving commitment to improving learning and achievement for all students, especially those who are furthest behind

At their best, professional learning communities embody the most positive features of distributed leadership, bringing the energy and ability of the whole community forward to serve the best interests of all students. But like the idea of facilitative leadership, which often hints at inclusion while secretly providing tightly controlled direction, professional learning communities can also be just a new elixir in the old bottles of delegation and direction. So it's important to also be clear about what professional learning communities are not, or at least what they shouldn't be:

- Professional learning communities aren't merely convivial and congenial, they are demandingly collegial in the levels of commitment and critical debate they require in order to address compelling problems of student learning.[84]
- Professional learning communities aren't just bunches of teams that sit down and analyze data together after school is over; they are a way of life that changes the entire school culture and in which emergent leadership comes together in rewarding and caring communities that inquire into the need for, then create improvements that benefit all students.
- Professional learning communities don't get fixated on achievement scores in narrowly defined curriculum areas like literacy and mathematics in the old basics but develop a strong focus on improving deep and broad student learning that also includes the new basics.

- Professional learning communities avoid obsessions with alignment in which improvement efforts and staff development initiatives are discouraged or forbidden outside of narrowly defined priorities; instead, they create focus and cohesion among a diverse community of teachers with demonstrable but differing skills and talents.

- Professional learning communities overcome schools' dependency on a restricted range of standardized scores and measurable results in favor of a broader and more intelligent use of multiple forms of evidence and accountability to steer and monitor improvement.[85]

- Professional learning communities can't be forced; they can only be facilitated and fed. Professional learning communities combine high emergence with progressive design. Mandating and legislating professional learning communities sacrifices emergence to the arrogance and overconfidence of imposed design, leading to changes in the designation of schools and districts as "learning communities" but to no real changes in their nature.

- Professional learning communities shouldn't be used as co-optative devices to implement unquestioned mandates for scripted literacy programs, for example, but should work and function as empowered communities that can develop evidence-informed local solutions that respond to diverse and differing students and their compelling learning problems. The point of professional learning communities is to commit to and fulfill essential principles and purposes, not to implement other people's specific program priorities.

- Professional learning communities don't confine their discussions to the technicalities of training strategies and achievement gaps, but, like Noumea Primary School, they engage in intelligent and ethical deliberations about what counts as achievement. These deliberations include courageous questioning and even creative subversion of the mandates and measurement tools that diminish that sense of achievement.

When it is ingrained and embedded, the strength of distributed leadership, like the interconnected roots of giant redwood trees, enables the school to withstand the tempestuous storms of questionable reform and to survive difficult successions of senior leadership. Indeed, some public sector literature suggests that the strong cultures that professional learning communities exemplify can inoculate organizations against mediocre successors.[86] At the extreme, then, strong cultures and communities of distributed leadership are not only emergent but are assertive and resilient.

Assertive Distribution

When Lord Byron Secondary School opened its doors to students in 1970, it was labeled as the most innovative school in Canada. Its principal, Ward Bond, created an environment that encouraged leadership from any quarter of the school and invited openness and advice from everyone on staff. One woman who, at the time of interview, was a director of education (CEO) for a neighboring school district, recalled, "It was significant that he was going to let women wear pantsuits. I just remember it being an issue for working women. You just had a sense that if you took something to him, an idea, it was going to be heard. I think that in three years we were willing to say as women 'We must go further.' I almost felt that was the ethos that was there—readiness to accept, and an invitation to proceed."

Ironically, none of the original formal leaders at Lord Byron were women. Perhaps because of the patriarchal value system that prevailed at the time, no women had applied. However, a critical incident related to Bond's departure from Byron after three and a half years spurred the women into their own leadership action.[87] To celebrate Bond's promotion, the male staff members organized a two-day, men-only stag party at farms a number of teachers owned in northern Ontario. The women were incensed that the men had excluded them from this symbolic event. One of them recalled, "We had always felt respected, and our individuality was important to us, and he was important to us as well." Another reflected on how the stag party "was the catalyst that got us talking together about not being part of decision making. It was a very symbolic representation of the fact that we, as women, were not considered part of the decision making because we were not in formal leadership positions. So we decided to set up our own leadership, encouragement, training, and support group, because we felt that other groups were not open to us. So it was a case of experiencing a need, talking about it, and doing something about it."

The Byron women organized an alternative event, to which they invited all staff members and their partners. The success of this event and the enjoyment of working together to achieve the goal led to subsequent meetings. The Byron Women's Group still meets about six times a year, even though everyone has moved on to other jobs and places. Over the years, these women have helped one another professionally and personally. They were there for one another at the birthing of babies and when they were pursuing promotion. Since there were initially no women department heads at Byron, for instance, they encouraged their colleagues to apply, and many of them did, successfully. Women and men alike discouraged sexist jokes and gender-based language at Byron.

The movement spread throughout the district. In the early 1980s, members of the group helped to found an organization in the district that dealt with gender-based issues in the region. One of its successes was a board policy on inclusive language and a review of curriculum to ensure gender equity. By the mid-1990s, women occupied a number of senior positions in the district office, and at least half of the district's secondary school principals were women. Over time, members of the women's group moved on to take up principalships, were appointed to senior district leadership positions, and were to be found in some of the highest-level leadership positions in the province. Their leadership was definitely taken, not given. It was asserted by the women. It was also accepted by Ward Bond, who had built a culture that enabled assertive leadership to flourish. This challenged his authority on occasions, but in ways that didn't compromise and, indeed, strengthened the overall mission and purpose of the school.

Assertive distribution of leadership means that teachers in a school feel free to challenge the principal or superintendent and are actively empowered to do so, provided their assertive leadership strengthens and does not undermine the overall vision for sustainable learning and improvement. This does not mean that critical voices should degenerate into curmudgeonly grumbles. Instead, assertive leadership moves distributed leadership to a higher, riskier, and more overtly political plane. It calls for courage and self-confidence among senior leaders, who must be able to endure, encourage, and empower assertive distribution of leadership that furthers the school's or system's goals (even though it may challenge the means). And it requires an activist orientation among teachers, who must be change agents committed to social and educational missions that unite them in confronting bureaucratic and political obstacles to socially just and educationally justifiable improvement and reform.

Governments and bureaucracies don't always occupy the high ground on change and reform. It's not just teachers who are resistant to change. Governments and administrators can be resistant too. In the mid-nineteenth century, it was assertive, indeed activist distributed leadership in the form of "the spontaneous efforts of the colored people" that started and ran hundreds of secret slave schools in the American South[88] and that, against Southern white suppression and in the light of their impatience in "wait[ing] for the coming of a white teacher" from the North, later set up "a class of schools got up and taught by colored people, rude and imperfect, but still groups of people, old and young, *trying* to learn."[89]

It was assertive distributed leadership that established the British Mechanics Institutes of the same period, providing scientific education for adult and adolescent males in the industrial working classes.[90] In the small textile town of Accrington, for example, where there were no secondary schools in the mid-nineteenth century, the Accrington and Church Industrial Co-operative Society, formed by the town's weavers under the motto "Organize and Educate," had forty students in 1873, who took examinations in "geometry, machine construction, drawing, mathematics, animal physiology, inorganic chemistry, magnetism and electricity, acoustics, light and heat, and physical geography."[91]

More recently, assertive distributed leadership motivated a generation of women, like those at Lord Byron, to seek out and achieve stronger representation in the world of educational leadership. It galvanized a group of mothers in Ontario to build a social movement that documented and publicized data on the largely negative impact of standardized educational reform policies on schools and students, which helped topple the government that had imposed them.[92] And assertive distributed leadership repeatedly emboldens successful leaders of schools in challenging circumstances—for example, Jenny Lewis and her colleagues at Noumea Primary School—to challenge government or district bureaucracies that impede their path to achieving authentic improvement and make it unnecessarily hard for them to engage with the varied cultures and intellectual differences among their diverse students.

The founding principal of Durant Alternative School, a high school in a northeastern U.S. city, believed that the school's original vision of fostering independent learning in real-life settings would survive only if teachers, students, and parents shared that vision. The principal emphasized dialogue and shared decision making, and the staff members came to believe that, in the words of one, "we were all administrators." Indeed, because of the principal's many other admirable and ethical qualities, teachers were prepared to cover for his more routine administrative shortcomings. Long after the principal's retirement, the teachers and other members of the school community continued to resist the standardizing policies of the district and state, holding fast to their founding vision by seeking waivers for their distinctive program.

Durant engages assertively with its environment in a pattern of mutual influence. In the past few years, the school's courageous new principal has activated his personal and professional networks and forged strategic alliances with the community in a tireless campaign to preserve the school's mission. He has written articles for local and state newspapers, appeared on radio and television programs, and supported students and parents, who, in a symbolic gesture of opposition to the strictures of increased testing, protested in straitjackets outside the district offices. He has organized conferences on the adverse effects of high-stakes testing and has worked assiduously with his allies and other innovative schools throughout the state to push for a group variance from the state tests, receiving for his efforts a temporary exclusion from state policy. Durant's story shows that, especially in an unhelpful reform environment, sustainable leadership is necessarily also activist leadership.

Durant's assertive and distributed leadership defends depth of learning as a shared responsibility that secures social justice for students and lasts over time. Its strong sense of purpose is passionately shared among its professional learning community, which is prepared, in activist terms, to try and reshape the environment that periodically threatens it. In such challenging circumstances, distributed leadership demands an assertive and activist orientation that advocates relentlessly for disadvantaged students against forces that deny them their due.

Hay Group Education's study of distributed leadership in England concluded that distributed leadership is given rather than taken.[93] This finding is not surprising, considering that educational leaders in that country had spent fifteen years working in a predominantly autocratic reform environment. The leading edge of distributed leadership must do more than project trends based on the evidence of a limited past. It's important, instead, to extend beyond the past, to develop and encourage assertive professional learning communities that are passionate about the purposes of learning and justice and prepared to argue, advocate for, and organize to protect and promote those purposes whenever they can. Provided the organization's core purposes remain intact, strong senior leaders needn't just tolerate widely distributed assertiveness; they can actively encourage it. Indeed, what pleasure or surprise is there for leaders if they are surrounded only by servants and sycophants?

Anarchic Distribution

The line between autocracy and anarchy is a thin one. Autocracies foment resentment and rebellion. Lacking government, anarchies give rise to lawlessness and disorder. Anarchies result from distribution by neglect.[94] Senior leaders who are never present, who can't maintain clarity or unity of purpose, who are weak or afraid, or who want only to be liked—all create a leadership vacuum that others are more than eager to fill. But, as in William Golding's fable *Lord of the Flies*, this kind of emergent leadership is often divisive and self-serving or even callous and cruel because there is no moral glue to hold it together.

Like weak or inexperienced teachers who inherit a class from a controlling colleague who has kept the lid screwed on too tight, transitions from leaders who are controlling to ones who are inexperienced or ineffectual provide optimum conditions for the emergence of anarchy. The shift from autocracy to anarchy can be frighteningly fast. At Stewart Heights, which we encountered in Chapter Two, Bill Andrews was not an autocratic leader, but the transition from the firm hand of his guided distribution of leadership and his passion for adversarial argument to first-time principal Eric West's wish to watch the existing culture and wait led to destructive political infighting, reassertion of departmental self-interest, and punitive purges based on a new code of student behavior on the part of the school climate team.

The specter of anarchy reminds us that assertive distributed leadership does not mean absence or abrogation of senior-level leadership. Improvement doesn't arise by accident; and democracy and justice aren't achieved by capitulating to the crowd. Anarchy isn't the answer for distributed leadership, but it is a consequence of ignoring the responsibilities of such leadership.

Conclusion

Leadership in a school is not limited to the principal or even its teachers. It stretches across individuals, communities, and networks and up and down organizational layers. No one has to distribute leadership in a school; it's already distributed. Leadership exists everywhere, across time and space—at lunchtime, between classes, after school and on weekends, and in the school's offices, classrooms, and playing fields. Distributed leadership can be good or bad, planned or serendipitous, focused or unfocused. Distributed leadership can enhance the sustainability of deep and broad learning for all students or disintegrate into the kind of turmoil that sucks the energy and enthusiasm out of students and staff. Distributed leadership can be guided by an inspirational leader like Jenny Lewis; develop and evolve organically, as it did at Blue Mountain School; emerge as a dynamic community of practice like the Byron Women's Group; or take on an assertive and activist character, as it did at Durant Alternative School. Alternatively, distributed leadership like that of Talisman Park's Circle group can sabotage a school's efforts at improvement, or it can destabilize the leadership of inexperienced administrators, as it did at Stewart Heights Secondary School.

Our continuum of distributed leadership shows that this kind of leadership can take many forms. We don't claim to have captured them all. Each pattern of distribution has strengths and weaknesses. Delegation might seem like a limited strategy for distributing leadership, but in a traditional school that is suspicious about change or a school that has experienced years of anarchy or autocracy, delegation offers a clearly structured and easily understood way to make a start. Facilitated leadership offers more deliberate and thoroughgoing distribution, but each of its forms also has its limitations. Guided distribution may be too leader-dependent; emergent distribution is sometimes prone to groupthink; and assertive distribution can easily tip over into anarchy.

Our own evidence suggests that emergent and assertive patterns of leadership develop most easily in new or especially innovative schools where the teachers are hand-picked and the learner-centered values are clear. The distribution of leadership in more traditional schools or in schools with young and transient staffs often has to be much more carefully guided—at least at the outset—although the senior leader's premature departure will always place the long-term sustainability of this pattern of distribution in jeopardy. Some sense of how to progress from one point to another on the scale of distribution is provided in Figure 3.2.

Anarchy
Avoid anarchy.

Assertive Distribution
Be even more steadfast and passionate about shared purposes and values. Stimulate wide-ranging debate about important proposals. Involve resisters early. Include and listen to minorities. Use processes that surface thoughtful divergence and disagreement. Demonstrate the value of learning from differences. Be prepared for criticism but insist on respectful dialogue. Keep your sense of humor. Ensure that the vigorous professional culture always moves you forward. Never abrogate responsibility. Always reaffirm your goals.

Emergent Distribution
Remain clear about purposes and values. Ensure that they are genuinely shared. Maintain a premium on relationships. Encourage staff to innovate. Develop a culture of professional entrepreneurship. Demonstrate trust. Step back from watching over all interactions and relationships. Learn to let go. Don't pour cold water on proposals when they are brought forward. Praise initiative. Celebrate good results.

Guided Distribution
Rely on more than your structures. Develop better relationships. Bring people together. Show interest in your staff members as people. Improve the quality of professional conversation. Concentrate on core purposes. Always remember food. Model the attentive behavior you expect of others. Be visible and vigilant, always steering conversation and relationships in a more productive and attentive direction.

Progressive Delegation
Extend and amend your structures, teams, and committees. Create new roles. Focus people's roles and responsibilities on learning and improvement. Use the new structures to restrict the veto of the old ones. Develop proper planning. Consult with your teams and committees. Audit the results.

Traditional Delegation
Hand over some power. Appoint good deputies, and seek and rely on their counsel. Respect their autonomy. Make sure they report to you regularly. Don't do everything yourself.

Autocracy

Figure 3.2. Stepping Up the Scale of Leadership Distribution

Whatever the starting point, an ultimate goal of sustainable learning and leadership is that, in time, the vast majority of schools will become authentic and assertive professional learning communities that will constitute the strong cells of systemwide improvement. Ultimately, leadership that stays centered on learning and that lasts over time is deliberately distributed leadership that stretches across a school or a system, is a genuinely shared responsibility, and is taken as much as it is given.

4

Justice
Others and Ourselves

From bitter searching of the heart,
Quickened with passion and with pain
We rise to play a greater part.

This is the faith from which we start:
Men shall know commonwealth again
From bitter searching of the heart.

We loved the easy and the smart,
But now, with keener hand and brain,
We rise to play a greater part.

The lesser loyalties depart,
And neither race nor creed remain
From bitter searching of the heart.

Not steering by the venal chart
That tricked the mass for private gain,
We rise to play a greater part.

Reshaping narrow law and art
Whose symbols are the millions slain,
From bitter searching of the heart
We rise to play a greater part.

> *Frank Scott (1899–1985), "Villanelle for Our Time," 1943.*

❖ PRINCIPLE 4

Sustainable leadership does no harm to and actively improves the surrounding environment by finding ways to share knowledge and resources with neighboring schools and the local community.

Unjust Leadership

Alicia Freeman is principal of one of the top high schools in the United States. Located downtown in a depressed rust belt city in the Northeast, Barrett Magnet High School has been through a lot. But as a result of its magnet status and the motivational power of its dynamic principal and her predecessor, Barrett now stands proud in the *U.S. News and World Report* high school rankings as one of the top 150 schools in the nation. Barrett is a classic turnaround story.

Barrett sits in one of its city's most concentrated areas of intense poverty. By the 1970s, the city and the school were in the throes of white and bright flight to the affluent suburbs. All but 5 percent of the school's population were from poor African American families. Student violence, poor attendance, low academic performance, and discipline problems were rife. By 1978, pressure from the neighborhood association led to the district and its superintendent renaming the school, assigning it a charismatic new principal, and eventually granting it magnet status in 1981.

With heightened outside interest and Barrett's new, inspiring identity, the school and its principal were able to attract talented and motivated faculty and administrators. Under Presidents Ronald Reagan and George H. W. Bush, magnet schools were encouraged to compete with other schools for students, and those at Barrett who didn't like the discipline or couldn't keep up the pace were assigned to other schools or asked to leave. The onset of legislated open enrollment that reduced Barrett's ability to select its incoming students only intensified its subtle and not-so-subtle ejection of students who didn't fit its unchanged and uncompromising expectations.

Like all magnets, Barrett was a force of powerful attraction— for motivated students, talented staff, and skilled administrators. The school became a showcase. Adoption of the prestigious International Baccalaureate program heightened its image of excellence. Local newspapers wrote glowing reports about it. President George H. W. Bush made a high-profile visit in 1989, and many other visitors came from far and wide to discover the secrets of its success.

When Barrett's founding principal resigned in 1986 because he refused to accept a transfer to another school, Alicia Freeman was appointed as his successor. An insider appointment, Freeman was liked and appreciated by most of the staff. Teachers admired her because she put students and instruction first, yet delegated well to others in serving their needs. In the words of a social studies teacher, "Mrs. Freeman is a very strong instructional leader and she has really, really . . . fought to keep . . . the integrity of this school where it should be." She believed in and perpetuated the school's magnet mission and steered the school through reapplying to the International Baccalaureate program in the late 1990s. Freeman was also successful in raising funds, and with strong achievement results to bolster her position, she was able to buffer the staff from unreasonable "flavor of the week" district demands.

For Freeman, the success of instructional efforts always had to be evident in measurable results. Teachers who got good results were praised by her; those who didn't were panned.

Performance evaluations as well as unannounced classroom visits and observations ensured that teachers never lost their focus on performance. Most teachers welcomed and supported the emphasis on examinations and standards. Some were closely involved with standards movements like America's Choice Schools and the National Center on Education and the Economy. They were critical of colleagues in other schools who seemed to treat standards and expectations for student learning less conscientiously. "I really think that the new state exam might wake up a lot of people and make teachers really do the job that they should have been doing for years," one of them said.

Not all teachers were followers of Freeman. Those who taught the special education students, whom the school was required to include because of open enrollment and federal legislation, quickly learned that their students were not part of the principal's or the school's mission nor beneficiaries of her favors. These students and their teachers were assigned to the basement of the building. If special education teachers questioned the elitist atmosphere, complained about their students' marginalization, or advocated for them too strongly, they quickly found themselves, in their words, "targeted" and "punished"—"stuck with classes that are the most difficult," reassigned to undesirable rooms on the periphery of the school, or "banished" from the school altogether. Barrett had developed impressive magnetic power, but it included the power to repel as well as to attract.

Barrett exemplifies many of the elements of sustainable leadership we have discussed so far. The school had a clear and persistent focus on high expectations and quality instruction (depth); it was one of our scarce instances of planned continuity that secured successful succession from one leader to the next (endurance); and although it wasn't awash with distributed leadership, Barrett's principal was always eager to delegate decision making broadly among her staff (breadth).

However, the positive force of Barrett's magnetic attraction was also a damaging one for its lower-status students and teachers, who didn't enhance its image or mesh with its mission. This was not the school's only problem. Barrett's fatal attraction harmed students and teachers in neighboring schools as well.

Few schools are islands. More and more parents are allowed and encouraged to choose between them. When parents can't or don't choose, their children get left behind. Outstanding teachers and leaders are drawn toward the most exemplary or highest-profile institutions, and at the same time, they are drained away from the rest. For every beacon or lighthouse school that attracts most of the local resources and attention, dozens of surrounding schools are treated more like outhouses—low-status places where districts dump their difficult students and weaker staff members. The more that school systems run on market principles of competition and choice, the tighter these interconnections among schools become.[1]

The fates of schools are almost always intertwined. What leaders do in one school affects the fortunes of students and teachers in other schools around them. Sustainability, therefore, is not only about the maintainability of initiatives within individual schools, but is also about being responsible to and for the schools and students in the wider environment that your leadership actions affect. Sustainability is ultimately and inextricably about social justice.

Sheldon High School shares the same city and district as Barrett Magnet High School, but that's all. Over time, the history of change efforts and the geography of competition have set the two schools on quite different paths, propelling them past each other in opposite directions. Sheldon's long-serving staff recalls that the school was the shining star of the district in the 1960s. At that time, more than 90 percent of the students were white. Teachers lived locally. While desegregation and school busing led to white flight to the suburbs and even some race riots in the school's cafeteria in the early 1970s, teachers were still able to maintain Sheldon's status as the top high school in the city by providing ten-week learning options and thematic courses on Vietnam, science fiction, slavery, sports literature, and black figures in national history. These engaged students' interests and connected with their lives, catering to the increasingly diverse student body.

All this changed in the 1980s. Further desegregation, the establishment of the city's first magnet school, and the introduction of enrollment policies that allowed parents to rank-order the schools they preferred for their children led to a second round of white flight as well as "bright flight" from neighborhood schools like Sheldon to the magnet schools beside and around them. Besides the loss of its best students to Barrett and the other magnet schools, Sheldon also had to contend with the busing of many poor African American students from a school on the opposite side of town, whose closure had been forced by the creation of the magnet schools. By the late 1980s, white students were very much in the minority, the number of students in poverty was rapidly rising, and the school's special education department changed from being the smallest unit, with just three teachers, in the late 1980s to the largest unit (twenty-five teachers) by the mid-1990s.

With Sheldon's lost reputation went its ability to attract outstanding staff. Veteran teachers became demotivated, increasingly unionized, and nostalgic for the 1960s and 1970s as students seemed to deteriorate, as six superintendents—often with contradictory agendas—rolled in and out of the district in a fifteen-year period, and as successively more autocratic and "iron-fisted" principals gave teachers little opportunity for leadership and treated them like "serfs." The district cared about social justice and tried to reverse the decline, but in 1986, when it proposed transferring Barrett's charismatic African American principal to Sheldon to help turn it around, he promptly resigned and, amid a storm of protest, moved out of the district altogether.

By the late 1980s, Sheldon's teachers found themselves teaching in extremely challenging circumstances. Meeting the state standards was much harder than in the magnet schools, and therefore the school's staff couldn't negotiate the curriculum discretion and flexibility enjoyed by teachers and students at Barrett. Standards turned into standardization. Innovative teachers became demoralized because they couldn't adjust to the needs of their students. "I'd much rather be trying to teach them a book or a story or something that they might enjoy," one English teacher said, "but we've got to prep them for the tests." Traditional teachers, meanwhile, found that the standardization process enabled them to become more traditional still. By the early stages of No Child Left Behind implementation, Sheldon's downward trajectory was moving it toward being designated an "underperforming" school, and its major challenge was now one of sheer survival: avoiding closure, being turned over to the state or a private company, or being replaced by a charter school.

The Barretts and Sheldons of this world are not unfortunate coincidences or historical accidents. They are interconnected and indivisible alter egos—like Jekyll and Hyde. The fortunes of one are perversely linked to the failures of the other. Self-centered leadership and improvement strategies that bring about success in one school only lead to failure in the schools around it. When we look at schools not as individuals but as interconnected systems, many of our current leadership and improvement strategies are unjust and unsustainable.

Schools and school leaders are on an uphill slope. Injustice is everywhere. When American schools were segregated by race, governments introduced busing and integration, only to see wealthy whites take flight to protected enclaves in the suburbs. Because people in many countries have historically separated themselves into different communities by class or race, turning their local schools into segregated institutions, some reformers suggested market choice and magnet school and charter school options so that minorities and the poor wouldn't be confined only to what their own neighborhoods could offer. However, market and magnet school strategies ended up exaggerating the injustices even further as the affluent parental "tourists" exercised their right to choose, while "vagabond" parents with few financial or social resources were left even further behind.[2]

Equity-based budgeting makes a sterling effort to equalize funding within school districts but can do nothing to rectify the even greater inequities between poor urban districts and their wealthy suburban neighbors.[3] School-business partnerships flourish more in affluent communities where parents have all the right connections, compared with poor neighborhoods that offer less return on business investments.[4] Professional learning communities prosper more strongly in schools with highly qualified teachers and with resources that can buy them the time to meet together.[5] Even efforts to reassign outstanding principals from privileged schools to impoverished ones meet with individual resistance, community protest, and threats to resign. In the face of this stubborn social and historical legacy, as we saw in the case of Sheldon and Barrett, the uphill slope of socially just leadership too often feels like an unscalable precipice.

Just Leadership

In 1759, Scottish economist and philosopher Adam Smith, most remembered for arguing in his *Wealth of Nations* that "the hidden hand" of self-interest that guided the market economy would also serve the general good, opined in another book, *The Theory of Moral Sentiments*, "The wise and virtuous man is at all times willing that his own private interest should be sacrificed to the public interest of his own particular order of society."[6]

When French aristocrat Alexis de Tocqueville visited and toured America in 1831, then wrote his influential treatise *Democracy in America,* he admired America's pursuit of liberty but wondered whether, in the face of the individualism that resulted, it could balance this properly with the demands and needs of equality. "There is no vice of the human heart that suits it as much as egoism,"[7] he warned. However, he noted, "When citizens are forced to assume responsibility for public affairs, they are necessarily removed from the milieu of their individual interests, and drawn away, from time to time, from looking at themselves."[8] Tocqueville understood that responsibility for public affairs set important limits on individualism and provided a foundation for justice.

In recent times, most Anglo-Saxon countries have experienced a resurgence of liberty over equality, of individual enterprise over social justice. Britain's Margaret Thatcher, the originator of this resurgence, famously declared that there is no such thing as society, there are only individuals. President George W. Bush proclaims the values and virtues of an "ownership society" in which more and more individuals will own their own property, pensions, medical care, and financial security. Yet this ownership society is little more than one in which everyone will be left to their own devices, fending for themselves with no thought for those who are less fortunate.

This return to *market fundamentalism* (as billionaire investor and social reformer George Soros has called it)—to the blind belief, even against the evidence, that the market, the operation of individual self-interest, is the best instrument of social development and public policy—has had an immense influence on educational reform strategies worldwide.[9] School choice; rankings of school performance; and competition between magnet schools, charter schools, and academies for the best students are the educational legacies of liberty without justice, of markets without morality, in which successful schools typically prosper at the expense of their sinking and underperforming neighbors.[10]

Yet market fundamentalism does not represent the end of social and educational history or the only future way for people to be. Leading social theorist Jeremy Rifkin contrasts the fading American dream and its emphasis on the lesser hunger of individual material advancement with the new European dream and its cosmopolitan commitment to addressing the greater hunger of improved humanity in an increasingly interconnected world: "The American Dream is far too centred on personal material advancement and too little concerned with the broader human welfare to be relevant in a world of increasing risk, diversity and interdependence.[11] . . . The European Dream emphasizes community relationships over individual autonomy, cultural diversity over assimilation, quality of life over the accumulation of wealth, sustainable development over unlimited material growth, deep play over unrelenting toil, universal rights and the rights of nature over property rights and global cooperation over the unilateral exercise of power."[12]

U.K. author and newspaper columnist Will Hutton observes that Britain is becoming too inclined to follow the American rather than the European economic and social model.[13] The American model, with its large, low-paid service sector and small, economically creative core, is accompanied by widening social and educational inequalities, reduced state supportiveness, unleashed economic competitiveness, and increased domestic indebtedness. The European model, by contrast, seeks to maximize everyone's educational and economic involvement and investment in a high-skill, high-wage economy that is strongly supported by long-term public investment in the economy and protected by welfare safety nets for those who need them.

Stanford educational historian David Labaree argues that committing to public education and the public good is not just a moral duty in a democracy; it also serves our individual and collective self-interest. It prevents us from sequestering ourselves in private schools, elite academies, and walled communities that anxiously shield us from the growing crime and mounting insecurity that widening inequalities send battering at our gates.[14] Money spent on public education now is money saved on supporting a burgeoning prison population in the years to come.

The challenge of educational leadership, therefore, is to commit to the public good as well as care for the private good of one's own students and their parents. It is to care for the students and teachers in neighboring schools whom your leadership choices affect, not just your own. As Arlie Hochschild reminds us, in the age of globalization, we are all connected in chains of care not only to friends and family around us but also to people far across the world whom we cannot see—to the exploited children who make our clothes or the impoverished communities who must live amid our exported waste.[15] Socially just and sustainable leadership is responsible leadership in the fullest sense. Jerry Starratt points out that educational leaders are responsible not just as professionals to their own students' learning but also as citizens, community members, and ethical human beings to all those whom their actions affect or might affect.[16]

Following the dramatic collapse of trust in the business sector and its selfish and self-destructive preoccupation with short-term shareholder value, leaders in the corporate and environmental sectors are finding creative and committed ways to take their public responsibilities seriously, to rectify the impact and damage they have exerted on the communities around them.

In *Cause for Success*, Christine Arena summarizes the enlightened environmental stance of a growing number of companies, including ten that she studied directly:

> "The capitalist doctrine that a company's singular function is to make as much money as possible—devoid of charity and divorced from society—is increasingly self defeating. The less credence a company gives to the social and environmental inequities surrounding it, particularly those inequities that its actions help to perpetuate, the less meaningful and invincible it tends to be. Inversely, the more a company operates with regard to the collective interest, the more it does something to improve people's lives and solve society's problems, the more indispensable and sustainable it ultimately becomes."[17]

When the city of Boston committed to its $14.6 billion Big Dig—one of the world's most massive construction projects, which has turned the city's ugly overhead skyways into hidden underground tunnels—its architects agreed that for every park, wetland, or green space the project destroyed, a new one would be created elsewhere in the city. Gary Erickson's Clif Bar corporation, described in Chapter One, makes a pledge that "a portion of the money we earn and the hours we work will always serve to support and improve environmental, social and cultural needs from our local to our global community."[18] This has meant not only avoiding the harm of expelling effluent into the neighborhood; it also meant that in 2003, almost twenty-four paid hours per employee per year were dedicated to the active good of worker-selected community service projects. Starting in 2006, the European Union will require all automakers to reduce waste and environmental impact by taking back the cars they once made. Anita Roddick's Body Shop has relentlessly and successfully campaigned for the release of international human rights advocates from prison and exposed the unethical business practices of large corporations overseas.[19] Corporate responsibility to the environment, the community, and the world beyond is increasing everywhere.

One way to think about the connection between sustainable leadership and social justice is through the concept of ecological footprint. Canadian environmentalist Bill Rees first defined *ecological footprint* as the impact and traces of our choices and consumption patterns on the fragile environment around us and on the amount of natural resources each of us draws on to live.[20] Because of affluent consumption levels, transportation use, waste production, and use of natural resources, rich and densely populated countries leave a bigger ecological footprint than poorer ones. The United States and Canada, for instance, have total ecological footprints of 9.7 and 8.8 hectares of resources used per person per year, respectively, while the ecological footprints of Brazil and Bangladesh are only 2.4 and 0.5 hectares per person.[21]

What ecological footprint does your leadership leave on the surrounding scarce resources of teaching and leadership talent available in the wider community? Does your district lure talented teachers and leaders away from the inner cities with higher salaries and other rewards? Does your oversubscribed school leave other schools only with the unwanted human "waste" of less-talented students that your selective strategies leave behind? Do you process and consume only the human resources of high-end students, teachers, and leaders or the financial resources of elite business partnerships, with no thought for what is left for everyone else? Sustainable and socially just leadership thinks about and takes responsibility for its ecological impact. It constantly seeks not only to reduce its negative environmental impact on others but also to have an actively restorative effect on them as well.

Becoming More Just

Outstanding and creative examples of social justice and socially just leadership are emerging not just in the environmental and corporate worlds but in education too. Many of them stretch beyond the individual school, distributing their leadership and its effects across many different schools—strong and weak, black and white, rich and poor. All children and schools are positively influenced by these leadership actions, rather than some of them suffering by default because leaders in successful schools are oblivious or indifferent to other students and schools that their actions affect. A few of the practical and positive directions for socially just and sustainable leadership are listed here.

1. *Paired schools*. Successful schools can coach struggling schools and help them to improve. It is best if the schools serve similar kinds of students and communities. Under the inspirational leadership of coordinator Dave Blackburn, Newport News School District in Virginia has pioneered just such a model of *paired schools*.[22] With district support, underperforming schools choose a higher-performing partner. More is involved than a small administrative team from the high performer moving in to evaluate and turn around its underperforming peer. Instead, the paired schools model promotes shared and distributed leadership. Counselors coach counselors; departments coach departments. Peer assistance is the key principle. And the learning runs in both directions, for even underperforming schools have pockets of excellent practice from which their higher-performing partners can benefit.

Paired schools, peer assistance, and shared leadership have raised the performance of students in the Newport News district. With the support of the Hope Foundation, these practices have been witnessed, coached, and spread to dozens of other districts across America.[23] Elsewhere—for example, in the United Kingdom or some American states—the power of this leadership and change model has been less impressive because it has been mandated as a quick-fix solution, with underperforming schools suddenly discovering that small evaluation and turnaround teams from high-performing schools elsewhere have been externally assigned to them to sort them out.[24]

2. *Networked districts*. Solving some of the social justice challenges to sustainable leadership may mean refuting the assumption of an essential bond between one child and one school. Under the English Specialist Schools Trust, for example, which already has over one thousand specialist secondary schools that will ultimately grow to a national majority, almost every school has its own specialty emphasis, perhaps in sports, technology, arts, or the environment.[25] For some communities, this kind of niche marketing will only motivate schools to hunt for the best students, leaving secondary schools in poorer communities with less talented academic students who have not been chosen elsewhere. But in rapidly improving Knowsley Education Authority near Liverpool, whose former director Steve Munby is now chief executive of England's National College for School Leadership, specialist schools are not being established in isolation, in competitive relationships to one another, but in interrelated and networked centers of learning.[26] In the morning, students will each be based in one school; in the afternoon, they will have access to all the varied learning resources of concentrated expertise across the district, developed in a collaborative and complementary way to enhance the learning power of all students and of all the institutions that can support them. Such networked learning communities, which are being encouraged on a more national scale by Britain's National College for School Leadership, are one of the most powerful ideas for using choice and diversity to undermine rather than exaggerate elitist competition and to bring about greater social justice.[27]

3. *Community consultation*. Schools of choice, purpose-built innovative schools, and charter schools can and should actively consult, contribute to, and avoid doing harm to the wider communities in which they are located. England's Specialist Schools Trust does this when it makes specialist status contingent on a plan to

contribute time and resources to the surrounding community.[28] One charter school we know of avoided raiding the best talent from nearby urban public schools by advertising its teaching positions only far beyond the district. Actively considering the needs of the community not only contributes to social justice and public good in the community, but it benefits the long-term reputation, viability, and sheer endurance of newly established schools themselves.

Blue Mountain School in Canada, which we encountered earlier, was established as a learning organization and community in 1994, with license to hand-pick its leaders and teaching community. Having seen other innovative schools fade over time because they failed to involve the surrounding communities, who then became suspicious of them, or to consult neighboring schools, who subsequently envied them, Blue Mountain took great care not to raid all the best teachers, leaders, and students from nearby schools. In consultation with the school district and other high school principals, its principal operated a quota system so the school would not draw disproportionately from any one school or age group of teachers in the district. By attending to the needs of other schools, the principal not only exercised responsibility for social justice but also avoided inviting envy and resentment from his neighbors.

Blue Mountain also consulted members of the community from its inception. Its parents council worked with the school to design the exit outcomes that it wanted students to have achieved by the time they left high school. All data, even disappointing or disturbing data, about achievement, behavior, or attendance, are also shared openly with the community. There are none of the secrets and surprises that undermine trust between schools and their communities.

4. *Collective accountability.* In early 2004, a number of schools in Birmingham Education Authority in England became concerned that individual school accountability was forcing them to compete with others, which undermined their collective capacity to learn and improve together. These schools therefore lobbied the government to pool their achievement scores, so that through collective accountability, schools of greater and lesser performance and advantage would be urged to work together to narrow their achievement gaps and improve their performance together—with direct benefit for the immediately surrounding community.[29]

Similarly, in the 1990s, in Melbourne, Australia, the principals of a group of contiguous high schools who had been spending their budgets on advertising for students in a system of competitive school choice, discovered that their advertisements were almost identical. In response, they exercised their courage and creativity to work together as a federation of schools dedicated to shared improvement for the whole community instead of frittering away their resources on enhancing their individual images.[30]

5. *Environmental impact assessment.* In North America and in many countries elsewhere, when a construction project is started or a new business is begun, its developers are legally required to undertake an environmental impact assessment of the construction's or the company's effects on the surrounding community. To sharpen the sense of social justice and increase sustainability of improvement and leadership across schools and not just within them, we propose that all newly established schools—academies, charter schools, beacon schools or just schools in new buildings—should undertake an environmental impact assessment of the effects of their physical design, market principles, and policies for selecting students and staff on surrounding schools and the community at large, so they not only avoid doing harm to other schools and communities but also make an active and socially just contribution to the wider public good.

Conclusion

The hardest part of sustainable leadership is the part that provokes us to think beyond our own schools and ourselves. It is the part that calls us to serve the public good of all people's children within and beyond our community and not only the private interests of those who subscribe to our own institution. Sustainable leadership means caring for *all* the people our actions and choices affect—those whom we can't immediately see as well as those whom we can. The hardest part of sustainable leadership asks us, in the words of Canadian poet Frank Scott, to draw on "the bitter searching of the heart," then "rise to play a greater part," not merely as managers of organizations or as professionals who produce performance results but also as community members, citizens, and human beings who lead to serve and promote the good of all.[31] Sustainable leadership is socially just leadership, nothing simpler, nothing less.

Diversity
Complexity and Cohesion

We need a new pedagogy, based on interactivity,
personalization and the development of autonomous
capacity of learning and thinking. While at the same
time, strengthening the character and securing the
personality.

Manuel Castells, The Internet Galaxy, *2001, p. 278*

❖ PRINCIPLE 5

**Sustainable leadership promotes cohesive diversity and
avoids aligned standardization of policy, curriculum,
assessment, and staff development and training in teaching
and learning. It fosters and learns from diversity and
creates cohesion and networking among its richly
varying components.**

Biodiversity

In 1988, a new word entered the English language: *biodiversity*.[1] By
1992, it was the subject of the Convention on Biological Diversity
at the Rio Earth Summit and an integral element of environmental thinking.[2] Its originator, Harvard scientist and double Pulitzer
Prize winner Edward O. Wilson, defined *biodiversity* as "the variety of

organisms considered at all levels, from genetic variants belonging to the same species to arrays of genes, families and still higher taxonomic levels; [it] includes the variety of ecosystems which comprise the communities of organisms within particular habitats and the physical conditions under which they live."[3]

Biodiversity, says Wilson, is organized into three levels: ecosystems (like rainforests or coral reefs), species (like algae or monarch butterflies), and the genes that make up individual heredity. Biodiversity represents the richness of the living world, in luxuriant rainforests or in lakes teeming with aquatic life. Biodiversity doesn't just include the number or scope of species, ecosystems, or genetic variability. It is the interdependence, interaction, and cohesion among the numerous elements of these systems that matter most.

Wilson argues that "every scrap of biological diversity is priceless, to be learned and cherished, and never to be surrendered without a struggle."[4] Species are worth preserving in their own right. Their protection also secures potential benefits for medical and scientific progress. But most of all, the shrinkage of diversity places species, ecosystems, and all of life itself in jeopardy, for the less biodiversity we have, the more fragile life in all its forms becomes.[5] Biodiversity is indispensable to environmental sustainability.

In ecological and evolutionary terms, biodiversity performs two vital functions: *resilience* and *flexibility* in the face of changes and threats. Canadian environmentalist David Suzuki explains that when a forest has great diversity of life within it, it bounces back more easily from blight, pests, flooding, or fire. "That's because the diverse species remaining in the surrounding areas can replenish the damaged parts."[6] Wilson puts the point starkly: "The more species living in an ecosystem, the higher [is] its productivity and the greater its ability to withstand drought and other kinds of environmental stress. Since we depend on an abundance of functioning ecosystems to cleanse our water, enrich our soil, and manufacture the very air we breathe, biodiversity is clearly not an inheritance to be discarded easily."[7]

Most artificial forests, whose only purpose is to produce timber, are not only aesthetically ugly and virtually bereft of birdsong, but they also have far less capacity to recover from disease and damage or from unpredictable changes in their environment. The same concepts apply to genetic diversity within a single species. Large and diverse populations help species respond to their changing environment and are crucial to species survival. When rare species like Siberian tigers shrink to very small numbers, the chance that they will reproduce successfully or be able to resist disease are gravely diminished by the lack of genetic variability that would otherwise make it possible for one gene, then another, to fight off an external threat.[8] Historically, some royal dynasties are infamous for the insanities and deformities that have resulted from excessive inbreeding within a tiny genetic pool. Pedigree dogs can be genetically selected to pure-bred perfection, but often at the cost of serious inherited health defects. The universal incest taboo and the prevention or discouragement of cousins from marrying each other are also ways that we preserve genetic diversity and protect the strength and future of the human species.

In the modern world, there are two great threats to biodiversity: (1) urban and industrial elimination of the natural environment and (2) large-scale, standardized practices of *monoculture*, single-crop cultivation in forests and farms. Together with the population growth that is behind them, these combined forces are extinguishing species at a rate of about 6 percent per decade,[9] destroying local knowledge and communities, and generally producing "a steep decline in biodiversity."[10] In the words of ecologist David Tilman, biodiversity is "nature's insurance policy against catastrophes. . . . By sustaining biodiversity, we help sustain ourselves."[11] Therefore, David Suzuki concludes,

> "If change is inevitable but unpredictable, then the best tactic for survival is to act in ways that retain the most diversity; then, when circumstances do change, there

will be a chance that a new set of genes, a species or a society will be able to continue under the new conditions. Diversity confers resilience, adaptability and the capacity for regeneration."[12]

Organizational and Cultural Diversity

Many of the principles of diversity that operate in the natural world apply to organizations and human societies as well. The most biologically diverse countries are also the most linguistically diverse ones.[13] World-renowned science writer Fritjof Capra urges us to bring about organizational and social change not by conquering, controlling, or interrupting nature, but by working with the natural design processes that also permeate human society. We need to understand, Capra says, that human organizations are also complex, living systems. "The principles of organization of ecosystems, which are the basis of their sustainability," he points out, "are identical to the principles of organization of all living systems"[14] . . . "To build a sustainable society for our children and future generations, we need to fundamentally redesign many of our technologies and social institutions so as to bridge the gap between human design and the ecologically sustainable systems of nature."[15]

A company is a living being, not a machine, says Capra. Its people get better by learning, evolution, and flexible adaptation. The companies profiled in Collins and Porras's *Built to Last* improved by engaging in diverse experimentation with new ideas, retaining those that worked when judged by evidence and experience and abandoning the rest.[16] Long-lived companies studied by Arie de Gues also exhibit the characteristics of living entities. They are open to the outside world, tolerant of new people and ideas, and able to adapt to new circumstances.[17] Atul Gawande's heart surgeons (described in Chapter Three) were most successful in learning the new techniques of microsurgery when their leader discussed problems openly and could entertain diverse ideas from many members of the team as difficulties and challenges repeatedly emerged.[18] In their book *Primal Leadership*, Daniel Goleman and his co-writers concluded that as well as being able to "resonate" with others around them, emotionally intelligent leaders are "more values driven, more flexible and informal, and more open and frank than leaders of old. They are more connected to people and to networks."[19] These leaders also value the richness of cultural diversity among their employees and find ways to capitalize on the collective intelligence of all their people. The regeneration of many cities, such as Detroit and Manchester, is occurring by first attracting the gay community, with its creativity and disposable income, into loft living, so that artists, young professionals, and new families follow close behind in mixed neighborhoods of growing prosperity and civility.

One of the key characteristics of living systems is the property and process of *emergence*. Capra expresses the idea of emergence as "the creation of novelty," which is often "qualitatively different from the phenomena out of which it emerged."[20] He illustrates his argument by describing the structures and properties of sugar. "When carbon, oxygen and hydrogen atoms bond in a certain way to form sugar," he notes, "the resulting compound has a sweet taste that is not in any of the separate atoms themselves."[21]

In the social world, invention and innovation arise in just the same way, through processes of emergence. Creativity emerges by putting disparate ideas together or by connecting different and diverse minds, or both. As coauthors of this book, for example, while the two of us share a common passion for public education, an interest in leadership and change, and a wish to connect theory and practice, we bring to this quest different backgrounds and talents as well as different metaphorical traditions and writing styles. We are British and Canadian, residents of Canada and of the United States, a historian and a sociologist, academics and administrators, and educators who previously taught in high schools and elementary schools. Although we devised a clear plan together before we began writing the book, our different orientations and the process of writing itself led to inevitable emergence. Each chapter affected another. New literature was discovered. Frameworks that seemed clear at the beginning turned out not to work at all.

Amid all this emergence, communication is vital if chaos is not to ensue. Although we live hundreds of miles apart, as coauthors, we communicate almost every day. We puzzle, worry, argue, and fret. We inspire and advise, affirm and admonish, reflect and react. This communication, together with a common purpose and a long-standing friendship, are what eventually gives our project cohesion, holds it together, moves us ahead. We ultimately enjoy our differences, even though they sometimes exasperate us. Without the purpose, the relationship, or the communication, the process of emergence—the detours and the differences—would ultimately have defeated us, and our book along with it.

The task of leadership, says Fritjof Capra, is to facilitate the process of emergence as we have described it and in doing so, to foster creativity. "This means creating conditions rather than giving directions, and using the power of authority to empower others."[22] Creating the conditions of emergence includes building "an active network of communications with multiple feedback loops"[23] and developing a culture that is "open to new ideas and new knowledge" and in which "continual questioning is encouraged and innovation is rewarded."[24] These cultures "value diversity"[25] and, in the words of Arie de Gues, welcome "experiments and eccentricities that stretch [our] understanding."[26]

In short, effective organizations in complex and unpredictable environments operate with the fluidity and adaptability of living systems rather than with the mechanical precision of well-oiled machines. Effective organizations are characterized by

- A framework of common and enduring values, goals and purposes

- Possession and development of variability or diversity in skills and talents

- Processes that promote interaction and cross-pollination of ideas and influences across this variability

- Permeability to outside influences

- Emergence of new ideas, structures, and processes as diverse elements interconnect and new ones intrude from the outside

- Flexibility and adaptability in response to environmental change

- Resilience in the face of and in response to threats and adversity

Denying Diversity

If ever there was an obvious candidate for flexible and adaptable leadership that could engage with diversity and appreciate how organizations operate like emergent and constantly evolving living systems, then educational leadership would be it. The purpose of schools is supposed to be learning. People are their products. The populations of schools are always changing and in many cases are becoming increasingly diverse. Two of the districts in which our work was located had over seventy languages spoken in their schools. The retirement of the baby boomer generation is leading to a massive demographic turnover and instability in the teaching force. In many countries, up to a third of new teachers leave the profession within three years. Principals and superintendents are also turning over at an alarming and accelerating rate. And the system is endlessly afflicted with repetitive change syndrome as successive governments assign mounting urgency and increasing priority to public education reform.[27]

Public education is full of diversity and surrounded by uncertainty. It is ripe for leadership that recognizes its strengths and vulnerabilities as a living system. Yet entirely the opposite has occurred.

Standardized education reform has managed public education like a machine. The rich diversity of urban classrooms and communities has been flattened by the imposed uniformity of curriculum content, one-size-fits-all literacy programs, strangulating testing regimes, and, in some American states, enforced elimination of bilingual instruction.[28]

Ted Sizer virulently criticizes the United States' No Child Left Behind legislation and Massachusetts's Education Reform Act of 1993 for "increased top-down regulation that leads to standardized practices imposed on populations that are not themselves standardized; and with assessments that sharply narrow the goal of a serious education to the ability to pass common standardized tests at a prescribed level."[29]

While the response of educational leaders to diversity has rarely been exemplary—for instance, the entire Canadian province of Ontario has almost no district directors (superintendents) of color, and in the United States, African American superintendents are largely found in the poor urban districts where students of their own race and ethnicity are concentrated—standardization makes dealing with diversity even harder. We saw evidence of this in the Introduction. Standardization, the educational equivalent of imposing monoculture in the natural world, has resulted in lost classroom creativity, restricted curriculum flexibility, stifled educational innovation, and diminished professional community.

In a study of fifty teachers' emotional responses to educational change, when we asked teachers what educational change meant to them, a number identified two starkly contrasting meanings:[30]

| "Keeping up with the times and changing our teaching routines and techniques" | vs. | Having "a political side to it all . . . [in which] there's a game going on and . . . politicians just seem to change like the wind |

"Things that you actually do yourself"	vs.	"People doing [it] to you"
"Change that is driven by myself and classroom teachers in collaboration to develop curriculum and better meet the needs of students"	vs.	"Change that is driven by people who have never been in the classroom"
"More emphasis on teacher as facilitator rather than as educator"	vs.	"[The minister] and cuts"
"If we are talking classroom practices, it depends on the issue"	vs.	"If we are talking politics, slash and burn"

Positive change, for these teachers, was self-driven, flexibly developed, connected to teaching and learning, and professionally current. Negative change was seen as driven by governments and bureaucracies that failed to understand classroom practice and even withdrew support from it so they could implement other, noneducational agendas. In some cases, these contrasts between good and bad were also ones of past and present:

> In the past, I would have described [educational change] as something good . . . that we are moving forward; we are implementing new and refreshing ideas. Nowadays, I would probably say we're heading in the wrong direction . . . [doing] what government wants us to do.

> Normally, you felt [educational change] was probably going to be a curriculum change that was designed to promote learning. Now educational change may be more a financially driven constraint.

The loss of diversity, resilience, and capacity to learn in a mono-cultural age of standardized reform is evident among several of the more innovative schools and leaders in our Spencer study.

> Durant Alternative School, which we encountered in Chapter Three, used to operate much like a living system. For a long time, this urban school literally had no walls. It connected itself to the community in several ways—for example, through the content of its interdisciplinary, student-centered curriculum, which was sometimes also taught by community members. When David, one of the school's principals couldn't efficiently manage the paperwork of the job, his staff, who valued other aspects of his leadership, spontaneously distributed responsibility for administrative tasks among themselves. Durant's compelling alternative vision of teaching and learning, its commitment to its students, and the highly collaborative nature of its staff community equipped it with great resilience that protected it for many years against the encroaching influence of standardization. But by the 1990s, the state curriculum had been narrowed and the testing increased to such a degree that Durant's resilience, rooted in the strength of its professionally diverse and flexible community, could no longer be sustained.
>
> Before standardization,
>
>> Part of our philosophical concept was to empower us as teachers to make decisions [about] what we're going to teach. So long as we follow the overall guidelines of the state and the Bradford Board of Education, empower us to set the curriculum, empower us to set the time when classes are, empower us to make every decision related to the operation of the school! Part of it was to share

that empowerment with the students, so they could, we could develop, quote, "ideally, a learning community."

After standardization, the added pressure of test preparation was

taking away my professional judgment as a teacher. I was trained at good colleges for both my bachelor's and my master's degrees. I was interned by a brilliant teacher. . . . I spent years learning how to teach, learning why kids learn, how they learn, what I can do to help that happen. Suddenly the state says, "No, none of that means anything. . . . We're going to tell you what to teach." And to me, that's saying, "All right, why don't we just get a videotape in here of somebody and they can do it," because it ignores so much about kids.

As we saw in Chapter Three, Durant was able to bounce back from these standardized setbacks, but they posed a constant threat to the school's responsiveness to its community and its capacity to deal effectively with external change.

During the same time period, other schools, in another country and with equal reputations for innovation, experienced a similar loss of professional diversity, flexibility, and capacity for emergent design. Even the leadership of highly innovative Blue Mountain School buckled somewhat during Ontario's era of highly standardized reform in the late 1990s. Facing budget cuts, staff reductions, and short time frames for implementation of required reforms, Linda White, the school's second leader, was seen as more tightly controlling than her predecessor. In one teacher's words, "I think we've gone from an organization that was kind of a shared responsibility, at least in appearance, to a very linear one now based on . . . [getting things done in] time. And [Linda] is fairly directive, and she likes to be in control of a lot of things, but she's also a humanist with you on that. But I think we've lost some of that shared responsibility because of outside direction." In conditions of standardized reform that disrespect diversity, distributed leadership rapidly turns into downloaded management.

Lord Byron Secondary School, birthplace of the feisty women's group of future influential leaders described in Chapter Three, opened with the expressed purpose of challenging the structures and practices of secondary education in Ontario in the 1970s. The philosophy, espoused by its first principal and adopted by the original staff, was stated this way by one staff member: "Our aspirations for Lord Byron are the development of a humane educational environment for students, a situation in which conduct and growth will develop from reason and mutual respect and trust."

Byron became the first semestered school in Ontario; its academic year was divided into two curriculum halves that were covered by four class periods per day. This restructuring of the school day enabled students to take a broader program from a wider diversity of courses than in conventional Ontario schools. Traditional department heads (most schools have twenty to twenty-two of these positions of responsibility) were replaced with ten chairpersons. This smaller leadership team worked out policy and procedures, while actual approval of school policy came from the staff. A model of differentiated staffing was agreed on with the teacher's union, enabling variations in class sizes that would release resources for other kinds of staff support, such as professional development, secretarial assistance, or high-quality materials. Staff members recalled the exhilaration, the tremendously hard work, and the public scrutiny of the thousands of visitors who came to this "school of the future" in its first five years.

Byron was the epitome of emergent design, with open physical architecture, flexible organizational structures, extensive communication, and an interdisciplinary curriculum. Within the framework of the school's compelling mission, the organization sponsored and successfully learned from professional diversity. A founding member of the school's women's group put it like this:

> We were into something together that was really powerful and created its own dynamics, and we bought our own excitement to it. It was a young staff, and when things got rolling a lot of stuff spun off. It was a school that operated on ideas that were significantly ahead of their time. A high level of collegiality was expected by people who were here. They simply assumed they worked in teams and partnerships. I haven't seen that degree of interdependence and influence until very recently at a school. . . . And I think that accounts to some extent for the increase in women's interest in leadership.

Over the years, Byron suffered the gradual attrition of innovative identity that has afflicted many schools of its type. It was difficult to fill the shoes of its founding charismatic leader, Ward Bond. Staff renewal was a challenge. The school was unable to be as open and "emergent" in relation to the needs and wishes of the external community as the teachers and administrators were with one another. Over time, other schools envied Byron, the community became suspicious of it, and the district started to withdraw its discretionary support.

But by the 1990s, the school was bouncing back. An ebullient and inspirational principal was succeeded internally by the assistant principal, Janice Burnley. She shared his student-centered philosophy and his commitment to staff involvement in decision making. With a new assistant principal, the leadership team was given a five-star rating by staff for making them part of the process of change. "Our administration is great," one young teacher declared. "They're right behind you all the time [with] any information you need." And their efforts were exemplified in results; the school is the second highest performer in the district on the newly introduced Grade 10 Literacy Test, for instance.

Yet by the late 1990s, cracks were again starting to show. Budget cuts, loss of middle-level leadership positions, resulting work-to-rule actions of teachers (in which teachers performed only the minimum duties required by their contract), and the overwhelming short-term implementation requirements of standardized reform all pressed the leadership team to be much more directive and less collegial than it preferred in order to achieve staff compliance. In the words of one of the school's most experienced teachers, outside forces had "knee-capped" the principal's ability to lead in the ways she wanted. For example, when the government required new approaches to assessment that a number of staff members were reluctant to embrace, the principal remarked, "What we have had to impose upon them is that you *will* become knowledgeable in computer areas, you *will* work on an electronic marks manager, and you *will* change your assessment and evaluation. If you're having trouble with this, we're here to help you. So that is laid on."

Sustainable leadership develops diversity, resilience, and human capacity within an organization. It enables people to adapt to and prosper in their increasingly complex environment. Repeated change efforts, like DDT spraying, increase eventual resistance to change after a deceptive early yield of promising results. Standardized scientific efficiency is often the enemy of creative and resilient diversity. It wreaks educational havoc through the dominance of an extensive and unsustainable monoculture of large-scale reform, producing overly simple systems that don't allow the shared learning and cross-fertilization that is necessary for healthy development. Standardized reform has destroyed too much diversity, threatening educators' capacity to acknowledge and adjust to the variable needs of their diverse students, to maintain improvement over time, and to respond resiliently when the next change or crisis comes upon them.

Restoring Diversity

In the environmental movement, the assault on and erosion of biodiversity is being questioned and challenged. Alternatives to raising cash crop productivity through monocultural practices and using large-scale chemical spraying and other standardized, environmentally harmful methods for eliminating pests are growing dramatically. Environmentalists and agriculturalists are increasingly working with communities around the world to promote sustainable farming development through crop mixing, crop rotation, and more natural methods of pest control rather than standardized farming, chemical pesticides, and endless encroachment onto marginal land.

Wangari Muta Maathai, the 2004 Nobel Peace Prize winner and assistant minister for environment, natural resources and wildlife for Kenya, has become a legend in her own time. She has addressed the need to restore biodiversity by establishing and coordinating an ambitious grassroots tree-planting movement. This iconoclastic leader had seen her country's topsoil, drainage systems, and livable land become seriously degraded by widespread deforestation. Among those who suffered most were tribal women who had to travel ever greater distances to collect firewood, leaving less and less time for them to be with their families, tend their crops, and provide stability as well as educational support in the home. Through her Green Belt Movement, Kenyan women have now planted more than 20 million trees across their country. This movement has empowered women, restored diversity, and enriched educational opportunities and family life.[31]

Restoring diversity is also possible in education. There can be no sustainable development without education—that is, without all community members having educational opportunities that improve their knowledge, strengthen their will, and develop their capacity to work with, restore, and get the best from the environment and the people around them. And there can be no worthwhile, widespread, and enduring educational improvement that does not acknowledge and activate the basic principles of sustainability within diverse communities. Short-term, imposed achievement targets, adequate yearly progress, monolithic curriculum prescriptions, and pervasive standardized testing don't define the end of history; a more sustainable and diverse world of learning and change beckons beyond them.

Almost everywhere, the tide is now turning. In Britain and Australia; in Singapore, Japan, and the juggernaut of China; and in international intervention agencies such as the World Bank, UNESCO, and the Organization for Economic Cooperation and Development, creativity, innovation, and flexibility are the new watchwords.

School-centered innovation, teacher-designed assessments, light-touch rather than heavy-handed accountability, greater curriculum flexibility, more personalized approaches to learning, and

increased collaboration and partnerships rather than ruthl[...]
school competition—these are the emergent policy direc[...]
countries that have experienced the overconfidence and ov[...]
of enforced standardization and are now beginning to pull back.
These developments don't portend a return to the unbounded and
inconsistent innovation movements of the 1960s and 1970s—to
the Julie Andrews curriculum, as one of us has called it, in which
"these are a few of my favorite things."[32] Instead, governments and
educators are beginning to work together to create systems that retain a common focus on and sense of urgency and consistency about
learning and achievement for all on one hand, while respecting and
encouraging the diversity and flexibility that makes systems strong,
resilient, and sustainable on the other. One of the most favored
solutions for creating this kind of synergy across schools and
throughout entire systems is professional networks.

Networked Diversity

Professional learning networks for teachers are based on the belief
as well as some evidence that "teachers learn best by sharing ideas,
planning collaboratively, critiquing one another's ideas and experiences and reducing the isolation encountered in most schools."[33]
Networks increase professional interaction and learning across
schools, and for those who participate in them, they generate excitement about teaching and learning.

Natural Networks

To understand the potential and pitfalls of professional networks, it
is important to grasp the nature of networks in general. Networks
have their origins in natural living systems. Bacteria are repeatedly
able to develop rapid resistance to drugs because of the effectiveness
of their complex communication networks.[34] Cells operate in networks, "using a constant flow of matter and energy to produce, repair and perpetuate" themselves.[35] Brains also work not like simple

circuit diagrams but through complex pathways of neural networks.[36] For Fritjof Capra, living systems are defined not by whether certain molecules are present but by "the presence of a self-generating network of metabolic processes."[37] These networks are behind "the spontaneous emergence of new order, which is the basis of life's inherent creativity."[38]

Technological Networks

Networks have not always provided the best, most efficient systems of human work and organization. The energy sources of water, coal, and steam gave rise to large factories, which had to be built close to those energy sources, concentrating people in great numbers in particular buildings and places and giving rise to the industrial and bureaucratic patterns of organization that have subsequently stifled so many of our schools.[39] The shift to networks as a viable and valuable form of organization in a society that conforms more to the operations of living systems in its workings is now made possible by changes in forms of communication and sources of energy. In his book *The Internet Galaxy*, Manuel Castells puts it like this: "As new technologies of energy generation and distribution made possible the factory and the large corporation as the organizational foundation of industrial society, the Internet is the technological basis for the organizational form of the Information Age: the network."[40]

The Internet itself evolved in an emergent way—"at the unlikely intersection of big science, military research and libertarian culture."[41] These influences gave the Internet and its predecessors "a *decentralized* network structure; *distributed* computing power throughout the nodes of the network; and *redundancy* of functions in the network to minimize the risk of disconnections. These features embodied the key answer to military needs for survivability of the system's flexibility, absence of a command center, and maximum autonomy of each node."[42] In the event of a nuclear attack, U.S. defense systems would not be made vulnerable by being concentrated in a single easily targeted communication center. Instead, the defense network was made resilient through redundancy, flexibility, and distributed autonomy.

Military purpose and countercultural individual freedom were among the strangest joint attractors that shaped the Internet's origins. Grassroots countercultures and nerdy graduate student communication channels helped define the genesis of the Internet through conference systems, bulletin boards, and other mechanisms. The culture's libertarian commitments to and beliefs in openness of access and information framed the Internet's basic network architecture, in which

- "Networking architecture [is] open-ended, decentralized, distributed and multidirectional."

- "All communication protocols . . . [are] open, distributed and susceptible of modification."

- "Governance of the network . . . [is] built in accordance with the principles of openness and cooperation that are embedded in the Internet."[43]

In the Soviet Union, where these libertarian values were absent, lack of openness locked up the nation's computer development within its military and security system and ultimately stunted the country's capacity for technological innovation and economic competitiveness. Networks were the nemesis of Cold War politics.[44]

Manuel Castells's masterly trilogy on the information age prophetically argued that "networks are the fundamental stuff of which organizations are and will be made."[45] "The morphology of the network," he suggested, "seems to be well adapted to increasing complexity of interaction and to unpredictable patterns of development arising from the creative powers of such interaction."[46]

Companies increasingly operate not only through vertical networks of suppliers and distributors but through horizontal networks of partnerships and strategic alliances within leaner, more flexible, and more decentralized management systems.[47] Universities use networks for learning, information, conferencing, instruction, and interchange of ideas. In private life, people turn to networks to access medical information, research their genealogy, and contact old school friends. Organizations employ networks for purposes as diverse as making financial investments, increasing voter registration, coordinating environmental protest, and engaging in global criminal activity. The purposes of networks may not always be desirable, but networks are an increasingly pervasive fact of modern life.

Educational Networks

While school systems have been slower than other organizations to catch on to the opportunities that networked learning and communication can provide, networks are not unknown to them. In the 1990s, over one hundred schools in Australia's National Schools Network agreed to establish waivers on union contract rules and government bureaucratic regulations so that they could generate innovative school practices that would also be interconnected across the network, especially at project meetings that brought together teachers from the schools. During the same period, the union-sponsored Creating a Culture of Change network in Ontario, Canada, offered facilitation support and interactive opportunities to schools that wanted to develop more collaborative approaches to school improvement.[48] Britain has created networks to connect schools participating in particular government initiatives such as Education Action Zones, Beacon Schools, or Excellence in Cities, and there is at least one influential school improvement network (Improving Quality of Education for All) that exists independently of government control.[49] As many as 40 percent of U.K. teachers claim to be part of a professional network.[50] In the United States, school improvement networks such as the Comer Schools, the League of Professional Schools, and the Coalition of Essential Schools, which include schools that subscribe to a set of common educational principles, are legion.[51] The United

States' National Writing Project brings together and connects thousands of enthusiastic teachers every year to communicate, share their practices, and explore how to improve the teaching of writing.[52] The Teacher Union Reform Network convenes and connects teachers who are advocates of meaningful reform, not merely opponents of others' reform strategies.[53] Action research, staff development, critical friends (peers who provide constructive feedback on one's teaching), and subject-based networks all perform similar functions.

Innovative as they are, many of these networks are more like clubs or groups. They comprise people who primarily gather together for face-to-face interaction at meetings or conferences. Like high school subject departments, they tend to have controlling hubs with spokes of communication that extend out to the rest of the network in simple and centralized pathways of influence instead of connecting through multiple nodes of interconnected influence that follow less predictable and geometrically precise patterns. What propels networks into another dimension of complexity and interconnectivity altogether is, as Castells points out, widespread access to and participation in technology-based interaction.

University of Toronto professor Barry Wellman has spent more than a quarter century researching the properties of communities and networks.[54] Founder of the International Network for Social Network Analysis in 1976, he currently studies the relationship between computer networks and social networks. Instead of living in densely knit groups in large public spaces, he says, we now work and live "in sprawling networks which we juggle several at any given time," connecting us to many groups while reducing our sense of strong attachment to any one.[55]

These networks vary a lot in their nature and form. Some are tight, some are loose. Some are broad and have many chains of connection. Others are small and have just a few.[56] Some are open to broad participation. Others are exclusive and closed. Networks may also be permeable to outside influences or tightly sealed from them.[57] But across all of them, instead of merely accessing particular networks occasionally, we increasingly live in and among them, says Wellman, participating in "networks of networks," as he first called them, throughout our lives.[58] Within these "network societies," the number of groups with which we interact multiplies, and the boundaries between them become more and more permeable.

The addition (not the substitution) of technologically assisted networks alongside face-to-face networks offers significant possibilities for leadership and change in education. Educational policy and leadership need no longer be excessively aligned and standardized in mechanical systems of linear and hierarchical decision making and curriculum delivery but can develop better architectures of leadership, innovation, and improvement on a substantial scale. Many efforts are being made to create educational networks of this kind. The more than one hundred schools participating in School-Net, sponsored by Industry Canada and working in partnership with government and with educational professionals, seek to sponsor innovative school efforts that also integrate information and communication technologies.[59] In England, the Primary Strategy Learning Networks will comprise 1,500 mini-networks with half a dozen small schools in each one,[60] and the Specialist Schools Trust is building a global network of innovative schools that will stimulate and share innovative practices together.[61]

One of the most extensive efforts to develop large-scale educational networks is the Networked Learning Communities initiative of the National College for School Leadership (NCSL) in the United Kingdom, which connects schools through e-learning and information exchange and through national and regional conferences and workshops.[62] One of the program's evaluators, Mark Hadfield, describes the initiative:

> This "network of networks" . . . currently involves . . .
> 5 percent of all schools in England. Currently there are
> 109 networks making a total of 1,259 schools. The net-

works [range] in size from a minimum of 6, with an ave
age of around 10. Not all of these are new networks.
Indeed . . . 60%, were already involved in some kind of
networking arrangement . . . under previous central government initiatives . . . [or] through the enthusiasm and
commitment of school leaders who came together with
other local schools for a variety of reasons. The NLC
programme has brought together these networks, old and
new, offering them a small amount of financial support
for three years, providing them with support from a central team of facilitators, researchers and administrators,
and creating opportunities and structures through which
they can learn from each other.[63]

The architect of Networked Learning Communities, former
head teacher David Jackson, argues that professional networks of
this kind

- Enable and encourage schools to share and transfer the
  considerable knowledge already in existence that can
  help children learn better. Individual schools have
  limited knowledge, but collectively they have almost
  as much as they need.

- Stimulate the professional fulfillment and motivation
  that comes from learning and interacting with
  colleagues in ways that help teachers be more effective
  with their own students.

- Capitalize on positive diversity across teachers and
  schools who serve different kinds of students or who
  vary in how they respond to them, instead of maintaining the negative diversity of cutthroat competition that
  prevents mutual learning and assistance or denying
  diversity altogether through imposition of standardized
  solutions.

- Provide teachers and others with opportunities for lateral leadership of people, programs, and problem solving beyond their own school setting.[64]

Other advantages of networked learning communities include the following:[65]

- They provide opportunities to draw on and develop evidence-informed, research-derived practices.[66]

- They promote innovation and its dissemination across large groups of interested schools.[67]

- They give teachers more of a voice in professional and school-based decision making.[68]

- They help personalize every school as a learning community, enabling them to adopt emergent solutions to their own needs, which are diffused and made available throughout the network, instead of being subjected to overly prescribed programs.[69]

- They are flexible and resilient in the face of crises or misdirected system initiatives that turn out to be unsuccessful, allowing new learning and fresh solutions to emerge and fill the gap that the false starts and failures have left behind.[70]

Network Limitations

Diverse networks are a promising alternative to monoculture and standardization, but by themselves, they are not a panacea. Michael Fullan is concerned that networks may not work well in areas of complex learning that require more expert input, may lead to sharing of beliefs and opinions rather than dependable knowledge, may lose focus and become self-indulgent ends in themselves, and may be insufficient for ensuring accountability.[71]

There are other concerns about educational networks. The scale of overall impact and involvement seems to be limited. Even the vast NCSL network still reaches only one in twenty of all the nation's schools.[72] The free, open and voluntary nature of networks that their libertarian roots demand also means that networks may suffer the fate of other innovation movements, appealing to as well as including only existing enthusiasts.[73] The enthusiasts then run the risk of overparticipating and burning themselves out.[74] Government attempts to secure cohesion and inclusion by funding and controlling professional networks, while often well-intended, eventually undermine the essential voluntarism and the libertarian foundation that sustains networks over time. The networks end up belonging to someone else rather than the people they serve. Governments are basically *analog*: rational, linear, and one-directional. Networks, however, are *digital:* they operate on multiple channels, in emergent systems of diverse and sometimes necessarily redundant communication. Analog systems cannot regulate digital ones.[75]

These difficulties are not specific to educational networks; they are inherent in the nature of networks themselves. Castells points to the essential dilemma in *The Rise of the Network Society:* "The performance of a given network will depend on two fundamental attributes of the network: its *connectedness*, that is, its structural ability to facilitate noise-free communication between its components, [and] its *consistency*, that is, the extent to which there is a sharing of interests between the network's goals and the goals of its components."[76]

Networks, in other words, face a fundamental tension between what Fullan calls *connectivity and cohesion.*[77] In Castells' words, "they have considerable difficulty in coordinating functions, in focusing resources on specific goals, and in accomplishing a given task, beyond a certain size and complexity of the network."[78]

Network Solutions

Despite all these difficulties, network dilemmas are manageable if they receive sustained attention from leaders at all levels. In the business world, Castells argues, networks work best when they have five fundamental features:[79]

- *Scalability* such that the number of components can be increased or decreased as required. Networks need not and should not have a fixed number of nodes.

- *Interactivity* in real or chosen time with all relevant parties that bypasses traditional vertical channels of communication.

- *Management of flexibility*, combining strategic guidance with multiple interactions.

- *Branding*, especially tight control over the nature and quality of the final end product.

- *Customization* rather than standardization, with responsiveness to customer preferences.

There are clues here as to what the solutions might be for educational networks. Networks can work as a sustainable pattern of leadership and change in a context of growing diversity when

- *They have a clear moral purpose* that people can unite around and that is connected to and focuses on all children's learning and success. Without this purpose, networks risk developing a self-indulgent life of their own and failing to sustain the commitment of their participants.[80]

- *They have clarity, focus, and discipline*; otherwise their members' efforts will dissipate and be short-lived.[81]

- *They have clear parameters and products* that "brand" what the network is meant to do and why it is important.

- *They are evidence-informed*, attentive to research, data, and verifiable knowledge, as well as experience and

intuition. If not, networks can become merely places
to pool ignorance, prejudice, and gossip.

- *Their cells or nodes are strong professional learning communities* that emphasize and develop capacity in the purposes
and processes of learning for children and adults. In
Louise Stoll and Lorna Earl's words, "networked learning
communities are professional learning communities that
operate across a broader landscape."[82] If network cells
are weak—that is, if they are not true professional learning communities—then they will not drive improved
practices but will perpetuate indifferent ones.[83]

- *They develop a "hacker" ethic* that promotes a culture
of autonomous projects, openly shared technical
knowledge, and a drive toward creativity. The network
should nurture "a culture of technological creativity
based on freedom, cooperation, reciprocity and informality as well as common good."[84]

- *They are actionable in real and chosen time*, supported by
portable technology that allows immediate access to
achievement data, research evidence, and professional
advice on a just-in-time basis (as at Noumea Primary
School in Chapter Three, for example).

- *They support and are supported by distributed, lateral
leadership* across and beyond schools, providing significant leadership opportunities beyond the separated
small worlds in which educators and their leadership
talents are often confined.

- *Their architectures are linked to remodeled school structures*, especially as children get older, so that learning
becomes more independent, personalized, and flexible
for students and so that teachers are no longer assigned

on a one-teacher, one-class basis, burdened with the custody of large groups, or unable to access their networks and networked learning in real school time.

- *They cannot be controlled; they can only be disturbed.* Government networks are an oxymoron. Governments are analog; networks are digital. Governments tend to go for linear alignment of policy, curriculum, staff training, and other elements, in order to achieve consistency and coherence. Networks, meanwhile, work by cohesion, constantly pulling diverse elements together. Governments deliver outcomes and standards in linear systems of delivery and implementation; networks develop outcomes in emergent systems of innovation. Government networks will always tend to fade or fail.

In Knowsley Education Authority in England, which we encountered in the previous chapter, former director Steve Munby has set up a collegiate (secondary school) for students aged fourteen to nineteen, in a partnership between the local education authority, secondary schools, the further education (community) college, and employers to offer more choice to older students. The *London Times Educational Supplement* reported that within the collaborative and inclusive approach to the education authority,

Every pupil joins it when they reach 14—Year 10 and 11 pupils can study outside their school at a new 14–16 vocational skills centre, at one of three learning centres, at a specialist [school] etc. . . . Last year, a third of the borough's Year 10 and 11, were engaged in learning outside their school and more children are now staying on in education after 16. . . . Over the next six years (with

Government money) the borough aims to bulldoze all 11 secondary schools and replace them with well-developed learning centres. . . ."We're not even going to call them schools," [Munby] says. "We just aim to knock the whole thing down and design from the outset what learning should look like in the 21st century."[85]

Knowsley shows that networked professional learning makes more sense when it is connected to networked school learning—to schools that are strong professional learning communities that work collaboratively and flexibly with the district.

Knowsley's networks meet several of the elements of sustainability at the same time, through an interconnected agenda:

- They give their students flexible, personalized learning across a network of learning centers.

- They do this within a context of distributed leadership that brings the schools "genuine collaboration, collective decision-making and just leadership," in Munby's words. Former head teachers (principals) provide leadership coaching for schools in difficulty, and staff are exchanged between schools when needs arise.

- The senior leadership climate is one of high expectation, high trust. "We had to have a relationship based on mutual trust" with head teachers, says Munby. "They had to believe in us and us in them."

- Deep learning and achievement for all students are taken seriously. Knowsley is starting to ascend in the national district rankings after being the worst performing authority in the country in 2001.

- Learning targets are common and agreed on, not enforced and imposed.

- The authority has an assertive relationship with national government, adopting its initiatives only if they "fit in with the exciting way we're working," says Munby, yet it still gains the government's respect; Knowsley is one of five case studies selected for inclusion in the government's National Strategy document.

  In Knowsley, networked learning is not an added process or a special project. Knowsley is a "networked society,"[86] something in which everyone works and lives. This society works because it is grounded in a clear and compelling purpose, a sense of urgency, a commitment to social justice in terms of supporting all children's learning, a high-trust culture of deliberately distributed leadership for the purpose of achieving agreed-on rather than enforced targets, and an inspirational belief in the power of the authority's people to achieve the goals of improvement together.

What, then, is the role of government in relation to networks? Should government leadership have nothing to do with networks at all? Are governments condemned only to endure or ignore them? On the basis of the arguments and evidence so far, we believe that governments do have a powerful role to play in supporting networked learning.

First, it is the role of government, with its people, to create and articulate a compelling and cohesive sense of moral purpose and, where justified, a climate of urgency for public education.

Second, governments need to establish accountability mechanisms that provide frameworks for network responsibility. This works best when accountability is collective and pulls schools and teachers together, and when it employs a "light touch"—testing when absolutely necessary, providing usable and interactive feedback whenever it can. Multiple forms of accountability also prevent networks from being squeezed into narrowly defined channels of teaching and learning.

Third, networks need strong cells. One of governments' greatest priorities in a networked learning society is to help to develop (not impose) professional learning communities.

Fourth, governments can and should provide resources to stimulate and support networks and their coordination and ultimately should hold them accountable for results, without micromanaging their activities or outcomes.

Fifth, networks need to be alternate structures of improvement; not additions to those that already exist. Networks require resource shifts, not resource additions; otherwise they will prosper only in optimistic eras of economic expansion and atrophy whenever times get tough. Governments need to reallocate resources away from the multimillion-dollar excesses of tested accountability, so they can build an increasingly strong and expanding network of strong and successful professional learning communities throughout their schools. Light-touch accountability systems like those being developed in the United Kingdom—with less emphasis on standardized tests and external inspection compared with teacher-developed assessments and school self-review—make this shift more feasible.

Networks are not everything. They should be a supplement to, not a substitute for strong face-to-face relationships. Zygmunt Bauman warns, "We talk these days of nothing with greater solemnity or relish than of 'networks'. . . only because the 'real stuff'— the closely knit networks, firm and secure connections, fully fledged relationships—have all but fallen apart."[87] "We seek rescue in 'networks,'" he says, because their "advantage over hard-and-fast bonds is that they make connecting and disconnecting equally easy."[88]

works are of no value unless they have strong pro-
...ing communities at their core. And professional learn-
...munities only have real strength if they are vibrant cultures
. people committed to common purposes and to one another rather than superficial teams that meet only to dispatch tasks and dis-
sect data.

Conclusion

Sustainability demands diversity. Alignment eliminates it. Competition corrupts it. Productive diversity requires less rather than more
testing, greater curriculum flexibility and creativity, explicit
acknowledgment of and engagement with the knowledge and learning needs of culturally diverse communities, personalized learning
rather than scripted instruction, focused cohesion instead of forced
alignment, and intelligent professional development rather than
paint-by-numbers in-service training. The leadership of organizations as natural systems wedded to modern networked communication patterns can help us work with rather than against the cultural
diversity of our students, the professional diversity of our teachers,
and the organizational diversity of our schools. Strong networked
learning communities that have a compelling sense of purpose and
work within clear parameters of collective, multiple, and light-touch
forms of accountability, are one of many strategies for restoring the
rich diversity that years of standardization have depleted or destroyed. In countries where people are increasingly diverse, our systems, schools, and leadership strategies need to be diverse, flexible,
and responsive. With professional dedication and sound leadership,
diversity can and should lead to cohesion, not confusion. Otherwise, standardized systems will offer the false dawn of short-term results as a misleadingly optimistic prelude to an unsustainable future.

6

Resourcefulness
Restraint and Renewal

We cannot solve the problems that we have created
with the same thinking that created them.

Albert Einstein

❖ PRINCIPLE 6

**Sustainable leadership develops and does not deplete
material and human resources. It renews people's
energy. Sustainable leadership is prudent and resourceful
leadership that wastes neither its money nor its people.**

Improvement and Energy

Improvement needs energy. Sustainable improvement needs sustainable energy that can be converted into human and material resources. But what resources? And how do we sustain these resources? There are two prevailing views on this issue. The first concentrates on the finite nature of planetary resources: fossil fuels are disappearing, greenhouse gases are intensifying, and we are running out of time and space. We have to stop producing and consuming more and more because within a century or less, more prosperous countries and their people will have reached the limits to growth. If we want to protect and preserve nature's legacy, along with our own survival within it, the people of more prosperous countries will have to restrain their appetites and start to come to terms with the meaning of *enough*.[1] The second position accepts the fact that our earth is fragile and imperiled but claims that it is still possible to meet the basic material needs and develop the human potential of everyone without damaging the surrounding environment, if we approach the problem with care and ingenuity.[2] The first position is that of *sustainability*; the second, that of *sustainable development*. Resourcefulness, we want to argue, entails being willing to recognize and respond to both visions of our relationship with the planet, its people, and their development.

Closed and Open Systems

The finite view of energy draws on an ironclad principle of physics: the second law of thermodynamics. This states that once energy is transformed, it is no longer a resource available for work in the future. The two laws of thermodynamics were first stated in 1865 by a German professor of mathematical physics, Rudolf Clausius. They are succinct.

1. The energy of the universe is constant.
2. The entropy of the universe tends to a maximum.[3]

Clausius invented the concept of *entropy*. Entropy measures the temperature of energy. As energy moves from high to low temperatures, it is not as capable of doing useful work. The energy spreads out; it is not as useful (even though it is still conserved); and so it tends toward disorder or increasing entropy.[4]

Entropy is nature's penalty for energy transformation.[5] Human and natural systems are in a perpetual state of dissipation until they reach equilibrium, at which point all the energy has been transformed and ultimately expended, resulting in death. A look in the mirror as we age gives evidence of entropy, as do air pollution and toxic waste. We can only slow down entropy, not stop it. So we exercise, recycle, donate money to poverty groups, and so on. For example, while recycling is an important way to slow down entropy, it also requires the expenditure of other energy sources. When we recycle newspapers, bottles, or cans, placing them in a plastic box provided by our municipality, a truck takes away the contents. But manufacturing the boxes, fueling the trucks, and running the recycling plant also require energy. Even then, the remnants and residues of the products and the machines that recycle them still end up in landfill sites. We might guzzle gas in large vehicles or conserve fuel in small ones; we might clothe ourselves in ever-changing fashions or prudently wear family hand-me-downs; we might write on brand new paper or rely on recycled products instead, but everything ends up as waste at the end of the line. This is the process of entropy and of design, production, and consumption processes that have a cradle-to-grave life cycle, just as we do.

The ecological implications of entropy for our optimal lifestyle and habits are clear and widely understood: slow down the damage, conserve fuel, reuse and recycle, be prudent and self-sacrificing, limit your appetites, do fewer bad things.

Nobel Prize–winning physicist Ilya Prigogine found this perspective somewhat depressing, and he also observed that living systems evolve in an opposite way from entropy: from simple to complex, from disorder to order. He suggested that some parts of the universe are closed systems, which behave in mechanical ways and are subject to the law of entropy. But most social and biological systems are open, exchanging energy, matter, and information with their environment. Open systems in nature include brains, immune systems, cells, and ant colonies.

In open systems, energy need not be dissipated but can be exchanged, replenished, and renewed, as it is among the practitioners of natural capitalism, whom we described in the Introduction, who try to convert the waste of one enterprise into a resource for a partner, reducing levels of waste (or entropy) almost to zero.[6]

In an even more creative vein, ecological and industrial design-ers William McDonough and Michael Braungart demonstrate that the manufacturing process can be designed as an open living system that transforms disorder into order.[7] In the case of shampoo pro-duction, for example, instead of asking how we can limit the nega-tive impact of chemical discharge from the production process, we should ask how the shampoo's by-products might actually improve the quality of the river. Indeed, the authors designed a product that not only worked as an effective shampoo but increased the quality of the waste leaving the factory compared with when it entered. Rather than cradle-to-grave design, McDonough and Braungart therefore propose an energy exchange model of cradle-to-cradle design, inspired by the natural processes of living systems as well as by technological ingenuity placed at their service. In this cradle-to-cradle approach, resources are never lost but are renewed and re-plenished in a way that promotes regeneration and improvement.

So there are two ways to understand and approach environmen-tal, organizational, and educational resourcefulness: *restraint* and *renewal*. Restraint urges us to do fewer bad things and avoid or limit actions that will wear out people or things. Renewal inspires us to do more good things and find ways to reenergize people or exchange energy more efficiently within the system. The problems in our work and our world arise when narratives of progress and change deny both of these ways to slow down entropy and renew or exchange energy.

Mechanical Waste

The dominant narrative of progress in the Western world and the scientific era has been the narrative of the machine. This narrative organizes the world as if it obeys universal physical laws of pre-dictable order and as if nature can be controlled through techno-logical mastery. It denies or diminishes the importance of entropy, operating on the assumption that resources of nature, as well as human labor and energy, can be used and exploited without limit, as if their availability were endless. In this mechanical narrative, progress is a ravenous machine of creative destruction, eating up everything in its path in order to create a better world ahead, oblivious to the natural and human waste it leaves strewn in its wake.

In the seventeenth and eighteenth centuries, the scientific method of Francis Bacon and the mathematical arguments of René Descartes and later of Isaac Newton laid the groundwork for this *mechanical view* of the universe by rejecting all other ways of knowing, such as intuition, ethics, and faith. These thinkers helped create a world that was viewed as rational, linear, and understandable through thought and reason.

The idea of a predictable, knowable universe based on unchanging laws impressed philosopher John Locke, who sought to discover the natural laws in humankind's social and economic activities. Locke rejected the church's teaching that the purpose of life was to prepare for the Last Judgment and asserted that the actual purpose of life was for people to look after their self- interest in the here and now. The job of governments and other institutions was to clear the path for people to achieve what they wanted in life, and if nature had to be exploited to enhance the well-being of people, so be it. There are clear echoes of John Locke among contemporary advocates of the ownership society. Even Frank Sinatra's motto, "He who dies with all the toys wins," has Locke's stamp.

In summary, in the mechanical narrative,

- There is a precise mathematical order to the universe and also to social and economic life.

- People must intervene to change nature's disorder into human order.

- People's self-interest depends on continual growth and development.

- Science and technology are the tools to achieve unlimited progress and growth.

These four principles have dominated our lives for over four centuries and still underpin economic development, political strategy, and top-down educational reform.

Together, these elements have unleashed the power of creative destruction that has produced capitalism, industrialization, modern city living, and globalized economic activity and lifestyles. The mechanical narrative has also created environmental degradation, provoked wars over resources, and wasted millions of human lives.[8] In practice, the mechanical narrative has denied and disregarded Clausius's theory of thermodynamics—the law of entropy, the price of progress. Inability to confront the law of entropy in standardized educational reform practice has also created waste in terms of human stress and burnout,[9] as well as loss of deep and broad learning, as the price of short-term targets and results.[10]

Janice Burnley was in her second year as principal at Lord Byron High School when she and her school had to confront the formidable challenges of implementing the government's far-reaching reform agenda in a context of dramatically reduced resources. Changes in the Ontario government's funding formula had cut the number of Lord Byron department heads from nine positions to just four. Each of the four leaders now had to attend to multiple areas of study—for example, one person had responsibility for physical education, art, music, drama, and technical education. The principal described this depletion of the school's middle-level leadership as "devastating." Burnley and her assistant principal had to assume many of the responsibilities previously performed by department heads, such as mentoring the eleven new teachers, teacher supervision, and community and district liaison. The assistant principal explained, "My typical day starts at 7:15 in the morning, phoning in for supply teachers [substitutes], covering classes, making sure that's in place. Seeing a bunch of kids as much as possible in between—I am not as visible as I would like. I feel bad, because I like to be in classes. My night finished last night at 10:30."

With only one full-time guidance counselor now remaining in the school, the administrators were "doing more guidance work than anything else." Some teachers had refused to contribute to extracurricular activities because of their workload, so Burnley sponsored a volleyball team, just to keep the program alive. Burnley felt "responsible for the world." "Every year I say I cannot work any harder, and every year I have to work harder. The support systems to make things happen are just not there anymore."

Burnley and her assistant tried to involve staff in decision making, but pressures of time and multiple, accelerating reform demands obliged her to be more directive and less collegial than she preferred. For example, the district required all schools to implement the Ministry of Education's new reporting system immediately. Although the technology was flawed, Burnley had to mandate in-service sessions for all staff. As a relatively new leader, she was not in a position to say "no" to her superiors, and she admitted to feeling "pretty isolated." She felt more and more like a manager for the government rather than a leader of her school. "The opportunities as an administrator to initiate changes, or even to get out in the hallways and into classes and network with kids and teachers are certainly restricted," she complained.

The denuded leadership structure forced staff to fend for themselves. The requirement to spend more time in class, the limitations on time outside class, and the overall intensification of work eroded the school's informal leadership. The government's determination to eliminate so-called waste in school district bureaucracies meant that the art teacher had to depend for subject assistance on the good will of colleagues in other schools and that the neophyte music teacher had to rely on a teacher from a neighboring school and a kind-hearted instrument repairman from a private firm.

Concern for the quality of their work and the welfare of their students permeated every conversation with teachers. There was a growing sense of powerlessness. With less resources of time and money, teachers constantly complained about outdated texts, computers that crashed, and the elimination of field trips and sports activities. "We are driven by computers and by the deadlines that somebody else sets," one teacher observed. As budget resources declined, human resources became depleted along with them. Within less than two years, the district's escalating resource crisis resulted in Lord Byron High School being merged with a nearby special education school.

Lord Byron's teachers and leaders were not alone. Teachers we surveyed in Ontario secondary schools felt "tired of being bashed," "beaten down," "browbeaten," "vilified," and "constantly criticized" by repetitive change and imposed reforms. Sixty-seven percent of them stated that since the reforms, they worked less collaboratively with their colleagues; 80 percent reported that their working relationships with school administrators had not improved; 43 percent pointed to reduced contacts with parents; and most tellingly of all, 88 percent indicated that they would be less likely to advise their own children to go into teaching.[11]

Caught between teachers' feelings of anger and distress and their own legal obligations to implement multiple reforms in a hurry, principals and assistant principals began to doubt themselves. "My whole life changed in a short time. Why am I feeling overwhelmed

by the political shift?" said one. "I'm implementing government policy I do not agree with," another remarked. One captured the feelings of most of his colleagues when he said, "The system is clearly
making you into *managers* but you have memories of how to be *leaders*. You are now feeling and acting like your teachers. You have
tried to pick up the slack of teachers' lack of involvement, but
you're beginning to behave as persons who are devalued and dis-
empowered."

Within five years, the government of Ontario had removed
resources from the public education system, returned millions of dollars to the taxpayers, imposed a demanding curriculum on students,
introduced a range of standardized tests, required teachers to teach
more students, and implemented an unwieldy computerized report
card. It did all this with alarming alacrity, reinforcing the fast school
philosophy of repetitive change. The complexity and speed of its
changes and the depletion of financial resources produced monu-
mental waste of emotional energy, confidence, commitment, and
trust among principals and teachers. The rage in the government's
machine had ravaged the educational environment on which its
rational model of progress had been inflicted.

Ecological Restraint and Renewal

There is a better narrative to guide our use of material and human
resources: a narrative of restraint and renewal. On one hand, the
quest and pressure to continually raise performance standards in
tested achievement at any price need not be so all-consuming. On
the other, ecosystems are also open systems that exchange energy,
matter, and information with their environment. They can renew,
restore, and rejuvenate. Losers can become winners, failures can
become successes, and the weak can become strong.

As we saw in the previous chapter, in ecosystems, everything is
connected to everything else. In *The Power of Full Engagement*, Jim
Loehr and Tony Schwartz argue that "the corporate body is a living,

breathing entity comprising individual cells of dynamic energy."[12] Fritjof Capra provides the same insight: sustainability "is not an individual property but a property of an entire web of relationships: it involves a whole community."[13] John Locke was wrong. So was Frank Sinatra. The purpose of life is not to amass all the toys for ourselves, but to restrain our appetites where we can and to grow and develop with others so that we can improve our environment along with the public good that benefits us all.

Restraint

Bill McKibben is one of the world's leading environmentalists. He issued some of the earliest warnings about global warming.[14] With great passion and a wealth of evidence, he has argued that the earth is already so despoiled that it will become a wasteland for all species, including humans, unless we change our patterns of production, consumption, and disposal. Many of McKibben's predictions, which were initially seen as extreme and alarmist, are now widely accepted scientific wisdom. In 2005, for example, over a thousand researchers from ninety-five nations, working with the World Resources Institute, undertook a worldwide ecosystem assessment, which concluded that human activity now seriously threatens the earth's ability to sustain future generations because of negative impact on the planet's basic circulation systems of air, water, and nutrients and on the fundamental diversity of life.[15]

Some energy resources are finite. Even with new discoveries and improved technologies of extraction, the worldwide supply of oil, like any mineral resource, rises from zero to a peak, and when consumption exceeds the possible rate of extraction, it then declines forever. In *Out of Gas*, David Goodstein prophesies that in just a few years, we will be at a point where "increasing demand will meet decreasing supply, possibly with disastrous results."[16] We are reaching the end of the age of oil, and if we are not careful, we will also be reaching the end of clean water, coral reefs, and fresh air. Out of time, out of options, out of gas—this is the future of energy and modern life, unless we can open up alternatives like hydrogen and wind power and severely restrain our consuming appetites and environmentally destructive behavior in the meantime.

The same issues apply in educational leadership and change. Loehr and Schwartz argue that there are four domains in which we need to conserve and renew energy: physical, emotional, mental, and spiritual energy.[17] Our energy and long-term effectiveness become depleted when we

- Have no time to sleep, relax, or exercise properly

- Feel constantly overwrought or emotionally disengaged from those around us in a world in which we have no time for proper relationships

- Are always having to think too quickly or superficially

- Are disconnected from and unable to pursue or fulfill our own morally compelling purposes

Attending to these energy deficits is partly within our control, Loehr and Schwartz argue. But they also acknowledge that some organizational and work environments are seriously and perhaps toxically energy-depleting. This type of environment has been abundantly evident in educational settings throughout our book, which has described fast school nations that are obsessed with

- A hurried and narrowing curriculum that allows no space for depth and breadth of learning or teaching

- Externally imposed and inescapable short-term achievement targets that turn teaching and learning into not a steady marathon nor a set of spurts and sprints but an enforced and everlasting hurdle race

- An accountability agenda of endless improvement that leaves schools more made over than Michael Jackson

- Subjecting schools to the repetitive change syndrome
  of bureaucratic overwork and innovation overload
  that produces exhaustion, insecurity, and lack of
  opportunity for reflection, replenishment, and renewal

- Shaming and blaming schools that are labeled as
  underperforming, leaving their teachers with
  diminished confidence and depleted commitment

These excesses of mechanically driven reform in an overly pressurized environment have led to epidemics of stress, loss of confidence, and emotional withdrawal on the part of teachers in many parts of the world.[18] The wasted contributions of teachers are reflected in the wasted lives of principals. A statewide survey of principals in Victoria, Australia, found that eight in ten principals experienced high levels of stress from the "unnecessary paperwork" and managerial nature of their jobs.[19] In the schools that we researched, only a few years after the onset of standardized reform, Eric West ended up in the hospital three days after his transfer to a new school following his stint at Stewart Heights; North Ridge's Diane Grant transferred to an elite girl's private school after taking her first full principalship in the public system; exemplary teacher leader Greg Allan took early retirement; Janice Burnley moved to another school; and after becoming exhausted by her efforts to turn around two schools in succession in a context of escalating reform requirements, Charmaine Watson opted for early retirement and the life of a graduate student.

In the age of standardization and in the push to meet short-term achievement targets, teachers and leaders have been treated by governments as if they are bottomless pits of energy. They are not. When a few educators fail to relax, regroup, and renew their energy, this is probably due to poor judgment and lack of balance among the individuals concerned. When entire systems experience heightened stress and depleted energy, it is a consequence of their exploitative attitudes toward essential human resources. Under these conditions, it is time for people and their governments to say "enough" (as the voters of Ontario did in 2003, when they elected a new government due to dissatisfaction with the educational and environmental record of the existing one) and to follow the example of system leaders who slow down the entropic process of depletion and waste by

- Infusing additional resources and extra energy into the system—as the governments of Ontario, British Columbia, and the United Kingdom did—for better buildings, smaller class sizes, increased numbers of support staff, and additional in-school time to prepare and plan[20]

- Replacing externally imposed targets with internally agreed-on targets for improvement

- Reducing the speed and scope of reform implementation and also the relentless and insatiable pace of expected improvement, accepting that there are human limits to the rate of progress (including how quickly educational standards can be raised)

- Replacing the emotionally depleting strategies of shaming and blaming underperforming schools and their teachers and leaders with supportive strategies that rebuild confidence, competence, and pride among the educators who will be responsible for arresting the decline in performance and for securing improvement

There are more than a few promising examples of school system leadership's being willing to rethink its approaches to school improvement and the use of resources:

- The British government has invested over £37 million in its Workplace Remodeling initiative, which recognizes the importance of teachers in raising educational standards by providing schools with the funds to hire, train, and deploy support staff to relieve teachers of administrative tasks, increase teachers' job satisfaction, and improve the status of the profession.[21]

- A new government in Manitoba, Canada, has reversed eleven years of top-down, mandated changes that left the province's school boards and educators feeling unappreciated and victimized.[22] It adopted a "better way," focusing on investing in teaching and learning, respecting all partners, building school capacity for improvement, developing classroom-based assessment expertise, and grounding its approach in the best available evidence and research.[23]

- The Bill and Melinda Gates Foundation is supporting reform efforts to reduce school size in communities across the United States. The foundation is seeking to harness students' and teachers' energy productively by giving teachers time to collaborate and strengthen their skills and by integrating technology into teaching and learning environments.[24]

- Despite its questionable commitment to imposing short-term targets, the Liberal government of Ontario has not only infused additional dollars into public education but also agreed to a settlement for peace and stability with key teachers' unions that restores much of the salary and planning time for working with colleagues that teachers lost under the previous government.

Thus, ecological renewal begins with the exercise of restraint—being less ruthlessly exploitative of teachers' and leaders' energy reserves and more prepared to conserve and replace some of their energy by injecting additional human and fiscal resources into the system.

Renewal

John Goodlad is one of the strongest proponents of school renewal. Now in his eighties, Goodlad is a cofounder and director of the Center for Educational Renewal at the University of Washington. The center strives "to advance the simultaneous renewal of K–12 schools and the education of educators within the larger context of education in a democracy."[25]

Goodlad distinguishes renewal from reform. Reform originates outside schools, "beyond time and space,"[26] and it doesn't "accommodate the nature and circumstances of schools."[27] Goodlad contends that traditional large-scale reform efforts assume that something is wrong and that systemwide restructuring must take place to create standardized "McSchools." Renewal, however, is ecologically grounded in the lives of schools and the people who work within them: "Schools are cultures seeking to maintain a state of equilibrium that allows them to function in the face of perturbations from without. They are ecosystems within larger ecosystems."[28]

Renewal, Goodlad argues, is a "cottage industry." It is about specific people and places that are linked to other cottage industries through common purposes and cultural ties. Each school becomes an ecosystem within a district ecosystem, and renewal occurs through networked interaction in which schools and districts work cooperatively towards common goals.[29] In a good school these interactions are healthy, enabling the school both to conduct its daily business effectively and to cope with exigencies. In a poor school, these interactions are unhealthy, making the conduct of business difficult. Bad schools are in a constant state of crisis or near crisis.[30]

The ability to maintain equilibrium while dealing with dissonance is essential to school renewal. Goodlad explains, "The language of school renewal is multidimensional, relatively free of good guys and bad guys and of ends, means and outcomes linearity. The language and the ethos are of the people around and especially in schools acquiring the efficacy and developing the collaborative mechanisms necessary to [produce] better schools."[31]

Since 1912, Eastside Technical School has provided vocational programs for generations of students in one of Ontario's most conservative cities. It quickly gained a reputation as a pioneer in vocational education and has remained on the leading edge throughout its history. One example was the development of the Television Arts Department in 1970, when radio and television broadcasting and programming became part of the curriculum. The first FM studio opened in November 1977, and students worked in Educational Television (ETV) studios and shops, running the *Good Morning Eastside Show* every morning. Students were fully involved in production of school television and radio programs and also worked at a local radio station. Business and visual arts programs as well as specific courses for nursing assistants and other careers drew a wide-ranging clientele.

Despite its exemplary record of preparing students for the workplace and its excellent reputation among provincial educators, Eastside's community thought the school was for students who couldn't succeed in a "real" school. Principals of the regular academic schools often used it as a dumping ground "for students who didn't fit." A former Eastside teacher recalled how many people had characterized the school with stigmatizing terms: "In the 50s, it was 'greasers,' in the 70s and early 80s, it was 'druggies' who attended Eastside." When a local newspaper named Eastside "Dope City," a number of teachers challenged it and forced a retraction.

In the 1980s and 1990s, stiff competition from other vocational schools as well as community colleges, along with district pressure to conform to conventional school structures, pushed Eastside's principal and his staff to improve their competitive standing in another way by developing creative policies and programs in music and entrepreneurship that ran counter to more conventional district directions. In the midst of all this, Eastside's staff continued to counter the negative "reputation it has not earned."

During the resource cutbacks of the mid- to late 1990s, Eastside was also able to compete with the expanding Catholic school system, which threatened to take its best students, by embarking on an ambitious reconstruction project to "rebuild, renew, and revitalize" the school. This renovation was a turning point in the school's fight to enhance its reputation. The nationally known art program is up and running again in new surroundings, and the technological labs and classrooms are filled with state-of-the-art resources. By the end of the 1990s, Eastside's staff was led by a core of aging but loyal teachers who had devoted their careers to addressing the educational needs of the kinds of students who came to the school. Despite the energy-depleting reform-based indignities of longer hours and increased workloads, they were able to take advantage of the government's relative indifference to vocational programs and focus on renewal and improvement of the school's image.

Teachers still fight against the negative stereotypes traditionally associated with Eastside Tech, but they have now adopted these labels proudly and are beginning to revel in the difference and in the freedom they afford to be more creative and more adaptive to the needs of the special and diverse student population they serve. Indeed, since the renovated school re-opened, there have been only positive articles in hitherto unsupportive public media about accomplishments by students at the school. Over a century, therefore, Eastside has managed to preserve its always imperiled identity through continual renewal of its purposes and programs.

Like Eastside, Blue Mountain School was never a "McSchool." This distinctive professional learning community, which we described in Chapter Three, faced the same kinds of resource reductions and external reform mandates as most schools around it, but with different results. Through multiple successions of leaders, turnover of staff, and corrosive reductions in time and personnel, Blue Mountain's professional learning community remained resilient enough to bounce back when the reform and resource environment eased after the election of a new government in 2003. One of the school's former department heads put it like this:

> Throughout the past six years, the formal and informal leaders who have remained at the school have succeeded in salvaging much of the student-centered nature of the school's program.
>
> There is no question that a lot of storms were happening. For a brief period of time, I believe that a specific faction of the old guard lost faith in the school's leadership. As an outsider to the school now, I can see a renaissance of support and energy, with the staff working more enthusiastically and progressively with the new administration team, working within system directions and initiatives that are building capacity for distributed leadership on many levels; in school-based projects as well as system work teams.

Durant Alternative School is another innovative institution with a distinctive identity that has had to endure endless assaults from an unsympathetic reform environment, but as we saw in earlier chapters, its response has also been resilient, for it has always been ready to reshape and renew itself in response to outside disturbances. In the late 1990s, when the school lost control of its own budget, for example, and of staff and resources as well, the students, teachers, and parents banded together to raise funds to compensate as best they could for this loss of district support. When the state required the school to conform to standardized state testing, the Durant community protested publicly in straitjackets and networked creatively with similar schools across the state to get a special dispensation for more innovative approaches to curriculum and assessment.

All three schools—Eastside, Blue Mountain, and Durant—undertook repeated renewal even in the face of a physically and emotionally depleting resource-poor environment resulting from standardized reform. While teachers in other schools became locked into downward spirals of disillusionment and demoralization in the 1990s, these schools preserved their innovative identities by actively resisting the excesses of standardization, networking with others who could support them, and creating new opportunities through program innovations that renewed teachers' energy and purposes.

These compelling cases point to seven fundamental principles of school renewal that cohere with the seven principles of sustainability:

- The schools recreated *deep and broad learning* experiences for their students and staff by constantly renewing the unique purpose and mission that distinguished them from other schools in their area. Blue Mountain was a deliberately designed learning organization; Eastside had a century-old commitment to marginalized students; and Durant had built its entire school around flexible student programs linked to individualized learning needs and connections with the community. Schools that stay focused on the integrity of their purpose and products, instead of simply implementing other people's purposes, are more able to renew their spiritual energy.

- The schools secured *endurance* over time by attending to successions of senior leaders and by retaining and rejuvenating a critical mass of teacher leaders through good times and bad. Schools that maintain some continuity of leadership from year to year and from one teacher generation to the next conserve the collective emotional energy that is otherwise expended on adjusting to constant changes of circumstances and personnel.

• The schools encouraged *breadth* by deliberately distributing leadership across their staff, even as principals came and went. Schools that distribute leadership widely spread the burdens, the learning, and the rewards that support staff emotionally and make them more resourceful intellectually.

• The schools promoted *social justice* by defending the distinctive needs of their disadvantaged students; by offering creative and challenging curriculum to ensure that more advantaged students who provided role models for their peers were not enticed away by school competitors; and by not actively undermining neighboring schools as they sought to renew themselves. Eastside and Durant had to struggle hard to preserve their existence and identities against the expansion of the Catholic system in Ontario and of magnet schools in New York State. Blue Mountain established its own learning community without impinging disproportionately on any one institution or age-group of teachers around it. Schools that fight for a broad mix of students provide the best support for their most disadvantaged students and avoid creating wasted lives. And schools that work with their neighbors rather than against them save energy that is otherwise expended in time-consuming and emotionally draining competitiveness.

• The schools honored their *diversity*. Eastside drew its students from across the city and opened its doors to anyone who would benefit from a vocational and technical education. Durant's mandate was to provide educational opportunities for students who found it difficult to succeed in a regular school structure, and Blue Mountain was a fully composite school that accepted all students in its increasingly multicultural community. Schools that honor their diversity ensure that their most marginal students are not cast on the waste heap; they preserve the student mix that maintains a diverse and productive community of learning, and they promote professional diversity that capitalizes on the school's existing intellectual resources.

• The schools benefited from physical and financial *resources*. The physical environment is an important resource for renewal. All three schools operated in relatively new or significantly upgraded facilities. Blue Mountain was bright, airy, and new, designed to promote student and teacher interactions in appealing public spaces as well as conventional classrooms and to integrate and promote modern communications technology. Eastside's overdue renovation in the mid-1990s helped to alter its forbidding image and attracted some high-achieving students. Durant's move to a better facility uplifted teachers and students in their quest to adapt their programs to changing conditions in the state. By contrast, schools like Sheldon, Stewart Heights, and Lord Byron that were trapped in downward spirals of demoralization and decline operated in old or overcrowded buildings with serious deficiencies. Schools need financial and physical resources (like decent facilities) as well as human ones in order to meet their learning obligations for all students. This is why initiatives like the United Kingdom's secondary school rebuilding program in economically impoverished communities is central to resourcefulness and renewal. Schools cannot starve their way to improvement.

• The schools attended to the *conservation* of their historical roots, traditions, and purposes. Each school had a rich and long-lasting sense of what and who it stood for as well as where it was going. School renewal requires passion and purpose that build on pride in the past: one of the most vital emotional and spiritual resources of all.

Enhancing resourcefulness is partly a matter of slowing down entropy, conserving energy, and in the drive for ever-escalating standards, sometimes being prepared to say "enough." Slowing the pace of change, improving the emotional tone of reform, injecting financial and building resources into the system, and generally exercising *restraint* in how far we go in exploiting people's reserves of energy—these are essential elements of resourcefulness. So too is commitment to replenishment and *renewal* among school and system leaders—renewal of purpose, learning, commitment, and emotional capacity through personal and professional development and sheer physical regeneration.

Renewal and restraint are not either-or choices in our challenge to develop resourceful, sustainable leadership. Renewal *and* restraint, exchanging energy *and* slowing down entropy, action by individuals *and* change in the system—all these both-and combinations are needed in our efforts to rethink sustainable leadership and improvement.

Three Sources of Renewal

The power of renewal can be observed by examining three sources of human resourcefulness in educational change: trust, confidence, and emotion.

Trust

If truth is the first casualty of war, then trust is the first fatality of imposed reform. Centuries ago, Confucius said that a government needs three things: weapons, food, and *trust*. If any of these have to be sacrificed, he said, the last of them should be trust.[32] Trust is an indispensable resource for improvement.

Effective organizations depend and thrive on trust. In relationships and organizations, trust amounts to people being able to rely on each other, so that their world and relationships have coherence and continuity. When we trust, we believe others will act in a reasonably predictable way, according to agreed-on or assumed expectations, in a context of shared understanding and assumptions of good faith—even and especially when we or they are absent.

In *Trust and Betrayal in the Workplace,* Reina and Reina describe three forms of trust:[33]

- *Contractual trust* is expressed through impersonal, objective, and often written agreements—in shared performance standards, agreed-on targets, clear job descriptions, homework contracts, and the like. Contractual trust requires us to meet obligations, complete contracts, and keep promises.

- *Competence trust* involves the willingness to trust oneself and other people to be competent and the willingness to provide sufficient support and learning opportunities for people to become competent. Delegating effectively and providing professional growth and development for others are strong indicators of competence trust.

- *Communication trust* is evident in human interactions that communicate shared understanding and good intentions. Clear, high-quality, open, and frequent communication are the hallmarks of communication trust. So too are sharing information, telling the truth, keeping confidences, and being willing to admit mistakes.

The opposite of trust is betrayal. Betrayal occurs when trust is absent or broken. Some acts of betrayal—unfaithfulness to one's partner or theft of a colleague's ideas, for example—are spectacular. But most betrayals are small, accumulated acts of inconsiderate behavior or mere thoughtlessness. In a study of trust and betrayal in teaching, we found that teachers felt they had been betrayed by colleagues when they didn't pull their weight, always taught the same thing, or complained about the union without going to its meetings (contract betrayal); when they were constantly dissatisfied with colleagues, couldn't delegate to them, and tried to script or micromanage everything they did (competence betrayal); or when they gossiped about colleagues and criticized or shamed them in front of others (communication betrayal).[34]

Trust is a resource. It creates and consolidates energy, commitment, and relationships. When trust is broken, people lessen their

...nt and withdraw from relationships, and entropy

...s.

...n their large-scale study of school reform in Chicago elemen-
...ry schools, Tony Bryk and Barbara Schneider determined that
"trust matters as a resource for school improvement."[35] In *Trust in
Schools*, they state that the presence of what they call *relational* trust
(similar to Reina and Reina's communication trust) has positive
organizational consequences in terms of "more effective decision-
making, enhanced social support for innovation, more efficient
social control of adults' work and an expanded moral authority to
'go the extra mile for children.'"[36]

When adults in a school work well together, with reciprocal and
relational trust, it increases energy for improvement that then benefits students and their achievement. Drawing on year-by-year
achievement data across the Chicago public school system from the
early to mid-1990s, Bryk and Schneider were able to identify the
top and bottom 100 improving and non-improving schools in terms
of year-by-year improvement. The relationships they discovered
between adult trust levels and improvements in achievement are
consistent and compelling:

> By 1994, much higher levels of trust, on average, were
> reported in schools that eventually would be categorized
> as academically improving than for those eventually cat-
> egorized in the non-improving group. These differences
> persist through 1997, with almost three-quarters of the
> non-improving schools in both reading and mathemat-
> ics offering negative indicators on the composite indica-
> tors of trust. . . . Schools reporting strong positive trust
> levels in 1994 were three times more likely to be cate-
> gorized eventually as improving in reading and mathe-
> matics than those with very weak trust reports. By 1997,
> schools with very strong trust reports had a one in two
> chance of being in the improving group. In contrast, the

likelihood of improving for schools with very weak trust reports was only one in seven. Perhaps most tellingly of all, schools with weak trust reports in both 1994 and 1997 had virtually no chance of showing improvement in either reading or mathematics.[37]

Trust in schools is essential. Yet we behave less and less like trusting societies. Improvement secured through cultures of shared understanding, joint commitment, and mutual responsibility is being replaced by compliance enforced by impersonal performance standards and abstract accountability. Onora O'Neill, presenter of Britain's annual Reith lectures on public radio, argues that in a world bereft of trust and awash with accountability, "professionals have to work to ever more exacting . . . standards of good practice and due process, to meet relentless demands to record and report, and they are subject to regular ranking and restructuring . . . [in ways that] damage their real work."[38] By moving from cultures of trust to contracts of performance, she says, we are "distorting the proper aims of professional practice"[39]—effective interaction with those we serve. Each profession, she argues, has its proper aim, and this "is not reducible to meeting set targets following prescribed procedures and requirements."[40] Indeed, she notes, change by contract not only diminishes trust but creates active suspicion, cynicism, and low morale.

Principal and author Deborah Meier amplifies this argument, pointing to government's pervasive distrust of teachers and schools: "We don't trust teachers' judgment so we constrain their choices. . . . We don't trust the public school system as a whole so we allow those furthest removed from the schoolhouse to dictate policy that fundamentally changes the daily interactions that take place within schools. . . . Social distrust plays itself out in education in the form of draconian attempts to 'restore accountability' through standardized schooling and increasing bureaucratization."[41]

Trust works. It improves organizations, increases achievement, and boosts energy and morale. Trust isn't easy. It is not blind faith, nor is it indifference. In Debbie Meier's words, trust is "hard won"; it is the essence of demanding professional commitment. Years of standardized reform have decimated political trust in teachers and the profession's trust of their governments in turn. In the words of one of the teachers we interviewed, "It is as though someone wishes to demonstrate how broken the system is by not providing the time or development to be successful."

Learning is poorly served by a low-trust environment. The bitterness of lost trust lingers like a stain. The legacy of teachers' distrust of their governments, for example, is seen in adversarial contract talks with political successors. In Ontario, the new minister of education acknowledges that teacher unrest "is simply the leftover of before," and that it will take the profession some time to heal from a "bruising experience." He speaks for many, perhaps, when he urges us "to leave that era behind us," and forge a better path.[42]

Confidence

A second source of energy is confidence. Harvard business professor Rosabeth Moss Kanter explains that confidence "consists of positive expectation for favorable outcomes. Confidence influences the willingness to invest—to commit money, time, reputation, emotional energy, or other resources—or to withhold or hedge investment."[43] Kanter conducted extensive studies of four types of businesses and sports teams—those that had long histories of either success or failure and those that had gone from rags to riches or vice versa. The key ingredient in successful businesses and winning teams, she found, is *confidence*—in oneself, in team members or colleagues, in the structures and policies of the organization, and in the external environment that provides resources.

Once lost, confidence is difficult to regain. A loss of confidence showed in the panicked response of Lord Byron teachers to the demands of a flawed reporting system, in the withdrawal from change of Talisman Park's cynical coffee circle, in Stewart Heights' teachers' lost belief in their students to improve their own behavior, and in the downward spiral of union-administrator conflict at Sheldon. In the confidence-sapping conditions of standardized reform, all these schools descended into what Kanter calls a *doom loop*, in which things got progressively worse.

"Decline is not a state, it is a trajectory," Kanter observes.[44] "Winning streaks are characterized by continuity and continued investment, losing streaks by disruption, churn, lurching, and lack of investment."[45] Kanter explains, "On the way up, success creates positive momentum. People who believe they are likely to win are also likely to put in the extra effort at difficult moments to ensure that victory. On the way down, failure feeds on itself. . . . The momentum can be hard to stop.[46]

Gill Helsby's study of the effects of large-scale reform on British teachers concluded that while teacher confidence is to some extent always a function of individual attitudes and local cultures, in general, "it is more difficult to retain a sense of professional confidence when responsibility for what teachers perceive as core areas of their work is reduced in favor of external prescription, when resources are lacking and when compliance is required rather than creativity."[47]

Confidence, Kanter explains, is the "sweet spot"[48] between despair and overconfidence. Overconfidence is "a person's certainty that his or her predictions are correct, exceeding the accuracy of those predictions."[49] Overconfidence is overpromising. It springs from excessive optimism. Some view it as arrogance. And arrogance is not the prerogative of the gifted, but the self-indulgent conceit of the vain and foolhardy.

Kanter describes how overconfidence among chief executives pushed and pressured employees of Gillette into having to meet increasingly unrealistic quarterly targets, with financially disastrous results. Overconfidence prompts government leaders to wage war in the false and tragic belief that the war will be quick and losses will be small. The Spanish Armada, the fall of Troy, and the debacle of Vietnam are all testimony to the overconfidence of "wooden-headed" leaders who were blind to the evidence, deaf to good ounsel, and oblivious to their own folly.[50] In *Overconfidence and War*, Dominic Johnson shows how governments are easily susceptible to "positive illusions"—exaggerated ideas of their own virtue and of their ability to control events and the future.[51] In education, overconfident governments extend the scope of their influence, shorten the time lines for improvement, and expect more to be produced with less. Yet all they create are teachers who eventually lose their confidence and spiral into doom loops of performance decline. The result is entropy and waste.

You cannot give people confidence; you can only gain it within yourself. Rebuilding the confidence of teachers in their leaders is a paramount priority. But more important still is the necessity of creating more optimistic conditions, in which teachers can regain confidence in themselves, setting them off on the winning streaks of improvement that their students so desperately deserve. In the words of Helen Keller, "Optimism is the faith that leads to achievement. Nothing can be done without hope and confidence."[52]

Emotion

Emotion is an indispensable source of human energy. Positive emotion creates energy; negative emotion saps it. There are many ways of understanding the role of emotions in organizations.[53] The best-known and most popular perspective is that of *emotional intelligence*. This view emphasizes the trainable skills and capacities of individuals in organizations to understand, articulate, and manage their own emotions as well as empathize with the emotions of others around them.[54] Here, we turn instead to a way of understanding emotion and its effects that connects the individual more closely to the organization.

More than two decades ago, sociologist Arlie Hochschild undertook a classic study of flight attendants. The resulting book, *The Managed Heart*, introduced a new concept: *emotional labor*. In the growing service economy, she said, more and more people were engaged not in manual or even intellectual labor but in emotional labor, in which they had to manufacture or mask their own feelings in order to create the feelings that the organization required in others. Emotional labor, Hochschild argued, "requires one to induce or suppress feelings in order to sustain the outward countenance that produces the proper state of mind in others."[55] For Hochschild, emotional labor requires people to trade part of their selves to motivate clients or subordinates, in exchange for financial reward or job security. Selling, consultancy, nursing, the work of flight attendants, and teaching are among the many occupations that involve this kind of labor.

Hochschild describes how the caring work of being a flight attendant—smiling, reassuring, being attentive—becomes increasingly difficult when profit-driven airlines downsize the staff and standardize the work operations so that flight attendants feel they no longer have the time or opportunity to interact with their passengers in the ways they would wish. As their work demands accelerate, some of them leave because the job loses its meaning and purpose for them; some of them burn out as they try to take on the new tasks while still retaining good relationships with passengers; and some of them become cynical, persuading themselves that passengers aren't worth caring for anymore.

Teaching and educational leadership also involve the extensive emotional labor of being responsible for motivating others and managing their moods and feelings. In Australia, Jill Blackmore discovered that women principals found themselves turning into emotional middle managers of unwanted and imposed educational reforms, motivating their staffs to implement the impractical and unpalatable policies of the government and losing something of themselves and their health in the process.[56]

Among the principals in our study, Charmaine Watson wanted to be inclusive of her teachers, but when reform demands took away their time, she found herself reduced to simply "modeling optimism." Eric West, with his counseling background, wanted to wait and understand the culture of his new school, but pressing reform demands undermined his humanistic approach, and his leadership ended in a hospital bed. Janice Burnley and Linda White found themselves becoming far more directive with their teachers than they wanted to be and transferred on when the opportunity arose. In a support meeting of fellow principals that we convened, North Ridge's new assistant principal, another former counselor, openly wept when he recalled how in the midst of a teachers' work-to-rule action, he had come in early every day to get the school and photo-copying machines ready for teachers' strictly timed arrivals, only to be besieged with a pile of written grievances from all of his staff, on the instructions of the union.

Yet these are not the inevitable consequences of emotional labor. Studies conducted after publication of Hochschild's landmark text show that emotional labor can be and often is positive, uplift-ing, and energizing when people identify with the kind of emotional work the job requires of them and when their working conditions enable them to perform their emotional work properly.[57] Detectives, for example, find the emotional labor of interrogating suspects ful-filling but experience the emotional labor of placating upset victims draining.[58] The same is true in education. In positive and support-ive working conditions, emotional labor is a labor of love.[59] It cre-ates energy.

The Alberta government and the province's teachers' union were at a standoff regarding the government's proposal to raise student performance. A new minister, along with a teacher's union executive who had always taken a forward-looking stand on improvement through professional development, decided to approach the problem another way.

In 1999, they jointly launched the Alberta Initiative for School Improvement (AISI). The program addressed issues of diversity and flexibility by "fostering initiatives that reflect the unique needs and circumstances of each school authority."[60] An injection of $68 million (Canadian) of resources annually was targeted for local improvement projects.

School improvement projects vary greatly and focus on areas as diverse as improving literacy skills, developing teachers' capacity to use differentiated strategies of instruction in their classrooms, building professional learning communities, improving home-school communication in Aboriginal communities, developing computer technology skills, increasing competency in particular subject environments, and enhancing the quality of school relationships. Cycles of improvement stretch over three years, and 90 percent of Alberta schools are now involved.

The initiative does not operate in a climate of imposed and accelerated government targets. Instead, schools establish their own targets, in terms of impact on student learning and satisfaction levels. Impressively, in this culture of shared targets, 90 percent of schools exceeded their baseline on the majority of measures every year. Over just three years, almost half the project schools improved student learning, and 57 percent improved levels of student, teacher, and parent satisfaction. And this is only the start.

The firm focus on student learning—the first principle of sustainability—is undoubtedly an asset to the initiative. The injection of needed resources into coordinating local support in networks of improvement rather than command-and-control systems of mechanical accountability also certainly helps. But it is the spirit of belief in, trust of, and support for schools and teachers to improve themselves that infuses human as well as financial energy and resources into the system. According to the project's first major report, "Brain research has shown that emotion drives attention, learning, memory and behavior. The emotional investment demonstrated by staff involved with AISI projects has resulted in renewed energy and excitement for school improvement. AISI promotes a culture of shared responsibility for continuous improvement in schools and jurisdictions that clearly align school improvement goals and classroom practices. Schools operating as learning communities actively engage both teachers and students in learning."[61]

AISI has a focus on learning and on building strong professional learning communities in ways that respond to and connect the diverse paths to improvement across the province. It takes a long-term, trusting view of improvement by valuing proximal as well as final measures that indicate progress toward greater student achievement. AISI slows down entropy by injecting additional resources into the system in a way that creates energy exchange and renewal, engaging the hearts, minds, and wills of all teachers in raising standards through *shared targets* that address authentic improvement in learning and not merely superficial gains in test scores. Imposed and impatient targets in a climate of resource reduction are energy-depleting. Shared targets in an environment in which resources are redirected to the schools that need them most, within a clear model of sustainable improvement, are energy-renewing. In the uncompromising oil territory of Alberta, shared targets and energy renewal are not flights of fancy but hard-nosed practical realities that make a real difference to students and schools.

The ingenuity of Alberta's Ministry of Education, the inspiring leadership of Blue Mountain's founding principal, the energetically resilient leadership of the principals at Durant, and the emotional satisfactions enjoyed by many of our leaders before the onset of standardized reform all exemplify the power of emotional labor as a positive and energizing leadership resource when work conditions and policy environments support it. It is time to end the collusion with cultures of fear and shame and the connivance with mechanical models of top-down implementation that deplete teachers' energy and to embrace instead the hope and optimism in people and professionals that are the lifeblood of educational change and renewal.

Conclusion

Five hours' flight time west of Chile, far out in the Pacific, is an island more than one thousand miles from any other landmass. "Discovered" by the Dutch on Easter Day, 1722, the tiny speck of Easter Island is scattered with huge stone monuments, some of which are seventy feet tall. The mystery of how such gigantic stone statues could have been moved and raised on an otherwise almost barren island lacking timber and rope was addressed by subsequent archeological discoveries.

The current burden of evidence and argument is that Easter Island was once a populous territory, thickly covered by forest and first inhabited by Polynesians. Rich in seafood, the island's ecology gave rise to a population of growing prosperity who cleared the best land for farming. Dividing into separate clans, the people began erecting monuments to their ancestors, each clan's carvings more grand and impressive than its neighbors'.

Over generations, this process of competitive status envy demanded that more trees be felled to make way for the statues to be dragged across the island and to provide the fiber and rope with which to pull them. By the fifteenth century, the last trees had been eliminated. In the grim decades and centuries that followed, the boats that gave the islanders access to fish and other seafood could not be repaired or replenished for want of wood. Sophisticated shelter could no longer be provided, so the diminishing population took refuge in caves and under stones. Captain James Cook described the remnant population he encountered as "small, lean, timid and miserable."[62] Famine, war, and possibly cannibalism were the end points of a society that had been complacent in prosperity, neglectful of sustainability, and driven apart by competitive envy.

The educational competition between modern societies for higher and higher performance standards, greater than any international competitors, at any cost to the value of what is actually being learned and at any cost to the teachers and leaders who are the substance and soul of the educational ecosystem, risks turning modern educational systems into Easter Islands of educational change, heedless of sustainability in the ruthless, short-term pursuit of competitive status.

An ecosystem is not a machine. Ecosystems value community interests over self-interests, diversity over sameness, and connectedness over individualism. They consist of interconnections and interrelationships.

Jeremy Rifkin tells us that the word *whole* is derived from the Old English word *hal,* which is also the root word in *health, hale,* and *heal.*[63] Sustainable leadership is healthy leadership. It is hale, and it heals.[64] Healthy organizations renew and recycle their resources; unhealthy ones exhaust and abuse them. Healthy organizations promote development and growth that respect the finite aspects of the earth's and our own ability to sustain life; unhealthy organizations are greedy organizations that exploit natural and human resources for the self-interest of a few. Dead leaders don't improve much. But when leaders feel energized and alive, there is almost no limit to what they can achieve. Resourcefulness gives them that chance. It is essential to sustainability.

Conservation

History and Legacy

I think immortality is the passing of a soul through many
lives or experiences, and such as are truly lived, used and
learned help on to the next, each growing richer, higher,
happier, carrying only the real memories of what has
gone before.

Louisa May Alcott, 1884

❖ PRINCIPLE 7

**Sustainable leadership respects and builds on the past
in its quest to create a better future.**

Combing and Recombining Elements from the Past

Most educational change theory and practice has no place for the
past. The arrow of change moves only in a forward direction.
The past is a problem to be ignored or overcome in the rush to get
closer to the future.[1] For those who are attracted, even addicted to
change, the past is a repository of regressive and irrational resistance
among those who like to stay where they are and are emotionally
unable to let go of old habits, attachments, and beliefs. Or the past
is a pejorative, a dim and dark age of weak or bad practice that
leaves negative legacies of regimented factory models of schooling

or uninformed professional judgment in teaching that get in the way of modernization.[2]

When change has only a present or future tense, it becomes the antithesis of sustainability. Sustainable development respects, protects, preserves, and renews all that is valuable from the past and learns from it in order to build a better future. Ancient environments, endangered species, cultural traditions, indigenous knowledge, and collective memory are defended and preserved because they are valuable in themselves and because they are a powerful source of learning and improvement.[3]

Change theory must get in touch with its past, as a few of its practitioners have already done.[4] Change theorists must learn to see resistance and nostalgia among more mature members of the profession not just as obstacles to change but as sources of wisdom and learning that can inform it.[5] They must work hard to build proposals for change upon legacies of the past instead of trying to ignore or obliterate them . Whenever changes are being considered, sustainable leadership should look to the past for precedents that can be reinvented and refined, and for evidence of what has succeeded or failed before. This doesn't mean living in the past, but it does mean valuing and learning from it.

Eric Abrahamson, the critic of repetitive change syndrome, urges us to find an alternative to what he calls *creative destruction*—the "need to obliterate the past to create the future"[6]—which leads to endless swings of the pendulum, increases in employee burnout, and unnecessary waste of accumulated expertise and memory. The alternative, Abrahamson proposes, is *creative recombination*.

Creative recombination operates like a good home workshop. It doesn't simply reuse or even recycle the past. It recombines the best parts of the past in a creative, craftsmanlike way that is resourceful yet also renewing, because the combination creates something new from what is already available. Instead of funding new structures, new technology, and new people, leaders of change without pain set about "finding, reusing, redeploying and recombining the mis-

From		To
Firing and rehiring	⟶	Redeploying the talent companies already have
Developing new communications	⟶	Plugging into and reinventing existing social networks
Inventing new values	⟶	Reviving and renewing existing values
Re-engineering new processes	⟶	Salvaging existing good processes
Complete restructuring	⟶	Reworking and rebuilding existing structures

Figure 7.1. Creative Recombination for Renewal

matched parts that the organization already has lying around its corporate basement."[7] Creative recombination, in other words, means transforming elements from the past, as shown in Figure 7.1.

Sustainable leadership and improvement is about the future *and* the past. It doesn't treat people's knowledge, experience, and careers as disposable waste but as valuable, renewable, and recombinable resources. While it should never blindly endorse the past, sustainable leadership should always respect and learn from it.

Wisdom and Memory

When the tsunami of South Asia swept across the Indian Ocean at the end of 2004, in its path were some of the oldest and most isolated aboriginal tribes in the world. Rescuers who reached the tribes fully expected that they would have been swept to their deaths. But most had successfully fled to higher ground. In at least some cases, they seem to have been saved by indigenous knowledge that was passed down through oral tradition.[8] Anthropologist Marish Chaudi, working with the Onge tribe on Little Andaman Island, for instance, states, "There's clear evidence that the aboriginals know about

> tsunamis and they know how to deal with them." Their indigenous knowledge, passed on as myth and story, refers to "huge shaking of ground followed by high wall of water."[9]

European tourists and even settlers who had inhabited the islands of the Indian Ocean for barely a few hundred years had considerable knowledge of the modern world but not the indigenous knowledge and collective memory that could protect them from the terror of a tsunami.

Dismissing the Past

In education and other walks of life, the changes and challenges we face are, thankfully, much smaller than a tidal wave. But whether they seem exciting or overwhelming, waves of innovation and reform still have a profound impact on schools. Many veteran teachers have seen these waves, or ones similar to them, come through before and have learned how to respond. But the experience, wisdom, and professional knowledge they have accumulated over the years is often dismissed as tired clichés (swinging pendulums, babies and bathwater), irrational resistance and cynicism ("tried that before, didn't work"), deceitful rationalization ("already doing it"), gross inflexibility ("over my dead body") or self-serving crassness ("I'm not giving up my best students/putting extra time in at my time of life/changing a thing just before retirement!") Because professional wisdom often challenges change and its advocates or tries to slow the change process down, it is regarded as an irritating obstacle to be ignored or eliminated rather than an assertive opportunity to be embraced and engaged.

Abrahamson describes how repetitive change syndrome, with its interminable downsizings, restructurings, and reengineerings, leads to massive hemorrhaging of staff and leadership and with it, a "loss of *organizational memory*" (italics added).[10] No one is left behind to celebrate the organization's tradition, to be a living bearer of its purpose and mission, to pass on the knowledge and expertise of how best to do things, or to show new recruits the shortcuts and the ropes.

When organizations shed too many senior people or middle-level leaders, they lose long-term effectiveness. When organizations whose work affects people's security, such as airlines or rail companies, fail to keep the bearers of their organizational memory, it can also lead to tragic loss of life. In the 1990s, when the railways in Britain were privatized and there was a widespread campaign to "eliminate waste" among middle and senior management, the resulting loss of engineering expertise on how to fix problems contributed to a series of fatal accidents, as well as to excessively cautious responses when the railways were subsequently subjected to hundreds of paralyzing slow-downs and closures because no one had the wisdom, memory, or experience that would have enabled them to make more judicious repair decisions.[11]

Instead of treating the elders of the education profession as toxic teachers and disposable waste, it's important to approach them as renewable and renewing resources who, like Greg Allan at Lord Byron High School, can raise the quality of their school's environment and its products through opportunities such as mentoring, continuous learning initiatives, and involvement in improvement.

In a study of the emotions of teaching, we asked fifty teachers how their age affected their response to change and whether teachers in other age groups reacted any differently. The results portrayed young teachers as enthusiastic and largely optimistic individuals who had learned the adaptability necessary to the survival of their generation in an occupational and social environment characterized by increasing insecurity. Toward the end of their career, as their body began to deteriorate, their experiences of repetitive educational change wore them down, and impending retirement weakened the grip that others had on them, many older teachers became more resistant and resilient in the face of change efforts outside the classroom, concentrating their remaining energies on a more relaxed sense of accomplishment within the classroom. In between, in the middle years of teaching, teachers retained but also reined back some of their enthusiasm, and with growing confidence, competence, and a sense of being established, they felt able to remain open to yet also selective about the change initiatives they adopted.[12]

These data point to a great opportunity for policymakers: take advantage of the shift toward younger teachers; their open attitudes toward change will be a better fit with reform policies. Get the right people on the bus, it seems, and the demographic divide between young and old can be turned into the demographic dividend of opportunity for change.[13] But will this demographic dividend yield automatic improvement? Our evidence suggests that while young teachers are more enthusiastic about and open to change than their older colleagues (partly because they have nothing in the past with which to compare it), they are also less competent and confident in implementing and even understanding change.[14] The absence of memory that creates openness to change is unavoidably accompanied by missing experiences that might otherwise put such change into perspective.

The project on teachers' emotions turned up another interesting finding. Teachers' own emotional responses to educational change don't always correspond to the responses that colleagues in other generational groups attribute to them. Older teachers exhibit more empathy toward younger colleagues (downward empathy) than vice versa. Younger teachers tend to make more simple and less generous assumptions about their older colleagues and underestimate their wisdom about change in the process. In educational systems now and in the future, youth will increasingly prevail over experience due to demographic turnover in teaching. But if upward empathy remains weak, this will lead to widespread misattributions about experienced teachers' orientations toward change that will marginalize their wisdom and expertise even further. More new teachers will not bring about greater improvement unless the generational differences in the profession are approached as a valuable asset rather than a disposable liability.

At Harvard University, Susan Moore Johnson and her colleagues have been studying the newer generations of teachers, who are entering the profession in great numbers at the beginning of the twenty-first century. One of the factors affecting whether new teachers remain in the profession is what kind of culture exists in the school where they take up their first position. Johnson and her colleagues identify three such cultures—novice-oriented, veteran-dominated, and blended. It's the novice-oriented culture that concerns us.[15]

When teachers get their first job, they may find themselves in an innovative, start-up setting like a charter school, a newly built school, or a reconstituted school that has been re-opened with a new staff. Principals often pack these schools with young recruits who are newly trained, energetic, and not yet tarnished by the cynicism of the system. At first, new teachers in these schools can feel they have fallen on their feet. Their appointments seem rewarding, even thrilling. They are surrounded by their generational peers. They are given opportunities to lead from the get-go, and there is no one to hold them back. These young, new teachers, it seems, can really make their schools rock. And so they can, for a while.

In novice-oriented cultures, teachers and their schools run on enthusiasm, adrenaline, and emotional intensity. New teachers have little access to the knowledge, memory, and wisdom of older colleagues that can help them find the shortcuts, direct them to existing resources so they don't have to produce all their own, or enable them to develop a little emotional distance or sense of perspective when they start to feel overinvolved with or overwhelmed by their children's emotional needs. Without access to professional wisdom and memory, teachers in novice-oriented cultures quickly burn out. This is also true on a larger scale; when systems and nations over-invest in youth as the answer, they find that they can easily recruit new teachers but that they just can't retain them.[16] Teacher wisdom and organizational memory has to be part of the solution to educational change, not just part of the problem.

Forgetting the Past

There are many reasons why organizations need to remember. There are also times when organizations need to forget. Smart organizations not only know the distinction but also understand when they have to make it.

Pablo Martin de Holan and Nelson Phillips undertook an illuminating study of the expanding Cuban hotel industry. New hotels, partnering with existing hotel chains outside Cuba, found themselves working with new people in a new culture. How would local Cubans adapt to the capitalist and consumerist hotel culture? How would hotel management staff be able to adapt their existing knowledge to the very different context of Cuban culture? What was important for each of them to remember, and what was it necessary to forget?

De Holan and Phillips identified four kinds of *organizational forgetting* in their Cuban case. These were based on whether the process of forgetting was intentional or unintentional and whether it applied to long-established or recently acquired knowledge (see Figure 7.2).

De Holan and Phillips summarized the options for organizational forgetting and their outcomes as follows: "Some companies forget the things they need to know, incurring huge costs to replace the lost knowledge. Other organizations can't forget the things they should and they remain trapped by the past, relying on uncompetitive technologies, dysfunctional corporate cultures, or untenable assumptions about their markets. Successful companies instead are

	New Knowledge	*Established Knowledge*
Accidental	Failure to consolidate **Dissipation**	Failure to maintain **Degradation**
Purposeful	Abandoned innovation **Suspension**	Managed unlearning **Purging**

Figure 7.2. Modes of Organizational Forgetting

Source: Adapted from P. De Holan & N. Phillips (2004), The dynamics of organizational forgetting, *Management Science,* 50(11), 1606.

able to move quickly to adapt to rapidly changing environments by being skilled not only at learning, but also at forgetting."[17]

Dissipation

Dissipation occurs when new knowledge comes into the organization but there's no will or way to make it stick, transfer it to others, or embed it in people's memory, so that it will last a long time and help the organization stay effective. Dissipation can be prevented by passing on and sharing new knowledge—something that charismatic leaders sometimes find hard to do. Practicing new techniques often and being directly coached and supervised in using them also makes a difference—as it did with Atul Gawande's high-performing heart surgeons, described in Chapter Three. De Holan and Phillips also describe how new knowledge is more likely to stick when it is explicitly connected to and makes sense in relation to people's existing or prior knowledge. Eastside Technical School in the previous chapter, for example, was repeatedly able to adapt innovations—such as computer technology—by connecting them to the school's long-standing experience and proud tradition of working outside of mainstream high school practice in technical and commercial education.

Degradation

A second kind of organizational forgetting, degradation, occurs when "well established knowledge is accidentally lost."[18] Knowledge degradation among professionals is common when there is "turnover of critical personnel" and there is "inability or unwillingness to create collective knowledge that would enable a successful collective action without their presence or immediate supervision."[19] Frequent leadership succession across almost all of the schools in our study made erasure of organizational memory or inability of incoming leaders to understand and draw on it an ever-present threat. High staff turnover presents similar difficulties, especially, as we have seen, in innovative schools in which distinctive goals, structures, and practices need to be reviewed and renewed every time new teachers arrive and existing ones leave. Sudden downsizing or elimination of alleged waste in middle management also can lead to degradation, as we saw with Britain's railways in the 1990s and as also occurred when management losses in the school districts in our study curtailed their capacity to support the principals in their schools.

Suspension

While a lot of organizational forgetting is accidental, some of it is quite deliberate, constituting a willful strategy to implement change and improvement. "Successful companies," say De Holan and Phillips, are "skilled not only at learning, but also at forgetting."[20] Jim Collins and George Porras identified one of the factors leading to long-standing success in business as the capacity of companies to engage in diverse experimentation, to know how and when to keep successful innovations, and to know when to drop the rest.[21] De Holan and Phillips call this kind of forgetting *suspension*.[22] Management guru Peter Drucker prefers the term *organized abandonment*.[23]

The purpose of organized abandonment, says Drucker, is to "free up resources that are committed to maintaining things that are no longer producing results."[24] With organized abandonment, the change leader puts everything "on trial for its life" on a regular basis.[25] Organized abandonment is called for when practices are tailing off in effectiveness or when they impede or crowd out the introduction of ones that are superior. If abandonment is just a vague intention, Drucker argues, it will never happen. It's too hard to let go of things spontaneously. Instead, organizations need to have regular abandonment meetings to make tough and focused decisions about what to leave behind so that there is space for innovation ahead.

In education, Brian Caldwell argues that abandonment should take place not just for Drucker's reasons of productivity and effectiveness but also to protect the fulfillment of cherished educational values such as equality of opportunity and rights of access.[26] Caldwell proposes organized abandonment of

- Curriculum that is outdated

- Pedagogies that no longer work

- Buildings whose designs are no longer appropriate

- Professionalism that has no regard for evidence or research

- Teaching and management tasks that can be handled by someone else[27]

For all the complaints about their flurries of new initiatives, a few governments, especially the United Kingdom, are addressing the need for organized abandonment in educational policy by, for instance, cutting back on the prescribed National Curriculum, offering exemptions to successful schools that use other designs, lightening the load of external accountability, reducing the impact of external testing on younger children and their teachers, transferring a hundred administrative tasks once handled by classroom teachers to other personnel, and bulldozing old buildings in poor communities to make way for new ones that are better designed to suit student learning today.[28]

It's easy and attractive to abandon tasks and practices you never wanted to do in the first place. Teachers in the Canadian schools in our study, for example, were delighted when work-to-rule action removed the demand for meetings. Some of them said that their classroom teaching had never been better. Others welcomed an end to the mandated policy of destreaming, or detracking, which, they felt, had been forcing them into new practices that were difficult and unfamiliar. But none of our schools and teachers were able to abandon practices they liked and found comfortable. For this to occur, a more organized, focused, systematic process is required.

A common school development technique for addressing organized abandonment is an exercise known as "Stop, Start, Continue," to which we add a fourth category, "Ignore/Subvert." After identifying what is valued and effective in the school (or other organization) and what is practiced frequently (or not), groups then decide to

- *Stop* activities that are practiced frequently but have little or less value compared with others (organized abandonment)

- *Start* highly valued initiatives that are currently practiced infrequently or not at all (through inventing, creative recombining, and so on)

- *Continue* highly valued activities that are already practiced frequently (this helps preserve organizational memory)

- *Ignore/Subvert* activities with little value or likelihood of effectiveness that have not been practiced so far but that external agencies have started to mandate (which makes resistance to change a constructive and thoughtful process of values preservation rather than a negative process of self-protection)

Although it's rarely easy to forget, organizational abandonment makes certain kinds of forgetting not only feasible but also deliberate and desirable.

Purging

Sometimes it is important to forget or at least to unlearn some of the things we have retained and remembered. Poor practices, bad habits, old ways of doing things that don't meet the needs of new cultures or new times—all of these are ripe for organizational purging. De Holan and Phillips describe how it was necessary for Canadian hotel partners not to treat their new Cuban location and its people like a suburb of Montreal and how Cuban service staff needed to provide the levels of customer service that foreigners liked, not ones that they enjoyed as customers themselves.[29]

Unlearning old practices in which we feel effective and exchanging them for new ones in which our initial competence is low is neither comfortable nor pleasant. People's temptation to cling to the past is both normal and understandable. All change involves loss, and when what is to be lost is comfort and competence, the loss will always be mourned and resisted.[30]

Purging of organizational memory is not productive, however, when the old and experienced are deliberately devalued—for example,

- When incoming principals push through pet programs without acknowledging the benefits and drawbacks or even the existence of similar programs and priorities that preceded their arrival[31]

- When repetitive change, hyperactive reform, and impatient implementation procedures pressure principals to force through changes without seeking input and feedback from experienced staff members about lessons to be learned from similar change efforts in the past[32]

- When narrow-minded reform practices in an overly aligned system make it hard for leaders to respect and listen to the voices of experienced teachers who have good reason to differ or doubt[33]

- When school and system leaders invest excessive faith in and award undue affirmation to inrushing tides of young teachers, for whom change promises only excitement and carries no sense of loss[34]

Whether what is to be unlearned or purged are ways of teaching literacy, attitudes toward assessment, procedures for communicating with parents, or approaches to running a school, two issues are crucial to address. First, have the areas for unlearning been diagnosed correctly, and is this unlearning educationally desirable or just politically expedient? Second, is the process of knowledge conversion, replacing unlearning with new learning, managed in a supportive or a traumatic manner? Schools and other organizations need to forget the right things in the right way. If the diagnosis or developmental processes of organizational forgetting are wrong, then schools and their leaders will quickly find themselves facing the formidable obstacle of teacher nostalgia.

Romanticizing the Past

Nostalgia is a peculiar and even perverse combination of memory and forgetting. Nostalgia comprises selective, distorted, and idealized views of the past that are contrasted against embittered experiences of the present. In Christopher Lasch's terms, nostalgia is "the abdication of memory."[35] Memory can involve reminiscence, recollection, and recall, but it is not necessarily sentimental. Nostalgia, meanwhile, is always sentimental. Yet not all sentimentality is nostalgic. The particular nature and also the cause of nostalgia is to be found in an unsatisfactory present that evokes a wish to remember and return to a more reassuring and idyllic past.

Not all nostalgic idealizations of the past portray only its positive features against a cruel or callous present. One popular genre of autobiography, represented in books like Frank McCourt's *Angela's Ashes* or Brian Woodruff's *The Road to Nab End*, portray the author's childhood past as one ridden with poverty, chaos, and cruelty. But in Dickensian fashion, these horrific histories are at least partially mitigated by moments of warmth, love, escape, and pleasure, and they are ultimately redeemed through their protagonists' capacity to triumph over the adversities they experienced. Those who recall having it hard; who refer to being dragged up rather than raised; who, as in the classic Monty Python sketch, lived in a shoebox and were glad of it are wistful about their pain and wary about or even resentful toward their successors who seem to have shared none of their suffering and who have had life too easy. Teachers whose recollection is less of a golden age than of a stone age during which they were thrown into their career at the deep end and had "classes from hell" exhibit some of these more complex characteristics of nostalgia.

Educational reformers paint negative images of the past for different reasons, but mainly to contrast them with heroic views of the present or the future. They may dismiss the past of teaching as one of lax progressivism, chaotic curriculum, or poor practice that justifies the imposed and overconfident prescriptions of government intervention to set the educational world right. If teachers are prone to idealize distorted images of ill-remembered pasts, reformers are more prone to anti-nostalgia that demonizes the past in order to justify their own responsibility for shaping the future.

In the face of years of imposed and overwhelming educational reform along with public disparagement of teachers as professionals, experienced teachers in the schools of our study grieved for the loss of working conditions that they remembered had once empowered them and enhanced their sense of status and value, and they were nostalgic for past school environments that were characterized by collegial trust, a sense of collective purpose, and students who were supported by their families, respected authority, and wanted to learn.

Teachers at Sheldon school in the northeastern United States remembered it as the jewel of the district in the late 1960s. They recalled, "Kids were more academically inclined. They were expected to pursue higher education. And a lot of them were on an academic track." Others remembered students who "really cared about what they were learning and took an interest in their studies." Baby boomer teachers remembered how, when they were just beginning their careers, they were "young, ambitious" and how they reveled in "being single and not having [outside] responsibilities." This made "it easier . . . to get involved" in ways that provided them with "connectivity" with their students and colleagues. In the face of standardized reform, successions of autocratic leadership, and "shams" of school-based planning teams, these teachers' idealism had evaporated in a climate of racial tension, diminished student interest in learning, and growing professional isolation among an aging faculty that had grown weary of top-down, sometimes contradictory mandates that robbed them of their independence and their voice.

Talisman Park Secondary School's coffee circle was the embodiment of embittered nostalgia. Its members recalled how students had changed from "mostly white kids" "having fewer problems" who "had a lot of money . . . and a lot of say in the running of the school." They had come from "comfortable homes," were "ready to learn and able to learn," and identified with the school's close family culture. In contrast, teachers felt that today's students, representing more diverse, less affluent backgrounds, had "far more to deal with" than earlier generations. Students from "single-family homes had problems just surviving, finding food, clothes." More students required support for English as a second language and, generally, students no longer saw the school as the social hub of their lives. Several teachers cited "increasing discipline problems," "poor work habits," and poor "short-term concentration." Another felt that students' attitudes toward authority had deteriorated because parents no longer provided their children with "the structure and guidance that they need." An English teacher with thirty-three years experience could not "imagine" today's students focusing their learning on the classics, such as Shakespeare. A colleague lamented the fact that "for the first time in history [the school] didn't have a senior football team because there were not enough kids from a background with an interest in football."

This hearkening back to a more glamorous "golden age" was prompted by teachers' current concerns that government reforms were "moving too fast" with "not enough time by any stretch of the imagination."[36] Teachers felt used as "scapegoats" for perceived failures in the public system. Others reported that "parents are anxious that their children will not measure up" and "don't want to be involved," reforms are "underfunded," "teachers lack control," "the reforms don't help students," it's a "mechanical process," and "there are too many unanswered questions."

The removal of resources due to budget cuts led the coffee circle and others to complain that there "was no money for the teachers to get upgraded," there were "no PD [professional development] days," "supply teachers were increasingly unavailable," "assistant department heads were eliminated," and teachers in fewer numbers expressed "interest in assuming department headships," since there was no longer any release time associated with these onerous middle management positions. Political nostalgia for greater professional autonomy, along with personal and social nostalgia for more amenable and motivated students coalesced as Talisman Park's teachers' embitterment with the present magnified their lost glories in the past.

As schools changed, social demands increased, resources shrank, and reform pressures started to bite, teachers across our study schools mourned the loss of schools as communities that were free from racial strife, students who came to class ready and able to learn, and stable communities that reflected and supported the values of schooling. Part of this sense of loss was for students and communities who were easier, better, just plain nicer to deal with in compared to the present context of growing cultural diversity, increasing poverty, and white flight that resulted in students who seemed too hard to reach and teach. In response to repetitive change syndrome, teachers also expressed political nostalgia for greater professional autonomy, status, and political voice and for the teamwork and ability to make professional decisions appropriate to students' needs, which teachers felt had been lost.

All nostalgia is a recollection of the past that is inflected and infected by an embittered experience of an unsettling present. The nostalgia for professional autonomy and lost missions is posed against a contemporary backdrop of reform, narrowed vision, standardization, and lost autonomy. The nostalgia for good, mainly white students who wanted to learn in a more professionally intimate environment contrasts with an uncomfortable present of classrooms characterized by growing racial diversity, increasing numbers of students in poverty, and a widening range of students with special educational needs.

Large-scale educational reform often fails because of its anti-nostalgic dismissal or derogation of teachers' professional past. This may appeal to public opinion and prejudice, but it also alienates the profession and dismisses the generational missions it holds dear. Anti-nostalgia is not only ethically contentious but also strategically problematic because it amplifies widespread resistance to change and intensifies entrenched and embittered nostalgia among the older teachers it perceives as being in the way. Repelled by the present, experienced teachers seek refuge by romanticizing the past.

Instead of inspiring experienced teachers to improve their practice, forced forgetting throws older educators back into the false memory of defensive nostalgia, wasting the wisdom of professional elders and turning them into demoralized teachers and disgruntled colleagues.

Renewing the Past

Overconfident reformers are prone to dismissing the past. Those who are the targets of reform are inclined to romanticize the past. The challenge that confronts them both is to preserve what they should from the past and learn from it whenever they can.

Preserving the past is a prime value of environmentalism. In England, William Wordsworth was one of the first to persuade his countrymen to seek nature and be inspired by it, rather than hold it in abeyance. In mid-nineteenth-century Massachusetts, on the cusp of the industrial age, America's "prophet of the conservation movement,"[37] Henry David Thoreau, took flight from the "lives of quiet desperation" endured by the rest of the masses, to live and write about months of abstemious existence in a rough and recycled cabin in the woods at Walden Pond. In "wildness," he proclaimed, "is the preservation of the world."[38] In 1870, John Muir, who would later found the world's first conservation society, the Sierra Club, walked into Yosemite Valley in California's Sierra Nevada, and there found "immortality."[39]

From these beginnings, a vast conservation movement grew—the Audubon Society, the national parks, the World Wildlife Fund, Conservation International, and countless other smaller organizations, all dedicated to the preservation of wilderness and biodiversity within the parameters of current institutions and economies.[40] To E.O. Wilson, this "conservation ethic is that which aims to pass on to future generations the best parts of the nonhuman world."[41]

Conservationism is not uncritical. For one thing, says Wilson, there is no noble savage. The Polynesian Maori, he points out, killed and ate the large flightless moa birds of New Zealand to extinction. The arrival of Aborigines in Australia quickly eradicated the largest mammals.[42] And at the time of Robin Hood, the decimation of England's forests forced the locals to purchase their own firewood from elsewhere so Britannia could use the available timber to put her navy to sea.[43]

Second, while conservationists believe in preserving the past, this does not apply to all of it: not, for example, to the thousands of feral pigs introduced into Hawaii that reduced the number of indigenous birds to just thirty-five species nor to the confusion of starlings all across America that spread like a plague after a collector who wanted to introduce to the country all the birds mentioned by William Shakespeare released one hundred starlings into the wild.[44] Even conservationists recognize that some things have to be discarded.

Third, even though conservationists preserve the past, the natural past is not as innocent, pure, and wild as they sometimes claim. In *Landscape and Memory*, historian Simon Schama rejects the simplistic view that nature is pure and that people sully it. Instead, he says, we bring myth and understanding from culture to our feelings and interpretation of awe and immortality when we see phenomena such as "cathedral groves" of giant redwoods in nature.[45] The cathedral groves are what we make of them as much as what they are in themselves. John Muir fled from his punitive father to find solace and a resurrection of sorts in Mother Nature. Nature was a refuge for his psyche and a kind of nostalgia for his soul. Yet we are part of nature, not a separate intrusion upon it. John Dewey, who delighted in demolishing unhelpful polarities, challenged the separation of "man and nature" that mechanical traditions of natural science had brought upon us.[46] "Man's" purposes and aims, he pointed out, "are dependent for execution on natural conditions. Separated from such conditions, they become empty dreams and idle indulgences of fancy."[47]

The moment we enter a wilderness, like an observer in a physics experiment, our very presence changes what we see. Neither is there a pristine wilderness, nor a perfectly harmonious relationship between the natural and the human that preceded the conquering arrival of industrialism and colonialism, although this fact does not excuse the scale of these movements' devastations.

What, then, can we learn from this more complex and less romantic understanding of the conservation ethic? How can it help us approach sustainability in our learning and our lives, as well as in the wilderness and the world? The most fundamental and far-reaching lessons, we believe, are the following:

- We should acknowledge the past, preserving the best, learning from the rest.

- Wildness, diversity, and disorder have richness and beauty that belong in our lives and our work. Micro-managed organizations are like obsessively manicured lawns. As Henry David Thoreau remarked, "reformers are the greatest bores of all."[48]

- Like nature, the past is neither pristine nor pure. It is important to recognize but not romanticize it.

- There is no Eden or Golden Age of history, nature, child-centered learning, or teacher-developed curriculum to which we can or should return.

- Our interpretations of the past are affected by our varying experiences and responsibilities in the present; the past should be understood together with others, not inhabited alone.

- We have always been part of nature and the past. They do not stand outside us. Nature and the past are not static. Our task is to bring past and present, nature and progress together, not keep them apart.

- When leaders and reformers dismiss or demean the
  past, they create embittered and resistant nostalgia
  among its bearers, who cocoon themselves within it.

- The point of progress is not to ignore or suppress the
  past but to learn from it and work with it when we can.
  William Wordsworth, England's great romantic poet
  and first conservationist, declared, "Let us learn from
  the past, to profit by the present, and from the present
  to live better in the future."[49]

These principles, and those who support them, become especially powerful when they are combined with other arguments and advocates in the environmental movement. For environmentalism is a social movement, a "creative cacophony" of diverse groups and different emphases, of passion for a common cause.[50] The strength of the environmental movement and of the project of sustainability to which it subscribes is that it includes traditional conservationists, privileged protectors of rural space and village life, Greenpeace eco-warriors, deep ecologists, ecofeminists, and many others. Find an unwanted motorway proposal in Britain that threatens that country's "green and pleasant land," and there too you will find not just young radicals resisting the bulldozers by tying themselves to treetops, nor only deep ecologists encamped in the fields, but also farmers, landowners, white-collared clergy and tweedskirted old ladies, all protecting the cause of conservation and the goal of sustainability beyond it. The strength and effectiveness of the environmental movement is to be found in its own diversity, focused on a common goal with relentless persistence. The staid and aging who embody the past play as powerful a part in that movement as the young and radical who agitate for its preservation.

Educational change movements and processes will benefit the more they are able to acknowledge and include the diverse constituencies of age, experience, role, culture, style, and orientation within and beyond the profession of teaching. Some past practices do have to be unlearned or forgotten. But not all of history is the enemy of modernization. The moment we begin to work with the past, not against or in spite of it, is the moment we will see an end to repetitive change syndrome and the widespread resistance that results from it. We close with a few ideas not just about how to be "less bad" and minimize the damage we do to conservation but also about how to actively incorporate and intelligently sift through the past in order to create a better future:

- *Organize annual or biennial retreats* to review and renew your school's or system's vision and reinvigorate its values, especially when there is high staff turnover.

- *Audit the organization's collective memory*, especially if you and many others have recently arrived. One way to do this is by drawing a time line and asking everyone to place their names along it at the point when they joined the organization. Then ask people to tell stories about critical incidents and important innovations they dealt with in their early years that still leave significant traces in the life of the organization today.

- *Compile an asset inventory* of the skills, knowledge, and resources of everyone in the institution, so they are no longer hidden in individual classrooms but are accessible to the entire community.

- *Instigate organized abandonment* through meetings specifically dedicated to discarding less-valued or less effective structures, processes, or practices in order to make room for new ones that are better.

- *Consider appointing principals and superintendents in midterm*, not at the end of the school year, so that they have time to learn the organization's culture and its history while it is up and running, before they address how to improve it in a more systematic way.

- *Tell stories* at meetings, retreats, and socials. Telling stories of people's experiences, especially shared ones, are ways to keep memories and what they stand for alive. If we don't talk about our collective memories, we will lose them.

- *Take mentoring seriously.* Don't overly revere the old; experience does not automatically bring either wisdom or graciousness. Even the young Thoreau judged that "the old have no very important advice to give to the young."[51] Yet most of us do have things to learn and can secure valuable support from good mentors. A central task of leadership is to organize mentoring, provide mentoring, and find mentoring for oneself. Not everyone's experiences are similar, and the match has to be right; otherwise, mentors quickly turn into tormentors.[52] But if there are enough values in common and enough differences to make it interesting, a good mentoring relationship is an excellent way to prosper from the past.

- *Keep good records.* When Toronto medical scientist Frederick Banting made a breakthrough, discovering how to produce insulin, he forgot to keep notes on the procedure. It took ages for him to discover the process all over again. Good records and comprehensive archives commit rules and procedures to the collective memory of the organization instead of allowing them to live in people's heads and disappear when those people leave. In the schools that we studied, the strongest and proudest school cultures were ones that kept the most comprehensive archives. These were schools that people wanted to remember. Weaker schools, like dysfunctional families, showed little interest in remembering and recording at all.

- *Create blended cultures.* Susan Moore Johnson and her colleagues found that the school cultures most likely to retain new teachers were those that blended youth with experience, so that new teachers could have opportunities for leadership, access to mentoring, and engagement in reciprocal learning with more experienced colleagues.[53]

- *Replace repetitive change with creative recombination,* so that innovations and reforms don't eliminate or insult the past but recombine the best parts of it in order to move forward effectively as well as efficiently into the future.

Conclusion

Sustainable leadership needs a rearview mirror as well as a driver's windshield. Without it, things will keep overtaking or rear-ending you. Sometimes the past is a point of pride, something to be honored. When there have been years of conflict, grievance, and mistreatment, as there have between some governments and unions, for example, the past may instead be something that needs to be healed. (This was the purpose of the Ontario government-union agreement for peace and stability in April 2005, for example.) If, as change leaders or change addicts, we do not face our past, even the painful parts of it, then we will find that, like people who were abused in childhood, we keep repeating the mistakes from it. This is the affliction of repetitive change that has assailed too many of us. Thankfully, as we have seen, this is avoidable. In the words of poet Maya Angelou, "History, despite its wrenching pain, cannot be unlived, but if faced with courage, need not be lived again."[54]

Conclusion: Sustainability in Action
A Meal, Not a Menu

Reformers are the greatest bores of all.

Henry David Thoreau

A Meal, Not a Menu

Sustainability is a meal, not a menu. You can't pick and choose. All the principles fit together. You have to eat all your "greens."

It's no use raising test scores if they don't reflect deep and broad learning. Heroic efforts to get everyone swiftly engaged in improving learning for all are of little value if they wear teachers and principals out. While initial success in implementing new initiatives can be gained by building them around enthusiasts and supporters, they will never spread across a school unless those who have concerns about them are included at the start. Single-minded pursuit of your own school's improvement goals will also be tarnished if they are achieved at the expense of schools around you.

Individual school improvement efforts should no longer be attempted or judged as a snapshot, in the short term, and with no regard for other schools elsewhere. Leadership and improvement efforts are interconnected and stretched out in time and space. This is the essence of their sustainability or unsustainability.

Our work with schools that are engaged in improvement efforts over many years and our research examining the record of educational

251

change in high schools over three decades, across many leaders and reform movements, has given us insights into and considerable evidence about which changes stay and which ones fade over time, and why.

The overall evidence is not uplifting. The vast majority of reform efforts and change initiatives—even the most promising ones—are unsustainable. Bill Andrews at Stewart Heights made significant progress in turning his school around but was lifted into the district office before his improvements had a chance to stick. Charmaine Watson at Wayvern secured dramatic gains in literacy scores within just two years by getting her staff to focus on authentic literacy for all students, but the enormity of the effort in an unsupportive reform environment meant that she and some of her key teacher leaders ran out of gas. And while the principals and teachers of Barrett Magnet High School were able to raise this urban school into the top 150 schools in the nation, the gains were made at the expense of the teachers and students at neighboring Sheldon High.

It's particularly important for us to be very clear about one of the most controversial issues in educational reform: targets. *Externally imposed, short-term achievement targets are incompatible with long-term sustainability.* This is where we part company from our colleague and friend, Michael Fullan, with whom we otherwise share so many areas of commitment and agreement on leadership, sustainability, and change. Fullan contends, "The new reality is that governments have to show progress in relation to social priorities . . . *within one election term* [typically four years]. Our knowledge base is such that there is no excuse for failing to design and implement strategies that get short-term results"[1]

Even by Fullan's own criteria, this argument falls short. Most parents in Britain (from which much of his evidence comes) are now opposed to standardized testing of younger children.[2] Alberta, Canada's most successful province in student achievement, is improving achievement through shared targets, not imposed ones.[3]

People around the world have shown themselves eager to support increased political investment in early childhood education, although the yield is not evident for years. And as we have seen throughout this book, even in their investment, consumption, and business practices, more and more people are searching for something more enduring and sustainable in their lives. Short-term targets may seem expedient to politicians and appealing to some parts of the public, but they undermine almost every other goal of sustainable improvement.

Until recently, Michael Fullan famously and repeatedly asserted that "you cannot mandate what matters to effective practice."[4] We agree with him. Still! Nothing has changed. Governments may want to assert and enforce the opposite, but, to change the wording slightly, "you cannot mandate short-term achievement targets to create effective practice." The collateral damage on all other areas of sustainability is just too great. This is not just intellectual quibbling; it is the lives and learning of children and their teachers and leaders that suffer most from these short-sighted practices.

Imposed, short-term achievement targets (or adequate yearly progress) transgress every principle of sustainable leadership and learning:

1. *Depth*. Short-term targets push most schools to focus on testing before learning; they put a priority only on learning that is easily measured; they narrow learning to the old basics, sacrificing breadth as well as depth, and by turning a sense of urgency into a state of fear and panic, they short-circuit teacher learning and replace it with paint-by-numbers training.

2. *Length*. Government ministers and the system leaders who implement their mandates frequently find they are unable to deliver the targets on time—and then their jobs are gone. Some do reach the targets by forcing or faking them, but the results quickly plateau once the system has run out of tricks. Leaders are cycled in

and out of schools with increasing frequency in the hope that a few will emerge who can produce miracle solutions, but accelerating succession only plunges schools into doom loops of performance decline.

3. *Breadth*. Acceleration and standardization of imposed change and its targets reduces teachers' time for working together and for learning from one another slowly and sustainably, as real learning communities. Distributed leadership turns into downloaded delegation along with artificial additives of stilted learning teams.

4. *Justice*. Target-driven forms of competitive accountability create disincentives for neighboring schools to share their learning and expertise. The desperate search for heroic stories of exemplary success also encourages systems to exalt highly improving schools at the expense of their neighbors, awarding them preferential allocations of interest, resources, and support.

5. *Diversity*. Imposed, short-term targets turn the deserved focus on deep standards into a damaging fixation with standardized testing. Standardization destroys and denies the diversity among students and teachers that is the source of their strength.

6. *Resourcefulness*. Improvement needs energy—energy that can be conserved and renewed, not used up and drained dry. High-speed implementation driven by short-term targets uses excessive energy, leaves no time for renewal, and causes people to run out of gas.

7. *Conservation*. Short-term targets force us to think and work in the present and future tense. Their creative destruction makes it hard for us to take the time to acknowledge, learn from, and recombine elements from the past, then move beyond them. Imposed, short-term targets turn us into innocent orphans who have been left no legacy and are cast into a world of repetitive and relentless change.

Like environmentalists, we don't believe that a record of failed sustainability in the past need condemn us to an unsustainable future. On the contrary, we are optimistic about the future of sustainable improvement, but not in the way that many governments and reformers are. They are usually supremely overconfident about their own power to manage and reform institutions and people but profoundly pessimistic about people's willingness or capacity to change themselves.

History is not on the side of the reformers. Thirty years of reform efforts in the high schools we studied are a testament to what octagenarian Seymour Sarason chillingly calls "the predictable failure of educational reform," which repeatedly fails to learn from its own past.[5] Reformers still cannot "mandate what matters" for effective practice in ways that matter, spread, and last.

Yet when people have a passion and a purpose that is theirs, not someone else's, and when their passion is pursued together and is sharpened by a sense of urgency or even guilt, there are no limits to what they can achieve. Civil rights, women's liberation, the end of apartheid in South Africa, and the quiet revolution in attitudes toward the environment all began with people, not policies, often against the opposition and entrenched resistance to change of governments.

We are optimistic about the power of parents to protect their children and promote common sense, like the Ontario mothers who persistently divulged the damaging effects of the government's standardized reform policies on teaching and learning in schools and helped bring its reign and policies to an end. We are optimistic about the mass of parents who can see when excesses of testing take the pleasure out of their children's learning and, like the majority of British parents, are able to pressure their governments to temper the extremes of targets and testing.[6] And we are optimistic about teachers' *seizing* leadership and not waiting for it to be given to them, like the Byron Women's Group, which rose to comprise some of the most influential and instructionally sophisticated senior leaders in their province.

There are ample grounds for optimism in all the schools in our study. Reasons for optimism are evident in the capacity of schools and their leaders to bring about long-term, lasting, measurable improvement when they are allowed and encouraged to put learning first; in the strength and achievements of true professional learning communities, in which all teachers in a school focus on learning and improvement together; in the striking success of sound succession management on the rare occasions when schools and systems pay proper attention to it; in the practical strategies that schools can and do adopt to assist their neighbors instead of being indifferent to their difficulties or profiting from their plight; in the courageous resilience of high-performing schools and their leaders when they protest against, secure waivers from, and find creative ways to maneuver around standardized excess; and in the hidden wisdom and untapped energy among dedicated and seasoned professionals that leaders know how to reuse, renew, and recombine instead of consigning it to the waste heap of allegedly outdated, unwanted, and "uninformed" professional judgment!

True sustainability is an integrated mission, not a pick-and-mix menu. It is ultimately optimistic and profoundly practical when it invests in people, works with rather than against the profession, and demands that governments act with moral purpose and have the courage to commit to sustainable improvement proposals, even if the results will only be evident after the immediate term of election.

Five Action Principles

For sustainability to be practical, it is important to grasp not just what sustainability looks like but also how to achieve it. To this end, drawing on the experience of environmentalism, sustainable business practice, and the evidence of our schools, we now outline five action principles for achieving sustainability in practice:

- Activism
- Vigilance
- Patience
- Transparency
- Design

Activism

Sustainable leadership is activist; it engages assertively with its environment. In the face of standardized reform, innovative schools tend to lose a lot of their edge. But the most resilient schools don't just react to external and unwanted pressures; they engage assertively with their environment. Activist leadership influences the environment that influences it by activating personal and professional networks, forging strategic alliances with the community, influencing the media by writing articles for newspapers, appearing on radio and television programs, and protesting openly against misconceived policies. Activist leaders are assertive leaders. Like Wangari Maathai in Kenya, Steve Munby in Knowsley Education Authority, Jenny Lewis in Australia, and the principal at Durant Alternative school, they have the courage to stand up to their superiors when their people's futures are at stake. It is when the environment is most unhelpful that sustainable leadership most needs to have an activist dimension. Anthropologist Margaret Mead perhaps put it best: "Never doubt that a small group of thoughtful committed citizens can change the world. Indeed, it is the only thing that ever has."[7]

Vigilance

Sustainable leadership is vigilant; it monitors the environment to check that it is staying healthy and not beginning to decline. In the nineteenth century, miners would enter coal mines with no way to tell whether they were inhaling poison gas. Methane had no odor, so it did not advertise its presence, and miners' robust bodies could absorb its toxic effects long enough for it to be too late to escape. So miners took tiny canaries, then rudimentary lamps invented by Humphry Davy down to the coal face, as sensitive devices that would detect the gas, giving early warning signs of environmental danger and deterioration. Nowadays, we look for signs of deterioration in our wider environment by monitoring population changes in sensitive species such as whales or frogs. While we can sometimes see the smoke and grime that is choking us, modern pollutants more usually work as invisible, silent killers. So in any environment, we need to use data, instruments, and measurements to check whether the situation is worsening, before it's too late, and also to ensure that it really is improving when we try to make it better.

Schools and school systems can also become toxic environments of wasted and seemingly disposable human potential. Sometimes the evidence is there for all to see—in crime, disorder, absenteeism, lack of learning, or loss of hope. But often the effects are more subtle, and like a frog in a bowl of increasingly heated water, as conditions deteriorate, not only might people be unaware of the deterioration, but many may even find it deceptively more comfortable. Results might improve, but only because of a few high achievers; teachers in a seemingly successful school might be coasting comfortably along while their motivated middle-class students jump through the exam hoops by themselves; governments might get rapid increases in test scores through heavy-handed reform measures, but motivation to stay in teaching or take up leadership roles might start to decline as a consequence.

Schools and leaders that practice sustainability therefore collect and review extensive and multiple sources of evidence and data to check that they are remaining healthy and not heading into decline, especially among their most vulnerable schools and student populations. They collect proximate measures of changes in teacher attitude and behavior or in student engagement as reassuring signs of progress toward long-term results in authentic student learning. Many kinds of data matter—test scores and achievement results; attendance and suspension figures; data on student satisfaction, engagement, and learning styles; data on teacher recruitment, retention, motivation, and morale; as well as qualitative samples of student work. What is important is that such data are used not only for marketing appearances or for appeasement of public opinion but also to ensure preservation and improvement of the overall learning environment. Holding schools in a town or a region collectively accountable can encourage and inspire them to assist one another in their improvement efforts. Continuing to collect standardized test data will maintain systemwide measures of effectiveness, but doing this through a *sample* rather than a *census* will also reduce the negative instructional impact on schools as well as the overall cost to the system. Sustainable leaders are vigilant leaders. They are hungry for data that warn them of the early signs of danger and that provide support and stepping stones on the path to improvement and success.

Patience

Sustainable leadership is patient; it defers gratification instead of seeking instant results. Sustainable leadership is patient and persevering. It invests urgently in improvement but does not expect or insist on instant success. Student achievement used to be seen as a product of delayed gratification, of a willingness to study hard and endure financial hardship, to resist the momentary temptations and distractions of adolescence in order to secure greater rewards in years to come. Sustainable school improvement also depends on habits of mind that are not impatient for rapid results.

Yet we no longer live in a world that values patience and permanence. Ours is, instead, a disposable society. In *Wasted Lives*, Zygmunt Bauman states, "No thing in the world is bound to last, let alone forever. Today's useful and indispensable objects . . . are tomorrow's waste. Nothing is truly necessary, no thing is irreplaceable. Everything is born with a branding of imminent death—everything leaves the production line with a 'use-by' date attached. . . . No step and no chance is once and for all, none is irrevocable. No commitment lasts long enough to reach the point of no return. All things . . . are until further notice and disposable.[8]

The disposable society is a society of wanton waste—of things that have planned obsolescence rather than being built to last, of mounting levels of personal debt that mortgage the future to satisfy the transient hungers of the present, of flexible labor that makes corporate loyalty obsolete, and of speed dating and instant messaging that replaces intimate conversation and lasting relationships.[9] The disposable society is also a society in which policies pander to opinion polls and appearances, driven by the need for instant impact, positive "spin," and quick-fix results. As disposable policies are repeatedly outstripped by their more fashionable successors in destructive cycles of repetitive change, they waste resources, human energy, and people's time. Imposed, short-term achievement targets in Britain and parts of Canada, along with demands for adequate yearly progress in America, are the epitome of wasteful, unsustainable policies that cultivate and capitulate to the craving for instant political gratification. Sustainable leadership resists these cravings. It is driven by an urgent need for immediate action but also by the ability to defer gratification for results in order to fulfill the moral purpose of authentic, lasting, and widespread success.

Transparency

Sustainable leadership is transparent; it is always open to scrutiny and inspection. Martha Stewart, Nick Leeson, Nortel, Enron, and WorldCom are names that symbolize and signal the end of an era of corporate and financial hubris, when share values and CEO salaries rose sky-high on the basis of shady practices, fuzzy numbers, insider trading, and outright corporate fraud. The new millennium marked a collapse of trust in an opaque and unaccountable world of business and finance that served itself at the expense of its clients and that duped the public into believing that economic progress had no limit and that the party would never end.

When corporations "spin" the numbers and cook the books, they threaten people's livelihoods—their savings, their pensions, and their jobs. When medical and environmental organizations disguise their difficulties, they end up burying their mistakes. Problems such as cover-ups of oil spills and nuclear disasters or failure to disclose damaging data about potentially lethal side effects of newly marketed drugs threaten not just livelihoods, but life itself.[10]

Corporate ethics meltdown and government "spin" have made people increasingly suspicious of the organizations that affect their lives. With growing access to and sophistication in using modern communication technology, determined and dedicated citizens can now act on their suspicions and pry information out of institutions, forcing them to be more open in their dealings. Sometimes this is a reluctant and grudging accommodation in the face of unrelenting external pressure. But increasingly, it is also a result of proactive efforts by leading companies to rebuild trust with clients and communities by sharing data openly, actively seeking feedback, and being honest about mistakes. Transparency is in; opacity is out.

David Batstone identifies transparency as one of his eight principles for creating and preserving integrity and profitability.[11] According to this principle, "A company's business operations will be transparent to shareholders, employees, and the public, and its executives will stand by the integrity of their decisions."[12]

An organization lacks transparency when it withholds sensitive data, hides its errors, communicates in impenetrable language, and presents only positive information about itself. Like fish, organizations that lack transparency and integrity rot from the head down. When schools finesse their test scores, when principals always unquestioningly support their teachers against parental complaints (even when the complaints are valid), when teachers try to avert criticism or even litigation from middle-class parents by being overly polite and insufficiently candid about their children's learning or behavioral difficulties, it is no excuse to say that everybody does it. Indeed, as Batstone argues, this "may be the best sign that you are in danger," that your whole culture is corrupt.[13]

Transparency is essential in sustainable organizations. But it is not for the lily-livered or fainthearted. When evidence emerged that someone had been tampering with Tylenol, the well-known pain medication, its producer, Johnson & Johnson, immediately pulled its product off the shelves of every distributor in North America to undertake safety checks. The company lost millions, and its stock dropped precipitously, but its fast and open actions engendered such levels of public trust that sales and stock value more than rebounded within the year.[14]

Blue Mountain School shared data openly with parents, including data that might arouse as well as allay anxiety. Data at Blue Mountain were not regarded as ways to fabricate favorable impressions or as means to pass conclusive judgments about failure or success. Instead, data and evidence provided opportunities for inquiry and conversation within the school's wider learning community. Increases in behavior and attendance problems, for example, were treated as opportunities to discuss the impact of the government's reform policies on teachers' time and on their ability to maintain their commitment to extracurricular activities in sports and other areas where strong relationships with students were normally cemented.

Sustainable leadership reaches out to communities. It invites direct engagement; two-way, jargon-free communication; and meaningful participation by students, parents, and communities in the life of the school. Sustainable leadership is honest and forthright about failures as well as successes. Because it aspires to greater integrity, sustainable leadership also advocates for and has no fear of increased transparency. Sustainable leadership wants to be seen in its true colors, not viewed through rose-colored glasses.

Design

Sustainable leadership is designer-made; it creates systems that are personalized for people's use and that are compatible with human capacity. All systems in nature are emergent and are the product of evolutionary adaptation. As humans, we are capable of designing even more complex structures than those of nature because of our abilities in language and conceptualization. But our efforts often disappoint. They impose outdated mechanical models that try to master and control nature rather than ecological or even designer models that work more effectively and harmoniously with diverse people and their local environments.

Sustainable leadership devises structures that take into account what Kim Vincente calls the *human factor*.[15] Vincente, an engineer at the University of Toronto, argues that technology should be tailored to suit people and their environment rather than expecting people to adapt to the technology. Vincente describes how we have created a mechanistic world that is capable of producing very complicated technology, alongside a human and natural world that constantly struggles to adapt and adjust. This is a classic case of Homer-Dixon's *ingenuity gap*—of human design not having the capacity to keep up with or resolve the problems it has created.[16] According to Vincente, the Chernobyl meltdown and its human and environmental tolls were the result of technology that was too complicated for people to have the capacity to respond effectively in an emergency.[17] As many as 98,000 preventable deaths in hospitals in the United States are caused by overly long work shifts, mistaken use of technology, or incorrect distribution of medications.[18] "No matter where we look, whether at everyday situations or complex systems, we see technology that is beyond our human capacity to control," Vincente says.[19] This technology includes hard technology like nuclear generators and water treatment plants and equally important soft technologies like complicated work schedules and instruction manuals.

Technology that acknowledges the human factor in schools enables teachers and leaders to use their energies to advance the learning of students. Noumea Primary School designed and used technology intelligently to inform teachers about their students' learning on an as-needed, just-in-time basis. The software was accessible, integrated, and easily learned, and it saved rather than consumed teachers' time. Blue Mountain School created structures such as large interdisciplinary workrooms that facilitated networked learning and cross-disciplinary instruction. The British government's workforce renewal strategy is designed to relieve teachers of unnecessary paperwork and administration so that they can focus on their students.

Technology that ignores the human factor and that disregards the natural principles of emergent design diverts precious energy away from the business of teaching and learning. For example, at the same time as the Ontario government imposed sweeping curricular and assessment changes on schools like Stewart Heights and Talisman Park, their school district also changed the entire structure of student administration. This technically flawed system would spit out incomplete or erroneous class lists and student attendance reports, erase information that teachers had meticulously typed, and generally frustrate teachers and principals who already felt harassed. The design problems were not merely technical. They were also human, resulting in two mechanical systems of top-down implementation that were oblivious to each others' demands and effects.

Sustainable leadership is well designed; it puts people first and is personalized to their needs. Technical systems such as reporting or student administration processes, attendance systems, and special education tracking procedures have to be user-friendly. Data management systems that can collate and disaggregate information about student performance, like those at Noumea Primary School, have to be widely and easily accessible for the right reasons, in the right way, at the right time. External accountability mechanisms should use a sample, not a census; should administer tests flexibly at a time of year that is appropriate for the child; and should involve high degrees of internal self-review alongside external judgment. The examples are many, but the principles are the same—basing improvement designs on ecological and human diversity, so that they create focus through cohesion rather than mechanical alignment.

If teachers need to trust their leaders as people, they also need to be able to trust the designed systems that define much of their work. Few of us would entrust our lives to airline pilots who acted as if their systems were always about to crash. And people are less likely to entrust the lives of their children to abstract, mechanical systems that are unwieldy and unresponsive to human needs. Sustainable leadership is therefore designer leadership—not standardized and mechanical but personalized, accessible, and flexible.

Spheres of Sustainability

What does and should sustainable leadership look like in the school, the locality, and the state or the nation? Our way of understanding this is not based on conventional models that use the machine metaphor of levels of influence, arranged hierarchically, in systems of professionally oppressive alignment. These models of abstract, hierarchical, systemic change are out of synchronization with the principles of natural and also ingenious design that are at the heart of the idea and practice of sustainability.

Instead, we see the school, the locality, and the state or nation interconnected in spheres of mutual influence, each one a network of strong cells organized through cohesive diversity rather then mechanical alignment and with permeable membranes of influence between the spheres. Leadership in each sphere has its own dynamic and responsibilities, but it is also intimately related to leadership in the others. This understanding of sustainable leadership is thoroughly grounded in the literature, theory, and practice of environmental and corporate sustainability; it is evident in our practical experience, grassroots research knowledge, and close improvement partnerships with schools and school districts; and it increasingly defines the leading edge of policy thinking and strategy in many parts of the world, including the United Kingdom, much of Australia, several provinces in Canada, and international and interventionist organizations like the Organization for Economic Cooperation and Development and the World Bank.

You cannot reconcile an authentic quest for sustainable improvement with an overconfident mechanical model of top-down change that is driven to address short-term targets and instant results. Instead, on the basis of our research and improvement efforts, we propose something more optimistic, more practical, and more authentically sustainable in purpose and design.

The Sphere of the School and Community

Sustainable school leadership begins with the moral purpose of product integrity. It puts learning first, before achievement or testing. Learning is the essential prerequisite to everything else. Learning that sustains is deep and broad, moving far beyond the basics of literacy and numeracy. It does not import prescribed literacy solutions from abroad into schools, systems, and provinces or nations whose literacy record is already among the strongest in the world.[20] Instead of waiting interminably until later, it reaches beyond the basics now, thus giving every child the opportunity to participate in the highest levels of the creative knowledge economy, not just the lower-level service jobs for which the basics will barely equip them. Learning that sustains is slow, and it sticks. It does not degenerate into a series of frantic performances designed to meet externally imposed short-term targets.

Sustainable school leadership for learning is not opposed to targets. It encourages and insists on targets developed together, as a shared and continuing responsibility, between teacher and student and among the teachers and parents in the school's community. Urging educators to invest in externally imposed targets for their own reasons doesn't count, for that is not high-class ownership of authentic improvement but low-grade rental of other people's agendas. Nor does "spinning" the external targets by saying they are "aspirational" count.[21] Shared targets are shared targets, nothing less. Governments and districts will need to work in partnership with schools to ensure that targets are neither excessively cautious nor overly ambitious, but at the end of the day, the targets need to be matters of joint commitment, not required compliance.

The leadership context for learning and shared target setting develops and renews a clear sense of moral purpose and vision; focuses on learning; is compatible with the basic principles of sustainability, which are articulated and modeled repeatedly; and collectively reviews them through retreats and other means on a cyclical basis.

Shared responsibility for learning and target setting demands distributed leadership and the creation of strong professional learning communities—the strong cells of a sustainable system. These do not require heroic principals, but principals who can help create a culture in which leadership is distributed in an emergent and even an assertive way, so that the community engages in evidence-informed and experience-grounded dialogue about the best means to promote the goals of deep and broad student learning for all. Urgency of action, patience in regard to results, integrity of purpose, focus of effort, trust among colleagues, respect for evidence, and grown-up norms of respectful dialogue are the cultural hallmarks of sustainable school leadership. Integrated data systems, like Noumea Primary School's, and assigned roles for information management (including access to educational research) provide the technical infrastructure that enables professional learning communities to function well.

Sustainable school leadership thinks beyond the present. It invests resources in training, trust building, and teamwork, whose effects remain long after the resources have disappeared. It takes succession seriously, incorporating a succession plan into the school's improvement plan and educating those who are responsible for appointing new principals about the school's succession needs. Sustainable leadership develops aspiring leadership from the first few months of a teacher's career and builds a culture of leadership, of veterans and novices working and learning together, in which succession management problems become easier to resolve. World-class leadership development schools are one venue in which long-term leadership development strategies might be pursued and achieved. Sustainable leadership addresses upcoming succession and the need to leave a legacy from the first days of a senior leader's new appointment, not as an afterthought when it is nearing its end. It encourages senior leaders to stay with improving schools until their efforts become embedded within the wider culture, yet also prepares their staff emotionally and strategically for the time when the senior leader will eventually leave.

Sustainable school leadership does not sequester itself within the four walls of its own building but reaches out to other schools, providing assistance and offering advice, especially to those whom its own improvement actions immediately affect. Sustainable leadership is thoughtful about meeting the needs of its own school without draining students, staff, or system resources from neighboring schools.

Sustainable school leadership is insistent about firm principles that endure, not fixed programs that eventually disappear. Sustainable school leadership recognizes that cultural and linguistic diversity requires instructional diversity, and it understands that teachers learn differently just as much as their students do. Mechanical leadership imposes one-size-fits-all, overly aligned programs with singular approaches to instruction. Sustainable school leadership acknowledges and promotes multiple forms of instructional excellence; expands teachers' repertoires by networking them together across classrooms, grade levels, and departments; and adds extra elements of research-informed instruction through training and development when the school does not yet possess them.

Sustainable school leadership conserves and also renews people's energy, including leaders' own. Sustainable leaders don't perpetuate repetitive change; instead, they build improvements on the ones that preceded them. Sustainable leaders are assertive and activist in their refusal to implement external and unsustainable agendas that damage students' learning. Sustainable leaders don't try to do everything themselves; their door is not *always* open; they do not work long hours into the night. Sustainable leaders demonstrate that their work can be compatible with life, a family, children; that their job is not the last refuge for a terminal workaholic. They renew their own energy by attending to their own learning, take time away from the school periodically, access emotional support from mentors and coaches, and are emotionally open about their mistakes as well as their triumphs.

Sustainable school leadership treats the past as a resource more than an impediment. Whenever it is about to embark on a new improvement initiative, sustainable school leadership audits the past, capitalizes on its assets, charts and learns from its collective memory, thoughtfully abandons what is no longer useful, and involves its memory bearers in the early stages of change, even and especially when their orientation to change is one of skepticism and resistance. Sustainable school leadership keeps alive the collective memory through compiling rich archives, storing digital photographs and other visual memories, engaging in rituals of celebration, properly honoring those who leave or retire, and engaging in storytelling that continually reinscribes the school's myths and values.

The Local Sphere of Sustainable Leadership

Students will always be the purpose and the focus of change. Schools, not governments, will always be its center, the place where improvement efforts are initially and ultimately concentrated. The task of systems is to support and provide resources for the schools, create cohesion among their efforts, provide parameters of purpose and a climate of urgency, and ensure effective monitoring and intelligent accountability. Locally, in a district or a region, therefore, sustainable leadership must

- Reassert the sequential priority of learning, then achievement, then testing

- Obtain the resources of in-school time, staff support, professional development, and opportunities for retreats, so that school staff can work together to become a stronger learning community

- Provide leadership coaches and process consultants to assist schools in becoming stronger learning communities

- Create leadership development schools to grow outstanding future leadership

- Establish technical and human systems for information and data management, including school-based data, locally accumulated data, and external research evidence

- Promote school-driven inquiry and review as paths to improvement

- Provide in-system mentors, retired leaders who serve as coaches, and regular support group meetings for serving principals

- Ensure that all schools have succession plans and that these are shared with the district; limit the excesses of succession frequency and abolish the practice of regular and mathematically predictable principal rotation

- Establish a process for teachers, administrators, district officials, and community members together to develop a commitment to shared improvement targets

- Develop multiple indicators of accountability and apply these collectively, not just individually, as an incentive for schools to assist one another

- Encourage and fund local networks for schools to share effective practices and improvement strategies

- Orchestrate focused and intensive instructional training initiatives in areas in which the system and its schools are not yet strong, to expand schools' repertoires and ensure that there is excellence to share among them

- Audit past policies and change experiences before embarking on fresh change initiatives

National, State, and Provincial Sphere of Sustainable Leadership

At the national level, sustainability must move from mechanical strategies of excessive alignment, command-and-control administration, and paint-by-numbers instruction to a systemic strategy that can create improvement through diversity in ways that spread and last and that can attract and retain the highest-caliber leaders, who will be responsible for it. In this sphere, the essential elements of sustainable leadership are

- Setting parameters of broad purpose appropriate to the economy and the society.

- Providing a resource environment that supports schools in becoming strong professional learning communities through relief from extraneous bureaucratic responsibilities; provision of classroom assistants and support staff; obtaining resources of in-school time for engaging in evidence-informed improvement; and providing financial incentives for school-based innovation, inquiry, and research.

- Requiring that all schools, like the schools in the Alberta Initiative for School Improvement, set their own demanding improvement targets and be transparently accountable for meeting them, though not summarily punished if they do not achieve them straight away. This process can be embedded in school-based reviews, improvement plans and succession plans.

- Reallocating substantial resources from mechanical and analog systems of standardized testing to digital systems of networked improvement and learning, in which schools create improvement in student learning and achievement through focused and networked teacher learning.

- Making resource savings possible by applying standardized testing for external accountability to a statistically
  reliable and valid as well as economically prudent and
  resourceful sample of students and schools, rather
  than an exorbitant and time-consuming *census* of all
  of them.

- Initiating and supporting programs for identifying and
  developing leaders throughout their career, from the
  first months of their teaching career.

- Saying "enough" to the imposition of short-term
  targets and to the waste of energy, people, and
  resources that they create in the system, and replacing
  them with locally determined targets for which
  educators have shared responsibility.

Last Word

Leadership isn't and shouldn't be easy. The sooner we all have a
chance to practice it, the better. It is hard to be a successful leader.
It is harder still to be a sustainable one. Sustainable educational
leaders promote and practice sustaining learning. Sustainable leaders sustain others as they pursue this cause together. Sustainable
leaders also sustain themselves, attending to their own renewal and
not sacrificing themselves too much as they serve their community.
Sustainable leaders stay the course, stay together, stay around, and
stay alive.

Most leaders want to do things that matter, to inspire others to
do those things with them, and to leave a legacy once they have
gone. Sustainable leaders are human. Sometimes they will let their
schools and themselves down. So will the systems in which they
lead. But sustainable leadership certainly needs to become a commitment of all school leaders. If change is to matter, spread, and last,

sustainable leadership that stretches across many leaders must now also be a fundamental priority of the systems in which leaders do their work. Sustainability is the first and final challenge of leadership. And it is the biggest challenge to the highest-level leaders of all—those in our national and state governments.

Ardent environmentalists have defined the leading edge of sustainability. More and more businesses are combining money with morality and are following close behind. After years of resource-depleting standardization in education, many governments are increasingly seeking more prudent and ingenious ways to secure lasting and widespread educational improvement for all their students. It is time for other governments to follow their lead and for schools to show that greater trust in and support for their own improvement abilities will not lead to loss of energy, urgency, or effectiveness. We cannot afford to waste the time and energy of our teachers and our leaders any longer. But most of all, we can tolerate no more wasted lives among our children. These two things are connected. We have an opportunity to leave behind the overconfident mechanical age of endless waste and enter a more sustainable era of hopeful renewal. It is an opportunity that must be seized. The lives of our children and the legacy we leave them depend on it.

Research Sources

Our work and analysis in this book draws on our Change Over Time? study for the Spencer Foundation, which was codirected by Andy Hargreaves and Ivor Goodson. The final report of the study is available:

Hargreaves, A., & Goodson, I. (2003). Change over time? A study of culture, structure, time and change in secondary schooling. Project #199800214. Chicago: Spencer Foundation of the United States.

Much of the detailed evidence from the study is available in a series of articles in a special issue of the journal *Educational Administration Quarterly* (2006, vol. 42, no. 1, pages unavailable) that is devoted to the project:

Hargreaves, A., & Goodson, I. Educational change over time? The sustainability and non-sustainability of three decades of secondary school change and continuity.

Goodson, I., Moore, S., & Hargreaves, A. Teacher nostalgia and the sustainability of reform: The generation and degeneration of teachers' missions, memory and meaning.

Fink, D., & Brayman, C. School leadership succession and the challenges of change.

Baker, M., & Foote, M. Changing spaces: Urban school interrelationships and the impact of standards-based reform.

Giles, C., & Hargreaves, A. The sustainability of innovative schools as learning organizations and professional learning communities during standardized reform.

Evidence from the Spencer project on the impact of standardization and the potential of professional learning communities is presented in two books:

Hargreaves, A. (2003). *Teaching in the knowledge society: Education in the age of insecurity.* New York: Teachers' College Press.

Goodson, I. F. (2004). *Professional knowledge, professional lives: Studies in education and change.* Buckingham, U.K.: Open University Press.

Our work on leadership succession and sustainability has been developed through a number of earlier papers and reports, and we appreciate the publishers' permission to draw on them here. In addition to the article by Fink and Brayman listed earlier, the other papers and reports include the following:

Hargreaves, A., Moore, S., Fink, D., & White, R. (2002). *An investigation of secondary school principal rotation and succession in times of standards-based reform and rapid demographics.* Toronto: Ontario Principals Council.

Hargreaves, A., & Fink, D. (2003). Sustaining leadership. *Phi Delta Kappan, 84*(9), 693–700.

Hargreaves, A., & Fink, D. (2000). Three dimensions of educational reform. *Educational Leadership, 57*(7), 30–34.

Hargreaves, A., & Fink, D. (2004a). Editorial statement: Sustaining leadership. In B. Davies & J. West-Burnham (Eds.), *Handbook of educational leadership and management* (pp. 435–450). London: Pearson Education.

Hargreaves, A., & Fink, D. (2004b). The seven principles of sustainable leadership. *Educational Leadership, 61*(7), 8–13.

Hargreaves, A. (2005). Succeeding leaders? *Kappa Delta Pi, 69*(2), 163–173.

Hargreaves, A. (2005). The changing world of leadership. *Kappa Delta Pi, 69*(2), 101–110.

Hargreaves, A. (2004). Developing leadership for succession. In M. Coles & G. Southworth (Eds.), *Developing school leaders: Creating tomorrow's schools.* London: Open University Press, 21–36.

Further reading on the practical realities of school leadership can be found in the following book:

Fink, D. (2005). *Leadership for mortals: Developing and sustaining leaders of learning.* Thousand Oaks, CA: Corwin Press; London: Paul Chapman.

Notes

Introduction

1. J. Goodall (2004, October 13), Curbing our appetites, *Globe and Mail* (Toronto), A27.

2. B. McKibben (1989), *The end of nature* (New York: Random House).

3. J. Gleick (1999), *Faster: The acceleration of just about everything* (New York: Pantheon Books); C. Honoré (2004), *In praise of slowness: How a worldwide movement is challenging the cult of speed* (New York: HarperCollins).

4. R. L. Nadeau (2003), *The wealth of nature: How mainstream economics has failed the environment* (New York: Columbia University Press); H. E. Daly (1996), *For the common good: Redirecting the economy toward community, the environment, and a sustainable future* (Boston: Beacon Press).

5. R. L. Carson (1962), *Silent spring* (Boston: Houghton Mifflin), 189.

6. Carson (1962), 189.

7. D. Suzuki & A. McConnell (1997), *The sacred balance: Rediscovering our place in nature* (Seattle: Mountaineer Books).

8. M. Castells (1997), *The power of identity* (Malden, MA: Blackwell).

9. J. Collins & G. Porras (2002), *Built to last: Successful habits of visionary companies* (rev. ed.) (New York: Harper Business Essentials), 2.

10. W. Greider (2003), *The soul of capitalism: Opening paths to a moral economy* (New York: Simon & Schuster), 117–118.

11. I. Jackson & J. Nelson (2004), *Profits with principles: Seven strategies for delivering value with values* (New York: Doubleday).

12. D. Batstone (2003), *Saving the corporate soul and (who knows?) maybe your own* (San Francisco: Jossey-Bass), 11.

13. P. Hawken, A. Lovins, & L. H. Lovins (1999), *Natural capitalism: Creating the next industrial revolution* (New York: Little, Brown).

14. Quoted in Jackson & Nelson (2004), 64.

15. Honoré (2004).

16. R. A. Heifetz & M. Linsky (2002), *Leadership on the line: Staying alive through the dangers of learning* (Boston: Harvard Business School).

17. S. Bowers (2004, November 22), Forget Maxwell House. Would you like a cup of Kenco Sustainable? *The Guardian* (Manchester, U.K.), 1.

18. W. Hutton (2002), *The world we're in* (New York: Little, Brown).

19. McKibben (1989).

20. Nadeau (2003); Daly (1996).

21. D. Reina & M. Reina (1999), *Trust and betrayal in the workplace* (San Francisco: Berrett-Koehler).

22. J. Cassidy (2003), *Dot con: How America lost its mind and money in the Internet era* (New York: Perennial Press).

23. M. Brewster (2003), *Unaccountable: How the accounting profession forfeited a public trust* (Hoboken, NJ: Wiley).

24. E. Abrahamson (2004), *Change without pain: How managers can overcome initiative overload, organizational chaos, and employee burnout* (Boston: Harvard Business School), 2–3.

25. A. Hargreaves (2003), *Teaching in the knowledge society: Education in the age of insecurity* (New York: Teachers College Press); I. F. Goodson (2004), *Professional knowledge, professional lives: Studies in education and change* (Buckingham, U.K.: Open University Press); A. Hargreaves & I. Goodson (2006), Educational change over time? The sustainability and non-sustainability of three decades of secondary school change and continuity, *Educational Administration*

Quarterly, 42(1); D. Fink & C. Brayman (2006), School leadership succession and the challenges of change, *Educational Administration Quarterly, 42*(1); C. Giles & A. Hargreaves (2006), The sustainability of innovative schools as learning organizations and professional learning communities during standardized reform, *Educational Administration Quarterly, 42*(1); M. Baker & M. Foote (2006), Changing spaces: Urban school interrelationships and the impact of standards-based reform, *Educational Administration Quarterly, 42*(1); I. Goodson, S. Moore, & A. Hargreaves (2006), Teacher nostalgia and the sustainability of reform: The generation and degeneration of teachers' missions, memory and meaning, *Educational Administration Quarterly, 42*(1).

26. National Association of Secondary School Principals (2001), *The principals' shortage* (Reston, VA: Author).

27. Hargreaves (2003).

28. L. Earl, B. Levin, K. Leithwood, M. Fullan, & N. Watson (2003), *Watching and learning* (Vol. 3) (London: Department for Education and Skills).

29. A. Hargreaves (2004, March 5), Drop the standards, *London Times Educational Supplement*, 14.

30. M. Fullan (2005), *Leadership and sustainability: System thinkers in action* (Thousand Oaks, CA: Corwin Press).

31. W. Mansell & P. White (2004, November 12), Stop test drilling, primaries warned, *London Times Educational Supplement*, 1.

32. B. Levin (2005), *Governing education* (Toronto: University of Toronto Press).

33. C. Alphonso & K. Harding (2004, December 8), Finland and Alberta spawn star students, *Globe and Mail* (Toronto), 5.

34. W. Mansell & R. Bushby (2004, November 26), Schools must join the crowd, *London Times Educational Supplement*, 112–113; C. Tayler (2004), *What makes a good school* (London: David Fulton).

35. Organization for Economic Cooperation and Development (2005), *Teachers matter: Attracting, developing and retaining effective teachers* (Paris: Author).

36. For more on the work of Lester Brown, the Worldwatch Institute, and the concept of sustainability, see D. Suzuki (2003), *The David Suzuki reader: A lifetime of ideas from a leading activist and thinker* (Vancouver, Canada: Greystone Books).

37. World Commission on Environment and Development (1987), *Our common future* (New York: United Nations General Assembly).

38. United Nations (2002, August 26), *Report of the world summit on sustainable development* (New York: Author).

39. W. L. Filho (2000), Dealing with misconceptions of the concept of sustainability, *International Journal of Sustainability in Higher Education, 1*(1), 9–19.

40. There is an important literature and set of initiatives on how education for sustainable development can improve the wider environment—for example, through global education initiatives in curriculum development, construction of more environmentally friendly and resource-conserving school buildings, and introduction of programs by UNESCO and other organizations to increase environmental awareness and responsibility in less developed countries. These are exceptionally important interventions, but this book addresses issues of sustainability in education and leadership in a more generic sense.

41. Fullan (2005).

42. A. Hargreaves & D. Fink (2003), Sustaining leadership, *Phi Delta Kappan, 84*(9), 693–700.

43. Hargreaves & Goodson (2006).

44. Collins & Porras (2002), 31.

Chapter One

1. N. Mandela (1994), *Long walk to freedom* (London: Little, Brown), 363.

2. A. de Gues (1997), *The living company: Habits for survival in a turbulent business environment* (Boston: Harvard Business School Press); M. Fullan (2001), *The new meaning of educational change* (3rd ed.) (London: Routledge/Falmer Press).

3. J. Collins & G. Porras (2002), *Built to last: Successful habits of vision-ary companies* (rev. ed.) (New York: Harper Business Essentials), 8.

4. I. Jackson & J. Nelson (2004), *Profits with principles: Seven strategies for delivering value with values* (New York: Doubleday), 32.

5. Collins & Porras (2002), 88.

6. D. Batstone (2003), *Saving the corporate soul and (who knows?) maybe your own* (San Francisco: Jossey-Bass).

7. G. Erickson & L. Lorentzen (2004), *Raising the bar: Integrity and passion in life and business: The story of Clif Bar, Inc.* (San Francisco: Jossey-Bass), 125.

8. Erickson & Lorentzen (2004), 25.

9. Erickson & Lorentzen (2004), 26.

10. Erickson & Lorentzen (2004), 25.

11. Erickson & Lorentzen (2004), 252.

12. Erickson & Lorentzen (2004), 253.

13. Mandela (1994).

14. C. D. Glickman (2002), *Leadership for learning: How to help teachers succeed* (Alexandria, VA: Association for Supervision and Curriculum Development). T. J. Sergiovanni (1999), *The lifeworld of leadership: Creating culture, community, and personal meaning in our schools* (San Francisco: Jossey-Bass).

15. L. Stoll, D. Fink, & L. Earl (2003), *It's about learning: It's about time* (London: Routledge/Falmer Press).

16. M. Knapp, M. Copland, & J. Talbert (2003), *Leading for learning: Reflective tools for school and district leaders* (Seattle: Center for the Study of Teaching and Policy, University of Washington).

17. Knapp, Copland, & Talbert (2003), 17.

18. P. Hallinger (1992), The evolving role of American principals: From managerial to instructional to transformational leaders, *Journal of Educational Administration, 30*(3), 35–48.

19. Glickman (2002).

20. J. Murphy (2002), Reculturing the profession of educational leadership: New blueprints, in J. Murphy (Ed.), *The educational leadership*

challenge: Redefining leadership for the 21st century—101st yearbook of the National Society for the Study of Education (Chicago: National Society for the Study of Education), 71.

21. K. K. Manzo (2004) Social studies losing out to reading and math, *Education Week*, 24(27), 1, 16.

22. R. Elmore (2002), Hard questions about practice, *Educational Leadership*, 59(8), 22–25.

23. C. B. Handy (1998), *The hungry spirit: Beyond capitalism: A quest for purpose in the modern world* (New York: Broadway Books), 13.

24. Handy (1998), 13.

25. Confucius (1998), *Confucius: The analects* (London: Penguin Books), 65.

26. J. Dewey (1944), *Democracy and education: An introduction to the philosophy of education* (New York: Collier-Macmillan) (original work published 1916), i.

27. J. Dewey (1963), How we think, in R. M. Hutchins & M. J. Adler (Eds.), *Gateway to the great books* (Vol. 10) (Chicago: Encyclopedia Britannica), 135.

28. L. Lambert (1998), *Building capacity in schools* (Alexandria, VA: Association for Supervision and Curriculum Development), 5–6.

29. B. Lingard, D. Hayes, M. Mills, & P. Christie (2003), *Leading learning* (Philadelphia: Open University Press), 10.

30. Education Queensland, in Lingard, Hayes, Mills, & Christie (2003), 10.

31. Education Queensland, in Lingard, Hayes, Mills, & Christie (2003), 11.

32. Handy (1998), 13.

33. This information was drawn from a range of quality newspapers.

34. R. Reich (2001), *The future of success* (New York: Knopf).

35. J. Delors, I. Al Mufti, A. Amagi, R. Carneiro, F. Chung, B. Geremek, and others (1996), *Learning: The treasure within—Report to UNESCO of the International Commission on Education for the*

Twenty-first Century (Paris: United Nations Educational, Scientific, and Cultural Organization), 86.

36. Delors and others (1996), 85.

37. Delors and others (1996), 86.

38. Delors and others (1996), 87.

39. On education for sustainable development, see United Nations Educational, Scientific, and Cultural Organization (2004), *United Nations Decade of Education for Sustainable Development, 2005-2014: Draft implementation scheme* (Paris: Author).

40. United Nations Educational, Scientific, and Cultural Organization (2004), 4.

41. A. Hargreaves (2000), Mixed emotions: Teachers' perceptions of their interactions with students, *Teaching and Teacher Education,* 16(8), 811–826.

42. D. Miliband (2004, January 8), *Personalized learning: Building new relationships with schools,* speech presented at the North of England Education Conference, Belfast, Northern Ireland; D. Hargreaves (2004), *Education epidemic: Transforming secondary schools through innovation networks* (London: Demos).

43. Bill and Melinda Gates Foundation (2005), *Making the case for small schools,* retrieved from www.gatesfoundation.org; see also A. Hargreaves & L. Earl (1990), *The rights of passage: A review of selected research about schooling in the transition years* (Toronto: Ontario Ministry of Education).

44. R. Callahan (1964), *Education and the cult of efficiency* (Chicago: University of Chicago Press).

45. J. Stein (2001), *The cult of efficiency* (Toronto: Anansi).

46. E. Eisner (2002), *The arts and the creating of minds* (New Haven, CT: Yale University Press), 13.

47. Organization for Economic Cooperation and Development (2003), *Learning from tomorrow's world: First results from PISA 2003* (Paris: Author).

48. For more discussion on cultures of performance standards, see A. Hargreaves (2003), *Teaching in the knowledge society: Education in the age of insecurity* (New York: Teachers College Press).

49. C. Brunner & M. Grogan (2004), Women superintendents and role conceptions: (Un)troubling the norms, in L.T.J. Kowalski (Ed.), *School district superintendents: Role expectations, professional preparation, development and licensing* (Thousand Oaks, CA: Corwin Press).

50. R. F. Elmore & D. Burney (1999), Investing in teacher learning: Staff development and instructional improvement, in L. Darling-Hammond & G. Sykes (Eds.), *Teaching as the learning profession: Handbook of policy and practice* (pp. 236–291) (San Francisco: Jossey-Bass); R. Elmore (2002), *Bridging the gap between standards and achievement* (Washington, DC: Albert Shanker Institute).

51. J. Spillane (2006), *Distributed leadership* (San Francisco: Jossey-Bass).

52. J. Lewis & B. Caldwell (2005), Evidence-based leadership, *Educational Forum, 69*(2), 182–191.

53. D. Hargreaves (2004).

54. B. Levin & J. Wiens (2003), There is another way: A different approach to educational reform, *Phi Delta Kappan, 84*(9), 660.

55. A. Hargreaves, L. Earl, S. Moore, & S. Manning (2001), *Learning to change: Teaching beyond subjects and standards* (San Francisco: Jossey-Bass).

56. On emotional literacy, see B. Harris (2004), Leading by heart, *School Leadership and Management, 25*(4), 391–404.

57. G. Claxton (1999), *Hare brain, tortoise mind: Why intelligence increases when you think less* (Hopewell, NJ: Ecco Press).

58. A. Hargreaves (2003).

59. T. Homer-Dixon (2000), *The ingenuity gap: Can we solve the problems of the future?* (New York: Knopf).

60. Claxton (1999), 4.

61. Claxton (1999).

62. Fullan (2001), 123.

63. Claxton (1999), 4.

64. R. Florida (2002), *The rise of the creative class and how it is transforming work, leisure, community and everyday life* (New York: Basic Books), 15.

65. Florida (2002), 15.

66. A. Hargreaves (2003).

67. Homer-Dixon (2000), 5–6.

68. M. Gladwell (2005), *Blink: The power of thinking without thinking* (New York: Little, Brown).

69. A. Gawande (2002), *Complications: A surgeon's notes on an imperfect science* (New York: Metropolitan Books).

70. A. Gawande (2004, November 23), The bell curve: What happens when patients find out how good their doctors really are? *New Yorker*, 17–20.

71. D. Hargreaves (1983), *The teaching of art and the art of teaching: Towards an alternative view of aesthetic learning* (Lewes, U.K.: Falmer Press).

72. With apologies to E. Schlosser (2001), *Fast food nation* (Boston: Houghton Mifflin).

73. D. Elkind (1993), School and family in the post-modern world, *Phi Delta Kappan, 77*(1), 8–14, 48.

74. Elkind (1993).

75. On the proliferation of cheating, see, for example, D. Hoff (2003), New York teacher caught cheating on state tests, *Education Week, 23*(10), 27; and British Broadcasting Corporation (2001), *Inquiry into school test cheats*, July 30, http://news.bbc.co.uk/l/hi/education/1464478.stm.

76. Spillane (2006).

77. Hargreaves, Earl, Moore, & Manning (2001).

78. C. Honoré (2004), *In praise of slowness: How a worldwide movement is challenging the cult of speed* (New York: HarperCollins).

79. M. Holt (2004, May), *The slow school: An idea whose time has come*, address presented at the Canadian Teachers' Federation Conference, Ottawa, Canada, 4.

80. Holt (2004), 7.

81. Honoré (2004).

82. Finnish schools were described by a Finnish official in C. Alphonso & K. Harding (2004, December 8), Finland and Alberta spawn star students, *Globe and Mail* (Toronto), 5.

83. *Excellence and Enjoyment* and other reports are summarized in Department for Education and Skills (2001, September), *Achieving success* (London: Her Majesty's Stationery Office).

84. Education Queensland, in Lingard, Hayes, Mills, & Christie (2003), 10–11.

85. Honoré (2004).

86. Claxton (1999).

87. For a discussion of the karaoke curriculum, see Hargreaves, Earl, Moore, & Manning (2001).

Chapter Two

1. World Commission on Environment and Development (1987), *Our common future* (New York: United Nations General Assembly).

2. S. Anderson & S. Stiegelbauer (1994), Institutionalization and renewal in a restructured secondary school, *School Organization*, 14(3), 279-293; M. B. Miles & A. M. Huberman (1984), *Innovation up close: How school improvement works* (New York: Plenum Press).

3. S. Anderson & W. Togneri (2002), *Beyond islands of excellence: What districts can do to improve instruction and achievement in all schools* (Washington, DC: Learning First Alliance).

4. K. Leithwood, D. Jantzi, & R. Steinbach (1999), *Changing leadership for changing times* (Birmingham, U.K.: Open University Press).

5. P. Gronn (1996), From transactions to transformations: A new world order in the study of leadership, *Educational Management and Administration*, 24(1), 7–30.

6. A. Hargreaves & D. Fink (2003), Sustaining leadership, *Phi Delta Kappan*, 84(9), 693–700.

7. Association of California School Administrators, Task Force on Administrator Shortage (2001), *Recruitment and retention of school leaders: A critical state need* (Sacramento: Author); National Clearinghouse for Comprehensive School Reform (2002, August), Planning for the succession of leadership, *NCCSR Newsletter*, 3.

8. D. Pounder & R. Merrill (2001), Job desirability of the high school principalship: A job choice perspective, *Educational Administration Quarterly*, 37(1), 27–57.

9. P. Early, J. Evans, P. Collarbone, A. Gold, & D. Halpin (2002), *Establishing the current state of leadership in England* (London: Department for Education and Skills); T. Williams (2001), *Unrecognized exodus, unaccepted accountability: The looming shortage of principals and vice principals in Ontario public school boards* (Toronto: Ontario Principals Council); K. Brooking, G. Collins, M. Cour, & J. O'Neill (2003), Getting below the surface of the principal recruitment "crisis" in New Zealand primary schools, *Australian Journal of Education*, 47(2), 146–158; P. Gronn & F. Rawlings-Sanaei (2003), Principal recruitment in a climate of leadership disengagement, *Australian Journal of Education*, 47(2), 172–185.

10. M. Roz, M. Celio, J. Harvey, & S. Wishon (2003), *A matter of definition: Is there truly a shortage of school principals? A report to the Wallace Foundation from the Center on the Reinvention of Education, University of Washington* (Seattle: Center on the Reinvention of Education, University of Washington).

11. J. Steinberg (2000, September 3), Nation's schools struggling to find enough principals, *New York Times*, A1, A4.

12. National Association of Elementary School Principals (2005), *NAESP fact sheet on principal shortage*, retrieved April 5, 2005, from http://www.naesp.org.

13. D. Pounder & R. Merrill (2001).

14. J. Howson (2005), *20th annual survey of senior staff appointments in schools in England and Wales* (Oxford, U.K.: Education Data Surveys).

15. Williams (2001).

16. Gronn & Rawlings-Sanaei (2003).

17. Brooking, Collins, Cour, & O'Neill (2003).

18. M. Fullan (2005), *Leadership and sustainability: System thinkers in action* (Thousand Oaks, CA: Corwin Press).

19. A. Bellow (2003), *In praise of nepotism: A natural history* (New York: Doubleday).

20. I. Kersner & T. C. Sebora (1994), Executive succession: Past, present and future, *Journal of Management, 20*(2), 327–373.

21. M. Liebman & R. A. Bauer (1996), Succession management: The next generation of succession planning, *Human Resource Planning, 19*(3), 16–29; E. Schall (1997), Public sector succession: A strategic approach to sustaining innovation, *Public Administration Review, 57*(1), 4–10; L. J. Eastman (1995), *Succession planning: An annotated bibliography and summary of commonly reported organizational practices* (Greensboro, NC: Center for Creative Leadership); J. P. Soque (1998), *Succession planning and leadership development* (Ottawa: Conference Board of Canada); W. J. Rothwell (2001), *Effective succession planning: Ensuring leadership continuity and building talent from within* (New York: AMACOM).

22. C. Borwick (1993), Eight ways to assess succession plans, *HR Magazine, 38*(5), 109–114; L. Clark & K. Lyness (1991), *Succession planning as a strategic activity at Citicorp* (Vol. 2) (Greenwich, CT: JAI Press); C. Getty (1993), Planning successfully for succession planning, *Training and Development, 47*(11), 31–33; M. Kets de Vries (1988), The dark side of CEO succession, *Management Review, 77*(8), 23–28; Liebman & Bauer (1996); M. Smith & M. White (1987), Strategy, CEO specialization, and succession, *Administration Science Quarterly, 32,* 263–280.

23. Soque (1998); Schall (1997); Liebman & Bauer (1996).

24. K. Farquhar (1994), The myth of the forever leader: Organizational recovery from broken leadership, *Business Horizon, 37*(5), 42–51.

25. W. Ocasio (1994), Political dynamics and the circulation of power: CEO succession in U.S. industrial corporations, 1960-1990, *Admin-*

istration Science Quarterly, 39, 285–312; Kersner & Sebora (1994); Y. K. Shelty & N. S. Perry, Jr. (1976), Are top managers transferable across companies? *Business Horizon, 19,* 23–28; A. Lewin & C. Wolf (1975), When the CEO must go, *Advanced Management Journal, 39,* 59–62; D. L. Helnich (1984), Organizational growth and succession patterns, *Academy of Management Journal, 17,* 771–775; G. Brady, R. Fulmer, & D. L. Helnich (1982), Planning executive succession: The effect of recruitment source and organizational problems on anticipated tenure, *Strategic Management Journal, 3,* 275–296.

26. Kersner & Sebora (1994).

27. Kets de Vries (1988).

28. Ocasio (1994); J. C. Santora & J. C. Sarros (1995), Mortality and leadership succession: A case study, *Leadership & Organizational Development Journal, 16*(7), 29–33.

29. National Academy of Public Administration (1997), *Managing succession and developing leadership: Growing the next generation of public service leaders* (Washington, DC: Author).

30. Financial Executive International (FEI) (2001), *Building human capital: The public sectors 21st century challenge,* www.fei.org.

31. K. Jackson (2000), *Building new teams: The next generation (A presentation)* (Perth: Government of Western Australia); Government of Western Australia (2001), *Managing succession in the Western Australia public sector* (Sydney: Author).

32. Financial Executive International (2001), *Building human capital: The public sector's 21st century challenge,* retrieved April 5, 2005, from http://www.fei.org.

33. Jackson (2000).

34. This point was first made in S. Sarason (1972), *The creation of settings and the future societies* (San Francisco: Jossey-Bass).

35. M. Messmer (2002), Grooming your successor, *Strategic Finance, 84*(6), 17–19.

36. Bellow (2003), 473.

37. Bellow (2003), 471.

38. Bellow (2003), 471.

39. Liebman & Bauer (1996), 16.

40. Smith & White (1987).

41. Ocasio (1994); Santora & Sarros (1995).

42. D. Hopkins (2001), *School improvement for real* (London: Routledge/Falmer Press); L. Stoll & D. Fink (1996), *Changing our schools: Linking school effectiveness and school improvement* (Buckingham, U.K.: Open University Press).

43. Stoll & Fink (1996).

44. S. M. Johnson (1996), *Leading to change: The challenge of the new superintendency* (San Francisco: Jossey-Bass).

45. Liebman & Bauer (1996).

46. G. Boris, N. Ashish, & N. Nitin (2004), The risky business of hiring stars, *Harvard Business Review, 82*(5), 92–101.

47. E. Wenger (1998), *Communities of practice: Learning, meaning and identity* (Cambridge, U.K.: Cambridge University Press).

48. D. Fink (2000), *Good schools/real schools: Why school reform doesn't last* (New York: Teachers College Press).

49. M. Weber (1978), *Economy and society: An outline of interpretive sociology* (Berkeley: University of California Press).

50. J. P. Spillane, R. Halverson, & J. B. Diamond (2001), Investigating school leadership practice: A distributed perspective, *Educational Researcher, 30*(3), 23–28; J. Spillane (2006), *Distributed leadership* (San Francisco: Jossey-Bass). We explore the theme of distributed leadership in detail in the next chapter.

51. Spillane (2006).

52. Schall (1997).

53. D. Fink & C. Brayman (2006), School leadership succession and the challenge of change, *Educational Administration Quarterly, 42*(1).

54. A. Lieberman & D. R. Wood (2002), *Inside the National Writing Project: Connecting network learning and classroom teaching* (New York: Teachers College Press).

55. National College for School Leadership (2002), *Making the difference: Successful leadership in challenging circumstances—A practical guide to what school leaders can do to improve and energise their schools* (Nottingham, U.K.: Author); Specialist Schools Trust (2003), *World class education: A challenge for every school* (London: Author); B. Portin, P. Schneider, M. DeArmond, & L. Gundlach (2003), *Making sense of leading schools: A study of the school principalship* (produced for the Wallace Foundation) (Seattle: Center on Reinventing Public Education).

56. C. Miskel & M. Owen (1983, April 11-15), *Principal succession and changes in school coupling and effectiveness,* paper presented at the annual meeting of the American Educational Research Association, Montreal; G. C. Gordon & N. Rosen (1981), Critical factors in leadership succession, *Organizational Behavior and Human Performance, 27,* 227–254; A. W. Hart (1998), *Principal succession: Establishing leadership in schools* (New York: State University of New York Press); J. J. Gabarro (1987), *The dynamics of taking charge* (Boston: Harvard Business School Press); D. E. Stine (1998, April 13-17), *A change of administration: A significant organizational life event,* paper presented at the annual meeting of the American Educational Research Association, San Diego, CA.

57. J. Reeves, L. Moos, & J. Forrest (1998), The school leader's view, in J. Macbeath (Ed.), *Effective school leadership: Responding to change* (pp. 32–59) (London: Paul Chapman).

58. A. Harris & C. Chapman (2003, January), *Democratic leadership for school improvement in challenging contexts,* paper presented at the International Congress on Effectiveness and School Improvement, Copenhagen; National College for School Leadership (2003).

59. Hay Management Consultants (2000), *The lessons of leadership* (London: Author).

60. R. MacMillan (2000), Leadership succession: Cultures of teaching and educational change, in N. Bascia & A. Hargreaves (Eds.), *The sharp edge of educational change: Teaching, leading and the realities of reform* (pp. 52–71) (London: Routledge/Falmer Press).

61. I. Saltzberger-Wittenberg, G. Henry, & E. Osborne (1983), *The emotional experience of learning and teaching* (London: Routledge Kegan Paul).

62. B. Beatty (2002), *Emotional matters in educational leadership: Examining the unexamined*, unpublished doctoral dissertation, University of Toronto; B. Beatty & C. R. Brew (2004), Trusting relationships and emotional epistemologies: A foundational leadership issue, *School Leadership and Management*, *24*(3), 329–356.

63. R. H. Ackerman & P. Maslin-Ostrowski (2004), The wounded leader and emotional learning in the schoolhouse, *School Leadership and Management*, *24*(3), 312.

64. D. Loader (1997), *The inner principal* (London: Falmer Press).

65. Loader (1997), 8.

66. Ackerman & Maslin-Ostrowski (2004), 312; P. J. Palmer (1998), *The courage to teach: Exploring the inner landscape of a teacher's life* (San Francisco: Jossey-Bass); C. James & U. Connolly (2000), *Effective change in schools* (London: Routledge/Falmer Press).

67. W. Shakespeare, (1966), *Complete works* (London: Oxford University Press).

68. Saltzberger-Wittenberg, Henry, & Osborne (1983).

69. Kets de Vries (1988), 23–24.

70. Farquhar (1994).

71. A. Hargreaves (2002), Teaching and betrayal, *Teachers and Teaching: Theory and Practice*, *13*(4), 393–407; D. Reina & M. Reina (1999), *Trust and betrayal in the workplace* (San Francisco: Berrett-Koehler); A. Bryk & B. Schneider (2004), *Trust in schools: A core resource for improvement* (New York: Russell Sage Foundation).

72. Farquhar (1994).

73. Santora & Sarros (1995).

74. Kets de Vries (1988).

75. A. W. Gouldner (1954), The pattern of succession in bureaucracy, in R. Merton (Ed.), *Reader in bureaucracy* (Glencoe, IL: Free Press), 339–351.

Chapter Three

1. B. Lingard, D. Hayes, M. Mills, & P. Christie (2003), *Leading learning* (Philadelphia: Open University Press).

2. *Historians rank presidential leadership in new C-Span survey* (2000), retrieved from http://www.americanpresidents.org/survey/amp022100.asp.

3. W. Ihimaera (2003), *The whale rider* (New York: Harcourt).

4. P. Hallinger & R. H. Heck (1998), Exploring the principal's contribution to school effectiveness: 1980–1995, *School Effectiveness and School Improvement, 9*(2), 157–191; P. Hallinger & R. H. Heck (1996), Reassessing the principal's role in school effectiveness: A review of empirical research, 1980-1995, *Educational Administration Quarterly, 32*(1), 5–44.

5. M. Copland (2003), Leadership of inquiry: Building and sustaining capacity for school improvement, *Educational Evaluation and Policy Analysis, 25*(4), 375.

6. J. O'Leary (2000, March 14), Another fresh start school head resigns, *Guardian* (Manchester, U.K.), 13.

7. The term *gallant leadership* is used in J. Spillane (2006), *Distributed leadership* (San Francisco: Jossey-Bass).

8. A. Gawande (2002), *Complications: A surgeon's notes on an imperfect science* (New York: Metropolitan Books).

9. Hallinger & Heck (1998).

10. J. Dewey (1977), Democracy and education, in J. A. Boydston (Ed.), *The middle works, 1899–1906* (Carbondale: Southern Illinois University Press), 231.

11. C. Barnard (1968), *Functions of the executive* (Cambridge, MA: Harvard University Press).

12. J. D. Thompson (1967), *Organizations in action* (New York: McGraw-Hill).

13. This discussion is based on Douglas McGregor's classic work *The Human Side of Enterprise* (New York: McGraw Hill), which was published in 1960. In 1981, William Ouchi, in his book *Theory Z: How*

American Management Can Meet the Japanese Challenge (Cambridge, MA: Perseus) suggested that the Japanese management system of the 1980s was a logical extension of McGregor's Theory Y. Ouchi's Theory Z assumes that workers have a strong loyalty to their organization and an interest in teamwork. Since they are already motivated to do a good job, he argues, they require more freedom and trust to become truly productive (p. 81). This view differs from McGregor's more managerial and less optimistic perspective, which suggested that Theory Y was a more productive way to motivate workers than the more authoritarian approach of Theory X.

14. M. Rutter, B. Maughan, P. Mortimore, J. Ouston, & A. Smith (1979), *Fifteen thousand hours* (London: Open Books).

15. J. M. Burns (1978), *Leadership* (New York: Harper & Row); D. McGregor (1960), *The human side of enterprise* (New York: McGraw-Hill); B. M. Bass (1985), *Leadership and performance beyond expectations* (New York: Free Press).

16. Burns (1978), 20.

17. K. Leithwood, D. Jantzi, & R. Steinbach (1999), *Changing leadership for changing times* (Buckingham, U.K.: Open University Press).

18. K. Leithwood (1993, October), *Contributions of transformational leadership to school restructuring,* paper presented at the convention of the University Council for Educational Administration, Houston, TX.

19. K. Leithwood & D. Jantzi (1999), Transformational school leadership effects, *School Effectiveness and School Improvement, 10*(4), 451–479.

20. Leithwood, Jantzi, & Steinbach (1999), 121.

21. K. Leithwood & D. Jantzi (2000), The effects of different sources of leadership on student engagement in school, in K. Riley & K. S. Louis (Eds.), *Leadership for change and school reform: International perspectives* (pp. 50–66) (New York: Routledge/Falmer Press), 56.

22. Leithwood, Jantzi, & Steinbach (1999).

23. Leithwood, Jantzi, & Steinbach (1999), 23.

24. Leithwood & Jantzi (2000), 61.

25. H. Silins & B. Mulford (2002), Leadership and school results, in K. Leithwood, P. Hallinger, K. S. Louis, P. Furman-Brown, P. Gronn, W. Mulford, & K. Riley (Eds.), *Second international handbook of educational leadership and administration* (pp. 561–612) (Dordrecht, Netherlands: Kluwer).

26. M. Weber (1978), *Economy and society: An outline of interpretive sociology* (Berkeley: University of California Press).

27. J. Lipman-Blumen (2004), *The allure of the toxic leader: Why we follow destructive bosses and corrupt politicians—and how we can survive them* (London: Oxford University Press).

28. H. Gunter (2001), *Leaders and leadership in education* (London: Paul Chapman); A. Harris (2001), Building the capacity for school improvement, *School Leadership and Management, 21*(30), 261–270; F. Crowther, S. Kaagan, M. Ferguson, & L. Hann (2002), *Developing teacher leaders: How teacher leadership enhances school success* (Thousand Oaks, CA: Corwin Press); A. Lieberman & L. Miller (2004), *Teacher leadership* (San Francisco: Jossey-Bass); J. MacBeath & P. Mortimore (2001), *Improving school effectiveness* (Buckingham, U.K.: Open University Press).

29. Lieberman & Miller (2004), 154.

30. S. Rosenholtz (1989), *Teachers' workplace* (New York: Longman).

31. D. Hopkins & D. Jackson (2003), Building the capacity for leading and learning, in C. Day, A. Harris, D. Hopkins, M. Hadfield, A. Hargreaves, & C. Chapman (Eds.), *Effective leadership for school improvement* (London: Routledge).

32. B. Malen, R. Ogawa, & J. Kranz (1990), What do we know about school-based management? A case study of the literature—A call for research, in W. H. Clune & J. F. Witte (Eds.), *Choice and control in American education* (Vol. 2, pp. 112–132) (New York: Falmer Press).

33. A. Harris (2002), *School improvement: What's in it for schools?* (London: Routledge/Falmer Press); M. Katzenmeyer & G. Moller (2001),

Awakening the sleeping giant: Helping teachers develop as leaders (Thousand Oaks, CA: Corwin Press).

34. N. Bennett, J. Harvey, C. Wise, & P. A. Woods (2003), *Distributed leadership: A desk study* (Nottingham, U.K.: National College for School Leadership), 6.

35. Crowther, Kaagan, Ferguson, & Hann (2002).

36. Lipman-Blumen (2004).

37. J. Oakes, K. H. Quartz, S. Ryan, & M. Lipton (2000), *Becoming good American schools: The struggle for civic virtue in educational reform* (San Francisco: Jossey-Bass); M. McLaughlin & J. Talbert (2001), *Professional communities and the work of high school teaching* (Chicago: University of Chicago Press).

38. M. Smylie, S. Conley, & H. Marks (2002), Exploring new approaches to teacher leadership, in J. Murphy (Ed.), *The educational leadership challenge: Redefining leadership for the 21st century— 101st yearbook of the National Society for the Study of Leadership* (Chicago: National Society for the Study of Education), 163.

39. B. Berry & R. Ginsberg (1990), Creating lead teachers: From policy to implementation, *Phi Delta Kappan, 71,* 616–621; L. Ingvarson (1992), *Educational reform through restructuring industrial rewards: A study of the advanced skills teacher* (Melbourne, Australia: Melbourne University).

40. M. Smylie (1997), Research on teacher leadership: Assessing the state of the art, in B. J. Biddle, T. Good, & I. Goodson (Eds.), *International handbook of teachers and teaching* (pp. 521–592) (Dordrecht, Netherlands: Kluwer).

41. L. Darling-Hammond, M. Bullmaster, & V. Cobb (1995), Rethinking teacher leadership through professional development schools, *Elementary School Journal, 96,* 89.

42. Katzenmeyer & Moller (2001).

43. Spillane is principal investigator of the Distributed Leadership Project, the longitudinal study of urban school leadership funded by the National Science Foundation and the Spencer Foundation.

44. P. Gronn (2000), Distributed properties: A new architecture for leadership, *Educational Management and Administration*, *24*(1), 23–24.

45. Spillane (2006).

46. I. Goodson (1996), *Studying school subjects: A guide* (London: Falmer Press).

47. Crowther, Kaagan, Ferguson, & Hann (2002), 21.

48. This argument is also made in J. Ryan (2005), *Inclusive leadership* (San Francisco: Jossey-Bass).

49. Hay Group Education (2004), *Distributed leadership: An investigation for NCSL into the advantages and disadvantages, causes and constraints of a more distributed form of leadership in schools* (London: Author), 4.

50. Hay Group Education (2004), 11.

51. A. Huxley (1931), *Brave new world* (London: Chalto and Windus).

52. A. Hargreaves (1994), *Changing teachers, changing times: Teachers' work and culture in the postmodern age* (New York: Teachers College Press); A. Hargreaves (2003), *Teaching in the knowledge society: Education in the age of insecurity* (New York: Teachers College Press).

53. See, for example, J. Blase & G. Anderson (1995), *The micropolitics of educational leadership* (London: Cassell), chap. 5.

54. One variation of autocracy is oligarchy. Oligarchy is government controlled by a small elite group. In a school, the principal and a few department heads from major subject areas might well dominate the school's policies.

55. We develop this case further in the next chapter on justice.

56. L. Stoll & K. Myers (1998), *No quick fixes: Perspectives on schools in difficulty* (London: Falmer Press).

57. L. Stoll & D. Fink (1996), *Changing our schools: Linking school effectiveness and school improvement* (Buckingham, U.K.: Open University Press).

58. Spillane (2006).

59. This case report is based on our visits to Noumea Primary School and on the principal's self-review in J. Lewis & B. Caldwell (2005), Evidence-based leadership, *Educational Forum*, *69*(2), 182–191.

60. Lewis & Caldwell (2005).

61. P. Gronn (2003), *The new work of educational leaders: Changing leadership practice in an era of school reform* (Thousand Oaks, CA: Sage).

62. Coordinated, collaborative, and collective distribution of leadership are discussed in Spillane (2006).

63. Crowther, Kaagan, Ferguson, & Hann (2002).

64. Crowther, Kaagan, Ferguson, & Hann (2002), 8.

65. Crowther, Kaagan, Ferguson, & Hann (2002), 8.

66. Crowther, Kaagan, Ferguson, & Hann (2002), 12.

67. Ryan (2005).

68. Lieberman & Miller (2004), 26.

69. R. E. Dufour & R. Eaker (1998), *Professional learning communities at work: Best practices for enhancing student achievement* (Bloomington, IN: National Educational Services).

70. D. Tyack & W. Tobin (1994), The grammar of schooling: Why has it been so hard to change? *American Educational Research Journal*, *31*(3), 453–480.

71. For example, M. Fullan (2003), *Change forces with a vengeance* (London: Routledge/Falmer Press); K. Leithwood & K. S. Louis (Eds.) (1998), *Organizational learning in schools* (Downington, PA: Swets & Zeitlinger); C. Mitchell & L. Sackney (2000), *Profound improvement: Building capacity for a learning community* (Downington, PA: Swets & Zeitlinger).

72. S. M. Hord (1997), *Professional learning communities: Communities of continuous inquiry and improvement* (Austin, TX: Southwest Educational Development Laboratory), 1.

73. J. Westheimer (1999), Communities and consequences: An inquiry into ideology and practice in teachers' professional work, *Educational Administration Quarterly*, *35*(1), 75.

74. L. Stoll (in press), Professional learning communities: A review of the literature, *Journal of Educational Change*.

75. A. Hargreaves & C. Stone-Johnson (2004, September), *Evidence-informed change and the practice of teaching*, paper presented at the

MacArthur Foundation Symposium on Evidence-Based Education Reform, Cambridge, MA.

76. R. A. Heifetz & M. Linsky (2002), *Leadership on the line: Staying alive through the dangers of learning* (Boston: Harvard Business School).

77. Dufour & Eaker (1998), 183.

78. Dufour & Eaker (1998), 183.

79. R. Evans (1996), *The human side of school change: Reform, resistance, and the real-life problems of innovation* (San Francisco: Jossey-Bass).

80. A. Bryk & B. Schneider (2004), *Trust in schools: A core resource for improvement* (New York: Russell Sage Foundation).

81. Hargreaves & Stone-Johnson (2004).

82. Westheimer (1999).

83. S. Anderson & W. Togneri (2002), *Beyond islands of excellence: What districts can do to improve instruction and achievement in all schools* (Washington, DC: Learning First Alliance).

84. M. Fielding (Ed.) (2001), *Taking education really seriously: Four years' hard labour* (New York: Routledge/Falmer Press).

85. M. Fullan (2004a), *The moral imperative of the principalship* (Thousand Oaks, CA: Corwin Press).

86. E. Schall (1997), Public sector succession: A strategic approach to sustaining innovation, *Public Administration Review, 57*(1), 4–10.

87. On critical incidents, see D. Tripp (1994), *Critical incidents in teaching: Developing professional judgment* (London: Routledge).

88. The quotation is from John W. Alward, the superintendent of the Freeman's Bureau who toured the South in 1865, in H. Gutman (1987), Schools for freedom: The post-emancipation origins of Afro-American education, in I. Berlin (ed.), *Power and culture: Essays on the American working class* (New York: Pantheon Books), 261.

89. Gutman (1987), 270.

90. B. Simon (1965), *Education and the labor movement* (Southampton, U.K.: Camelot Press).

91. E. Stones (1960), The growth of technical education in nineteenth century Accrington, *Transactions of the Lancashire and Cheshire Antiquarian Society, LXX*(29).

92. Hargreaves (2003).

93. Hay Group Education (2004).

94. Hay Group Education (2004).

Chapter Four

1. S. Powell, T. Edwards, G. Whitty, & V. Wigfall (2003), *Education and the middle class* (London: Open University Press).

2. Z. Bauman (1998), *Globalization: The human consequences* (Oxford, U.K.: Basil Blackwell).

3. W. Ouchi (2003), *Making schools work: A revolutionary plan to get your children the education they need* (New York: Simon & Schuster).

4. H.-J. Robertson (1998), *No more teachers, no more books: The commercialization of Canada's schools* (Toronto: McClelland & Stewart).

5. M. McLaughlin & J. Talbert (2001), *Professional communities and the work of high school teaching* (Chicago: University of Chicago Press).

6. A. Smith (1809), *The theory of moral sentiments* (12th ed.) (Glasgow: R. Chapman) (original work published 1759).

7. A. de Tocqueville (2000), *Democracy in America* (Indianapolis, IN: Hackett) (original work published 1839), 109.

8. Tocqueville (1839/2000), 207.

9. G. Soros (2002), *George Soros on globalization* (New York: Perseus Books).

10. Powell, Edwards, Whitty, & Wigfall (2003).

11. J. Rifkin (2004), *The European dream: How Europe's vision of the future is quietly eclipsing the American dream* (New York: Jeremy P. Tarcher/Penguin), 3.

12. Rifkin (2004), 3.

13. W. Hutton (2002), *The world we're in* (New York: Little, Brown).

14. D. Labaree (1988), *The making of an American high school: The credentials market and the central high school of Philadelphia, 1838-1939* (New Haven, CT: Yale University Press).

15. A. R. Hochschild (2000), Chains of love, in W. Hutton & A. Giddens (Eds.), *On the edge: Living with global capitalism* (pp. 130–146) (London: Jonathan Cape).

16. R. J. Starratt (2004), *Ethical leadership* (San Francisco: Jossey-Bass).

17. C. Arena (2004), *Cause for success: 10 companies that put profits second and came in first: How solving the world's problems improves corporate health, growth, and competitive edge* (Novato, CA: New World Library), xvi.

18. G. Erickson & L. Lorentzen (2004), *Raising the bar: Integrity and passion in life and business: The story of Clif Bar, Inc.* (San Francisco: Jossey-Bass), 125.

19. A. Roddick (1994), *Soul: Profits with principles: The amazing success story of Anita Roddick & the Body Shop* (Three Rivers, MI: Three Rivers Press).

20. D. Suzuki (2003), *The David Suzuki reader: A lifetime of ideas from a leading activist and thinker* (Vancouver, Canada: Greystone Books).

21. Suzuki (2003).

22. See D. Blackburn (2003), *School leadership and reform: Case studies of Newport News paired-school model,* occasional paper, Newport News Schools, Newport News, VA.

23. The Hope Foundation Web site is at http://www.communitiesofhope .org/ (retrieved April 5, 2005).

24. W. Mansell (2004, March 12), Heads offended by "shotgun marriage," *London Times Educational Supplement,* 4.

25. H. Wilce (2004, November 19), Prophet of the specialist schools, *London Times Educational Supplement,* 12.

26. J. Whittaker (2004, October 15), Take a risk and talk to heads, *London Times Educational Supplement,* 18.

27. National College for School Leadership (2003), *Why networked learning communities?* (Nottingham, U.K.: Author); D. Jackson

(2003), *Like no other initiative* (Nottingham, U.K.: National College for School Leadership).

28. C. Taylor & C. Ryan (2004), *Excellence in education: The making of a good school* (London: David Fulton).

29. J. Kelley (2004), Winners who sign up with losers, *London Times Educational Supplement,* April 2, http://www.tes.co.uk/search/story/id=393265.

30. A. Hargreaves & D. Fink (2003), Sustaining leadership, *Phi Delta Kappan,* 84(9), 693–700.

31. F. Scott (2004), Villanelle for our time, printed and sung on L. Cohen, *Dear Heather* (CD, Columbia Records).

Chapter Five

1. E. O. Wilson & F. M. Peter (1988), *Biodiversity* (Washington, DC: National Academy Press).

2. E. O. Wilson (2002), *The future of life* (New York: Vintage Press).

3. E. O. Wilson (1992), *The diversity of life* (Cambridge, MA: Belknap Press), 393.

4. Wilson (1992), 32.

5. Wilson (1992).

6. D. Suzuki (2003), *The David Suzuki reader: A lifetime of ideas from a leading activist and thinker* (Vancouver, Canada: Greystone Books), 46.

7. Wilson (1992), 23.

8. D. Suzuki & A. McConnell (1997), *The sacred balance: Rediscovering our place in nature* (Seattle: Mountaineer Books), 133.

9. Wilson (1992).

10. Suzuki (2003), 200.

11. D. Tilman, quoted in D. Suzuki (2003), *The David Suzuki reader: A lifetime of ideas from a leading activist and thinker* (Vancouver, Canada: Greystone Books), 76.

12. Suzuki & McConnell (1997), 138–139.

13. "Babel runs backwards" (2004, December 29), *The Economist*, http://www.clta-gry.org/article/endangeredlanguage.html.

14. F. Capra (2002), *The hidden connections: A science for sustainable living* (New York: HarperCollins), 100.

15. Capra (2002), 99.

16. J. Collins & G. Porras (2002), *Built to last: Successful habits of visionary companies* (rev. ed.) (New York: Harper Business Essentials).

17. A. de Gues (1997), *The living company: Habits for survival in a turbulent business environment* (Boston: Harvard Business School Press).

18. A. Gawande (2002), *Complications: A surgeon's notes on an imperfect science* (New York: Metropolitan Books).

19. D. Goleman, R. E. Boyatzis, & A. McKee (2002), *Primal leadership: Realizing the power of emotional intelligence* (Boston: Harvard Business School Press), 248.

20. Capra (2002), 41.

21. Capra (2002), 41.

22. Capra (2002), 122.

23. Capra (2002), 122.

24. Capra (2002), 123.

25. Capra (2002).

26. de Gues (1997).

27. E. Abrahamson (2004), *Change without pain: How managers can overcome initiative overload, organizational chaos, and employee burnout* (Boston: Harvard Business School).

28. T. Wiley & W. E. Wright (2004), Against the undertow: Language-minority education policy and politics in the "age of accountability," *Educational Policy, 18*(1), 142–168; P. Gandara (2000), In the aftermath of the storm: English learners in the post-227 area, *Bilingual Research Journal, 24*(1-2), 1–13.

29. T. Sizer (2005, February 20), The unidentified business of education reform, *Boston Globe*, D1.

30. A. Hargreaves (2004), Inclusive and exclusive educational change: Emotional responses of teachers and implications for leadership, *School Leadership and Management, 24*(2), 287–309.

31. W. Maathai (2004), *The Green Belt Movement: Sharing the approach and the experience* (New York: Lantern Books).

32. A. Hargreaves (2003), *Teaching in the knowledge society: Education in the age of insecurity* (New York: Teachers College Press).

33. W. Veuglers & J. M. O'Hair (Eds.) (in press), *School-university networks and educational change* (Maidenhead, U.K.: Open University Press/McGraw-Hill).

34. Capra (2002), 29.

35. Capra (2002), 31.

36. Capra (2002).

37. Capra (2002), 67.

38. Capra (2002).

39. It was actually the Chinese who first invented bureaucracy, but industrialization led to its spread across the modern world.

40. M. Castells (2001), *The Internet galaxy: Reflections on the Internet, business, and society* (Oxford, U.K.: Oxford University Press), 1.

41. Castells (2001), 17.

42. Castells (2001), 17.

43. Castells (2001), 29.

44. Castells (2001).

45. M. Castells (1996), *The rise of the network society* (Oxford, U.K.: Blackwell), 168.

46. Castells (1996), 61.

47. Castells (2001).

48. N. Bascia & P. L. Shaw (1994), Creating a culture of change: A work in progress, *Orbit Magazine, 24*(4), 2–5.

49. D. Hopkins, A. Harris, & D. Jackson (1997), Understanding the school's capacity for development: Growth states and strategies, *School Leadership and Management, 17*(3), 401–411.

50. C. Day, M. Hadfield, & M. Kellow (in press), Network learning and the democratising power of action research, in W. Veuglers & J. M. O'Hair (Eds.), *School-university networks and educational change* (Maidenhead, U.K.: Open University Press/McGraw-Hill).

51. D. E. Muncey & P. J. McQuillan (1996), *Reform and resistance in schools and classrooms: An ethnographic view of the Coalition of Essential Schools* (New Haven, CT: Yale University Press); C. Glickman & C. F. Hensley (1999), *A guide to renewing your school: Lessons from the League of Professional Schools* (San Francisco: Jossey-Bass).

52. A. Lieberman & D. R. Wood (2002), *Inside the National Writing Project: Connecting network learning and classroom teaching* (New York: Teachers College Press).

53. Teacher Union Reform Network (2005), *Transforming teacher unions to become agents of reform*, retrieved April 5, 2005, from http://www.gseis.ucla.edu/hosted/turn/turn.html.

54. B. Wellman & S. D. Berkowitz (1988), *Social structures: A network approach* (Cambridge, U.K.: Cambridge University Press).

55. B. Wellman & S. D. Berkowitz (1988), 197.

56. Wellman's Web site is at www.class.utoronto.ca/wellman/vita/index.html (retrieved February 22, 2005).

57. D. Hargreaves (2004), *Education epidemic:Transforming secondary schools through innovation networks* (London: Demos).

58. Wellman & Berkowitz (1988); J. Lima (1997), *Colleagues and friends: Professional and personal relationships among teachers in two Portuguese secondary schools,* unpublished doctoral dissertation, Universidade Dos Acores, San Miguel, Portugal.

59. See the SchoolNet Web site at http://www.schoolnet.ca.

60. M. Fullan (2004b), *System thinkers in action: Moving beyond the standards plateau* (London: Department for Education and Skills and National College for School Leadership), 10.

61. See the Specialist Schools Trust's iNet Web site at http://www .sst-inet.net (retrieved April 5, 2005).

62. D. Jackson (2003), *Like no other initiative* (Nottingham, U.K.: National College for School Leadership).

63. M. Hadfield (in press), From networking to school networks and "networked learning": The challenge of the networked communities learning program, in W. Veuglers & J. M. O'Hair (Eds.), *School-university networks and educational change* (Maidenhead, U.K.: Open University Press/McGraw-Hill).

64. D. Jackson (2004, January 6–9), *Networked learning communities: Characteristics of "networked learning"—what are we learning?*, paper presented at the annual conference of the International Congress for School Effectiveness and Improvement, Rotterdam, the Netherlands.

65. Veuglers & O'Hair (in press); Day, Hadfield, & Kellow (in press); D. Hargreaves (2004).

66. Day, Hadfield, & Kellow (in press).

67. Day, Hadfield, & Kellow (in press).

68. Veuglers & O'Hair (in press).

69. Association of California School Administrators, Task Force on Administrator Shortage (2001), *Recruitment and retention of school leaders: A critical state need* (Sacramento: Author).

70. C. Giles (2005), *Change over time: Resistance, resilience and sustainable education reform*, unpublished manuscript, Buffalo: University of Buffalo, State University of New York.

71. Fullan (2004b).

72. Hadfield (in press).

73. D. Hargreaves (2004).

74. D. Hargreaves (2004).

75. Castells (2001).

76. Castells (1996), 171.

77. Fullan (2005).

78. Castells (2001), 2.

79. Castells (2001).

80. Day, Hadfield, & Kellow (in press).

81. D. Hargreaves (2004); D. Hopkins (2003), Understanding networks for innovation in policy and practice, in Organization for Economic Cooperation and Development, *Networks of innovation: Towards new models for managing schools and systems* (Paris: Author).

82. L. Stoll & L. Earl (2004), Making it last: Building capacity for sustainability, in B. Davies & J. West-Burnham (Eds.), *Handbook of educational management and leadership* (London: Pearson Education).

83. D. Hargreaves (2004).

84. Castells (2001), 50.

85. J. Whittaker (2004, October 15), Take a risk and talk to heads, *London Times Educational Supplement*, 3.

86. See Wellman's Web site at http://www.chass.utoronto.ca/~wellman/.

87. Z. Bauman (2004a), *Identity* (Cambridge, U.K.: Polity Press), 69.

88. Bauman (2004a), 93.

Chapter Six

1. B. McKibben (2003), *Enough: Staying human in an engineered age* (New York: Times Books).

2. D. L. Meadows, D. H. Meadows, J. Randers, & W. Behren (1972), *The limits to growth* (London: Earth Island).

3. D. Goodstein (2004), *Out of gas: The end of the age of oil* (New York: Norton), 95.

4. Goodstein (2004), 93.

5. J. Rifkin (1981), *Entropy: A new world view* (New York: Bantam Books).

6. P. Hawken, A. Lovins, & L. H. Lovins (1999), *Natural capitalism: Creating the next industrial revolution* (New York: Little, Brown).

7. W. McDonough & M. Braungart (2002), *Cradle to cradle: Remaking the way we make things* (New York: North Point Press).

8. Z. Bauman (2004b), *Wasted lives: Modernity and its outcasts* (Cambridge, U.K.: Polity Press).

9. R. Evans (1996), *The human side of school change: Reform, resistance, and the real-life problems of innovation* (San Francisco: Jossey-Bass).

10. A. Hargreaves, L. Earl, S. Moore, & S. Manning (2001), *Learning to change: Teaching beyond subjects and standards* (San Francisco: Jossey-Bass).

11. For more details, see A. Hargreaves (2003), *Teaching in the knowledge society: Education in the age of insecurity* (New York: Teachers College Press).

12. J. Loehr & T. Schwartz (2003), *The power of full engagement: Managing energy, not time is the key to high performance and personal renewal* (New York: Free Press), 23.

13. F. Capra (2002), *The hidden connections: A science for sustainable living* (New York: HarperCollins), 214.

14. B. McKibben (1989), *The end of nature* (New York: Random House).

15. See the World Resources Institute Web site at http://www.wri.org/.

16. Goodstein (2004), 17.

17. Loehr & Schwartz (2003), 8–9.

18. S. Dinham & C. Scott (1997), *The Teacher 2000 project: A study of teacher motivation and health* (Perth, Australia: University of Western Sydney, Nepean); G. Troman, & P. Woods (2000), Careers under stress: Teacher adaptations at a time of intensive reform, *Journal of Educational Change*, *1*(3), 253–275; G. Helsby (1999), *Changing teachers' work: The reform of secondary schooling* (Milton Keynes, U.K.: Open University Press); A. Hargreaves (2003), *Teaching in the knowledge society: Education in the age of insecurity* (New York: Teachers College Press).

19. P. Gronn & F. Rawlings-Sanaei (2003), Principal recruitment in a climate of leadership disengagement, *Australian Journal of Education*, *47*(2), 172–185.

20. Teachernet (2005), *School workforce remodelling*, retrieved from www.teachernet.gov/uk/wholeschool/remodelling/.

21. Teachernet (2005).

22. B. Levin & J. Wiens (2003), There is another way: A different approach to educational reform, *Phi Delta Kappan*, 84(9), 660.

23. Levin & Wiens (2003), 664.

24. Bill and Melinda Gates Foundation (2005), *Making the case for small schools*, retrieved from www.gatesfoundation.org.

25. J. Goodlad (1997), *Beyond McSchool: A challenge to educational leadership*, retrieved February 12, 2005, from Center for Educational Renewal Web site: www.nas.edu/sputnik/Goodlad.htm.

26. Goodlad (1997).

27. Goodlad (1994), *Educational renewal: Better teachers, better schools* (San Francisco: Jossey-Bass), 218.

28. Goodlad (1994), 218.

29. Goodlad (1994), 217.

30. Goodlad (1994), 219.

31. Goodlad (1997).

32. Confucius (1998), *Confucius: The analects* (London: Penguin Books), 64.

33. D. Reina & M. Reina (1999), *Trust and betrayal in the workplace* (San Francisco: Berrett-Koehler).

34. A. Hargreaves (2002), Teaching and betrayal, *Teachers and Teaching: Theory and Practice*, 13(4), 393–407.

35. A. Bryk & B. Schneider (2004), *Trust in schools: A core resource for improvement* (New York: Russell Sage Foundation), 121.

36. Bryk & Schneider (2004), 22.

37. Bryk & Schneider (2004), 110–111.

38. O. O'Neill (2002), *A question of trust: The BBC Reith lectures 2002* (Cambridge, U.K.: Cambridge University Press), 49.

39. O'Neill (2002), 50.

40. O'Neill (2002), 49.

41. D. Meier (2003), *In schools we trust: Creating communities of learning in an era of testing and standardization* (Boston: Beacon Press).

42. Canadian Press (2003, March 2), Kennedy blames Tories for teacher work-to rule, *Toronto Star*, www.torstarreports.com.

43. R. M. Kanter (2004), *Confidence: How winning streaks and losing streaks begin and end* (New York: Crown Business).

44. Kanter (2004), 95.

45. Kanter (2004), 139.

46. Kanter (2004), 139.

47. G. Helsby (1999), *Changing teachers' work: The reform of secondary schooling* (Milton Keynes, U.K.: Open University Press), 173.

48. Kanter (2004), 8.

49. Kanter (2004), 72.

50. B. Tuchman (1984), *The march of folly: From Troy to Vietnam* (New York: Knopf).

51. D. Johnson (2004), *Overconfidence and war* (Cambridge, MA: Harvard University Press).

52. H. Keller (1990), *The story of my life* (reissue ed.) (New York: Bantam Classics).

53. A. Hargreaves (1998), The emotions of teaching and educational change, in A. Hargreaves, A. Lieberman, M. Fullan, & D. Hopkins (Eds.), *The international handbook of educational change* (Dordrecht, Netherlands: Kluwer).

54. D. Goleman (1995), *Emotional intelligence* (New York: Bantam Books).

55. A. R. Hochschild (1983), *The managed heart: The commercialization of human feeling* (Berkeley: University of California Press).

56. J. Blackmore (1996), Doing "emotional labour" in the education marketplace: Stories from the field of women in management, *Discourse: Studies in the Cultural Politics of Education, 17*(3), 337–349;

B. Beatty (2002), *Emotional matters in educational leadership: Examining the unexamined,* unpublished doctoral dissertation, University of Toronto.

57. B. E. Ashforth & R. H. Humphrey (1993), Emotional labour in service roles: The influence of identity, *Academy of Management Journal, 18*(1), 88–115.

58. B. Stenross & S. Kleinman (1989), The highs and lows of emotional labour: Detectives' encounters with criminals and victims, *Journal of Contemporary Ethnography, 17*(4), 435–452.

59. S. Fineman (Ed.) (2000), *Emotion in organizations* (London: Sage).

60. Alberta Learning (2004), *Improving student learning: Alberta Initiative for School Improvement* (Edmonton, Canada: Author), 8.

61. Alberta Learning (2004), 5.

62. Captain James Cook, quoted in R. Wright (2004), *A short history of progress* (New York: Carroll and Graf), 61. See also J. Tainter (1988), *The collapse of complex societies* (Cambridge, U.K.: Cambridge University Press); J. Diamond (2005), *Collapse* (New York, Penguin Books).

63. J. Rifkin (1981), *Entropy: A new world view* (New York: Bantam Books).

64. *Hale* means "vigorous and healthy," as in *hale and hearty.*

Chapter Seven

1. A. Hargreaves & I. Goodson (2004), *Change over time? A report of educational change over 30 years in eight U.S. and Canadian schools* (Chicago: Spencer Foundation).

2. M. Fullan (2003), *Change forces with a vengeance* (London: Routledge/Falmer Press).

3. The contributions of indigenous knowledge to medical science provide an especially compelling example, given that this indigenous knowledge as the legitimate intellectual property of the communities that have long possessed it has often been disregarded by Western research institutions.

4. K. S. Louis & M. B. Miles (1990), *Improving the urban high school: The what and how* (New York: Teachers College Press); S. Sarason (1971), *The culture of the school and the problem of change* (Boston: Allyn & Bacon).

5. I. Goodson, S. Moore, & A. Hargreaves (2006), Teacher nostalgia and the sustainability of reform: The generation and degeneration of teachers' missions, memory and meaning, *Educational Administration Quarterly, 42*(1).

6. E. Abrahamson (2004), *Change without pain: How managers can overcome initiative overload, organizational chaos, and employee burnout* (Boston: Harvard Business School), 23.

7. Abrahamson (2004), 10.

8. However, indigenous knowledge did not always seem to be responsible for people's escape from the tsunami, and accounts about its importance are somewhat conflicted. Revealing that history and news have many interpretations, especially in the Internet age, not all the accounts of this phenomenon appear reliable. The *Bangkok Post,* for example, originally reported that the Moken people, or sea gypsies, on Thailand's South Surin island were protected by indigenous knowledge passed on by elders whose myths recounted how "one day the navel of the sea would suck all water and spit it back in the form of waves. Many people would die" (Karnjarsya Sulering [2005, January 28], Andaman sea gypsies heeded pre-tsunami signs: Wisdom of the sea, *Bangkok Post*). *Thai Nation* similarly reported Moken elders stating, "If the water recedes fast, it will come back fast and will reappear in the same quantity as which it disappeared" (Phang Nga [2005], Saved by old wisdom: Gypsies know their sea, *The Nation,* Thailand). Yet *The Nation* misreported the Moken people as "the Morgan people." This mistake was transferred via Associated Press to many other Web sites, including CTV Canada (2005), Thai "sea gypsies" save village from tsunami, retrieved February 25, 2005 from http://www.ctv.ca/servlet/articlenews/story/ CTVNews/1104556665753. Further investigation by the *New Yorker* revealed that when Moken people were asked about this folklore after they were rescued, they "seemed perplexed." In the words

of one older woman, "We just saw the wave coming and ran" (Postcard from Thailand: Sea gypsies [2005, January 24], *New Yorker*, retrieved February 25, 2005, from http://newyorker.com/talk/content/?050124ta-talk-griswold). The account presented in our text appears more anthropologically reliable. See, for example, S. Bhaumik (2005, January 20), *Tsunami folklore saved islanders*, retrieved February 2, 2005, from http://news.bbc.co.uk/1/hi/world/south-asia/4181855.stm.

9. Bhaumik (2005).

10. Abrahamson (2004), 3. For previous work on organizational memory in education, see K. S. Louis & S. Kruse (1999), Creating community in reform: Images of organizational learning in schools, in K. Leithwood & K. Louis (eds.), *Organizational learning in schools*. The Netherlands: Swets & Zeitlinger, 17–46.

11. C. Wolmar (2001), *Broken rail* (London: Aurum Press).

12. A. Hargreaves (in press), Educational change takes ages, *Teaching and Teacher Education*.

13. J. Collins (2001), *Good to great: Why some companies make the leap . . . and others don't* (New York: HarperCollins); M. Fullan (2002, March 18-19), *The role of leadership in the promotion of knowledge management in schools*, paper presented at the meeting of the Organization for Economic Cooperation and Development, Oxford, U.K.

14. Hargreaves (in press).

15. S. M. Johnson (2004), *Finders and keepers: Helping new teachers survive and thrive in our schools* (San Francisco: Jossey-Bass).

16. Organization for Economic Cooperation and Development (2005), *Teaching matters* (Paris: Author).

17. P. M. De Holan & N. Phillips (2004a), Managing organizational forgetting, *Sloan Management Review, 45*(2), 7.

18. De Holan & Phillips (2004a), 3.

19. P. M. De Holan & N. Phillips (2004b), The dynamics of organizational forgetting, *Management Science, 50*(11), 1606.

20. De Holan & Phillips (2004a), 7.

21. J. Collins & G. Porras (2002), *Built to last: Successful habits of visionary companies* (rev. ed.) (New York: Harper Business Essentials), 2.

22. De Holan & Phillips (2004b).

23. P. Drucker (2001), *Management challenges for the 21st century* (New York: HarperCollins), 74.

24. Drucker (2001), 74.

25. Drucker (2001), 74.

26. B. J. Caldwell (2000), A "public good" test to guide the transformation of public education, *Journal of Educational Change*, 1(4), 307–329.

27. Caldwell (2000).

28. Teachernet (2005), *School workforce remodelling*, retrieved from www.teachernet.gov/uk/wholeschool/remodelling/.

29. De Holan & Phillips (2004a); De Holan & Phillips (2004b).

30. R. Marris (1974), *Loss and change* (London: Routledge Kegan Paul).

31. A. Hargreaves, L. Earl, S. Moore, & S. Manning (2001), *Learning to change: Teaching beyond subjects and standards* (San Francisco: Jossey-Bass).

32. A. Datnow, L. Hubbard, & H. Mehan (2002), *Extending educational reform: From one school to many* (London: Routledge/Falmer Press).

33. A. Gitlin & F. Margonis (1995), The political aspect of reform, *American Journal of Education*, 103, 377–405.

34. Johnson (2004).

35. C. Lasch (1991), *The true and only heaven: Progress and its critics* (New York: Norton), 82.

36. See also Goodson, Moore, & Hargreaves (2006).

37. E. O. Wilson (2002), *The future of life* (New York: Vintage Press), 14.

38. H. D. Thoreau (1951), *Walden* (New York: Norton), originally published in 1854.

39. B. McKibben (1989), *The end of nature* (New York: Random House).

40. Wilson (2002), 73.

41. Wilson (2002), 131.

42. Wilson (2002), 131.

43. S. Schama (1996), *Landscape and memory* (New York: Vintage).

44. Wilson (2002), 71.

45. Schama (1996), 282.

46. J. Dewey (1916), Education as a necessity of life, in *Democracy and education* (New York: Free Press), 282.

47. J. Dewey (1903), Democracy and education, *Elementary School Teacher*, 4(4), 285.

48. Thoreau (1951), 4.

49. Quote attributed to William Wordsworth, 1770–1850, http://chatna.com/author/wordsworth.htm.

50. M. Castells (1997), *The power of identity* (Malden, MA: Blackwell), 112.

51. B. McKibben, *Walden: Lessons for the millennium* (Boston: Beacon Press), 23.

52. A. Hargreaves & M. Fullan (2000), Mentoring in the new millennium, *Theory into Practice*, 39(1), 50–55.

53. Johnson (2004).

54. M. Angelou (1993, January 20), *The inaugural poem: On the pulse of morning*, poem presented at the inauguration of President William Clinton, Washington, DC.

Conclusion

1. M. Fullan (2005), *Leadership and sustainability: System thinkers in action* (Thousand Oaks, CA: Corwin Press), 25.

2. M. Shaw (2004, April 9). End testing of infants: Seven is too young for tests say parents in TES poll, *London Times Educational Supplement*, 1.

3. Alberta Learning School Improvement Branch (2004), *Improving student learning: Alberta Initiative for School Improvement* (Edmonton, Canada: Author), http://www.saee.ca/policy/D_030_111_LON.php. Similar work on networks for performance-based school improvement is emerging in British Columbia; see J. Halbert & L. Kaser, *The network of performance-based schools*, www.npbs.ca (retrieved June 22, 2005).

4. M. Fullan (1993), *Change forces: Probing the depths of educational reform* (London: Falmer Press), 21.

5. S. Sarason (1990), *The predictable failure of educational reform* (San Francisco: Jossey-Bass).

6. Shaw (2004).

7. This widely used quotation has an unclear and unidentified single source but is widely believed to have been made as an aside in an interview and has since been disseminated more widely. See www.interculturalstudies.org/Mead (retrieved June 22, 2005).

8. Z. Bauman (2004b), *Wasted lives: Modernity and its outcasts* (Cambridge, U.K.: Polity Press), 96.

9. Bauman (2004b).

10. E. Brubaker (2000), Walkerton: Government's three deadly mistakes, *National Post Online*, May 31, http://www.canada.com/national/nationalpost/index/html. D. Tapscott & D. Ticoll (2003), *The naked corporation* (Toronto: Viking Canada), 6, 20, 58.

11. D. Batstone (2003), *Saving the corporate soul and (who knows?) maybe your own* (San Francisco: Jossey-Bass).

12. Batstone (2003), 51.

13. Batstone (2003), 57.

14. Tapscott & Ticoll, 22.

15. K. Vincente (2003), *The human factor: Revolutionizing the way people live with technology* (Toronto: Knopf Canada).

16. T. Homer-Dixon (2000), *The ingenuity gap: Can we solve the problems of the future?* (New York: Knopf).

17. Vincente (2003).

18. Vincente (2003).

19. Vincente (2003), 27.

20. See P. Tymms (2004), Are standards rising in English primary schools? *British Educational Research Journal, 30*(4), 477–494, for a critique of the British target-driven literacy strategy.

21. As, for example, in the language of Britain's chief inspector of schools, David Bell; see D. Lepkawske (2004, August 27), Ministers shun pleas to axe 2006 targets, *London Times Educational Supplement,* 1.

Index

TITLES IN THE JOSSEY-BASS
LEADERSHIP LIBRARY IN EDUCATION SERIES

Ann Lieberman, Lynne Miller
Teacher Leadership

Teacher Leadership is written for teachers who assume responsibility for educational success beyond their own classrooms by providing peer support, modeling good practice, or coordinating curriculum and instruction. It offers cases studies of innovative programs and stories of individual teachers who lead in a variety of contexts. It shows how to develop learning communities that include rather than exclude, create knowledge rather than merely applying it, and provide challenge and support to new and experienced teachers.

ISBN 0-7879-6245-7   Paperback   112 Pages   2004

Robert J. Starratt
Ethical Leadership

In *Ethical Leadership*, Robert Starratt—one of the leading thinkers on the topic of ethics and education—shows educational leaders how to move beyond mere technical efficiency in the delivery and performance of learning. He explains that leadership requires a moral commitment to high quality learning, based on three essential virtues: proactive responsibility, personal and professional authenticity, and an affirming, critical, and enabling presence.

ISBN 0-7879-6564-2   Paperback   176 Pages   2004

James Ryan
Inclusive Leadership

This is an innovative and groundbreaking book about the powerful new idea of inclusive leadership. The culture of schools and the diversity of those who lead them have not kept pace with the growing diversity in the student population. James Ryan's work focuses on leadership as an intentionally inclusive practice that values all cultures and types of students and educators in a school. He looks upon leadership as a collective influence process to promote inclusion. In four chapters, Ryan provides an overview of the topic, a summary of research, examples of good practice, and guidelines for the future.

ISBN 0-7879-6508-1   Paperback   192 Pages   Fall 2005

Michael Fullan
Turnaround Leadership

ISBN 0-7879-6985-0   Paperback   128 Pages (approx.)   Spring 2006

James Spillane
Distributed Leadership

ISBN 0-7879-6538-3   Paperback   112 Pages (approx.)   Spring 2006

Geoffrey Southworth
Learner-Centered Leadership

ISBN 0-7879-7553-2   Paperback   128 Pages (approx.)   Fall 2006